John Indermaur

The student's guide to the law of real & personal property

John Indermaur

The student's guide to the law of real & personal property

ISBN/EAN: 9783337733094

Printed in Europe, USA, Canada, Australia, Japan

Cover: Foto ©ninafisch / pixelio.de

More available books at **www.hansebooks.com**

THE
STUDENT'S GUIDE

TO THE LAW OF

REAL & PERSONAL PROPERTY.

BY

JOHN INDERMAUR, Solicitor,

First Prizeman, Michaelmas, 1872;

AUTHOR OF "PRINCIPLES OF COMMON LAW," "MANUAL OF EQUITY," "MANUAL OF PRACTICE,"
"THE STUDENT'S GUIDE TO TRUSTS AND PARTNERSHIP," "THE STUDENT'S
GUIDE TO COMMON LAW," ETC., ETC.

AND

CHARLES THWAITES, Solicitor,

First Prizeman, June, 1880; Reardon Prizeman; Scott Scholar; Conveyancing Gold Medallist, Etc.;

AUTHOR OF "A GUIDE TO CRIMINAL LAW," ETC., ETC.

THIRD EDITION.

LONDON:
PRINTED AND PUBLISHED BY GEO. BARBER,
"LAW STUDENTS' JOURNAL" OFFICE,
16 & 17, CURSITOR STREET, CHANCERY LANE, E.C.
1893.
Price Ten Shillings.

ADVERTISEMENT TO THIRD EDITION.

THE Second Edition of this Guide was published in March, 1889, and has now been out of print for some time. The Authors have therefore prepared this Edition, in which the whole matter has been thoroughly reconsidered and revised, and a selection of Questions and Answers at past examinations given down to, and including, the last Bar Final. Many former Questions and Answers have been eliminated, and every endeavour has been made to avoid repetition and keep the work within a reasonable compass. The work forms the Fourth of the series of Guides to the Bar Final, the first being on Trusts and Partnership, by Mr. Indermaur, a Second Edition of which has been published; the second on Criminal Law by Mr. Thwaites, of which a Third Edition has been published; the third on Common Law and Practice by Mr. Indermaur, of which a Second Edition has been published; and the fifth on Specific Performance and Mortgages, by Mr. Indermaur and Mr. Thwaites.

Mr. INDERMAUR, assisted by Mr. THWAITES, continues to prepare Students, both in class and privately for the Bar Final Examinations, Solicitors' Final (Pass and Honours) Examinations, and the Solicitors' Intermediate Examinations. Particulars on application, personally or by letter, to Mr. Indermaur, 22, Chancery Lane, W.C.

May, 1893.

CONTENTS.

	PAGE
I. THE COURSE OF READING	1
II. EPITOMES OF STATUTES—	
(1.) Epitome of the Conveyancing Act 1881.	6
(2.) ,, ,, ,, 1882.	22
(3.) ,, ,, ,, 1892.	27
(4.) ,, ,, Settled Land Act 1882.	29
(5.) ,, ,, ,, 1884.	39
(6.) ,, ,, ,, 1890.	41
III. LIST OF IMPORTANT STATUTES	45
IV. TEST QUESTIONS ON THE LAW OF REAL AND PERSONAL PROPERTY	48
V. DIGEST OF QUESTIONS AND ANSWERS ON THE LAW OF REAL AND PERSONAL PROPERTY—	
(1.) Introductory	59
(2.) Tenures, Estates, &c.	65
(3.) Life Estates, Settled Land Acts, &c.	69
(4.) Estates Tail	81
(5.) Devolution on Death	85
(6.) Ownership	93
(7.) Future Estates and Interests	98
(8.) Uses and Trusts	116
(9.) Alienation *Inter Vivos*	122
(10.) Wills	134
(11.) Husband and Wife—Settlements	147
(12.) Incorporeal Hereditaments	155
(13.) Copyholds	162
(14.) Leaseholds, &c.	166
(15.) Mortgages, &c.	173
(16.) Title and Miscellaneous Points	182

THE STUDENT'S GUIDE

TO THE LAW OF

REAL & PERSONAL PROPERTY.

I.—THE COURSE OF READING.

THE design of this Guide is to assist law students in general, and in particular those reading for the Bar Final Examination. We propose to give our readers general advice and assistance by suggesting what they should read, furnishing them with certain material to read, giving a set of test questions, and finally concluding with a digest of questions and answers framed from the actual questions hitherto asked at the Bar Final.

The Council of Legal Education have now prescribed a course of study for the Bar Final which they estimate will cover a period of two years. The following is a condensed copy of the prospectus issued in 1892 :—

Regulations.

1. Candidates for the Pass Examination will be examined at their option in *any three* of the following subjects, in addition to Roman Law—
    I. Elements of the Law of Real and Personal Property.
    II. Elements of the Law of Contracts and Torts.
    III. Principles of Equity, Trusts, and Easements.
    IV. Procedure and Evidence.
    V. Constitutional Law and Legal History.

Such Candidates will *also* be examined in *one* of the following group of subjects, A, B, C, such group to be selected by the Candidate—

A { Purchases and Leases.
    Mortgages.
    Settlements and Wills.

B { Negotiable Instruments.
    Agency in Mercantile Contracts.
    Contracts of Sale of Goods.

C { Administration of Assets on Death.
Specific Performance.
Partnership and Winding-up of Companies.

2. Candidates for Honours will be examined in all the above subjects.

3. Up to January, 1894, both for Pass and Honours Examinations the above subjects will be examined upon so far only as treated in the lectures and classes since January, 1892; and after January, 1894, so far only as treated in the lectures and classes during the two years preceding each Examination.

The Honours Examinations in connection with the Bar Final are now held twice in each year. They are open to students who are under 25 years of years. At each such examination one studentship of £105 yearly for three years is awarded and certificates of honour are also awarded, and a pass certificate entitling to call to the bar without further examination may be awarded to any candidates who do not get honours. We understand that a student who has passed the Bar Final can subsequently sit for the Honours Examination before he is called.

The student who desires to attain a thorough knowledge rather than to merely satisfy the very reasonable demands of the examiners will find the following a good course of reading:—

1. Read Williams' Real Property.
2. Read Williams' Personal Property.
3. Read Goodeve's Modern Law of Real Property.
4. Read Goodeve's Law of Personal Property.
5. Make a separate reading of the Conveyancing and Settled Land Acts.
6. Read Smith's Compendium of the Law of Real and Personal Property.
7. Read Tudor's Leading Cases on Conveyancing.
8. Read the portions of Elphinstone's Introduction to Conveyancing and of the dissertations in Prideaux's Conveyancing, referring to some of the Precedents.
9. Specially analyze and consider the Statutes, of which a list is given in this work (*post*, page 45).

We think that the works might well be read in the order above detailed; but certainly, to conclude, Williams' Real Property and Williams' Personal Property, or Goodeve's Real Property and Goodeve's Personal Property should be read again.

With regard to Tudor's Conveyancing Cases, if the student should not be able to read the whole work, we give a list of the most important cases, and would remark that the notes to these cases are even more important than the cases themselves:—

        Alexander v. Alexander.
        Bowles' (Lewis) Case.
        Braybroke (Lord) v. Inskip.
        Cadell v. Palmer.
        Corbyn v. French.
        Elliott v. Davenport.
        Fox v. Bishop of Chester.
        Gardner v. Sheldon.
        Griffiths v. Vere.
        Hanson v. Graham.
        Morley v. Bird.
        Pawlett v. Pawlett.
        Richardson v. Langridge.
        Shelley's Case.
        Stapleton v. Cheales.
        Sury v. Pigot.
        Tyrringham's Case.
        Viner v. Francis.
        Wild's Case.

The really industrious student will read these cases and notes from "Tudor," but in doing so, he will find it an advantage to have by him "Indermaur's Epitome of Leading Conveyancing and Equity Cases," which contains all the above; and, having read the particular cases and notes in the large volume, he can then turn to the Epitome and read that, and, very likely, may be able to add to the notes there. In default of reading the large work, a perusal of the cases and notes in the Epitome will be of service.

With regard to the Conveyancing and Settled Land Acts the student should read any good edition, say Wolstenholme and Turner, or Hood and Challis. If time permit, he will find the notes following the various sections of great service. Some of the sections are long and complicated, and an Epitome of the Acts will manifestly be of service. We have therefore given such an Epitome (see *post*, page 6), and this should be studied in conjunction with the Acts; the condensation of the sections will tend to impress their provisions on the student. Some students may perhaps only find time to go through the Epitome, though here and there they will find it necessary to refer to the Acts.

Smith's Compendium is a hard work, and one upon which it will be found very useful to take notes during the reading. The student who does not care to tackle Smith, but wishes to read something besides Williams and Goodeve will find a perusal of Edward's Compendium of the Law of Property in Land repay him well for the time spent on it.

As to taking notes, they are useful in moderation, but great moderation should be observed. It is useless to put down in a note-book a lot of points merely for them to stop there and not be remembered.

With regard to our list of Statutes, a great many of them will be found sufficiently touched upon in the works we have set for the student's reading, but if time permit, it will be found very advisable to also consider them separately, either by reference to the text books, or, in some cases, to the Statutes themselves, and, to save time, an epitome of them will be found extremely useful. We recommend Marcy's Epitome of Conveyancing Statutes; and as to the Conveyancing and Settled Land Acts, we have already dealt with them specially, and given in this work our own Epitomes of them (see *post*, page 6).

Thus, then, we have mapped out for the student what we consider a very thorough course of reading. We wish now to deal with students who have not time, or who are not willing, to go through so much, and to these we would say, omit Smith's Compendium and Tudor's Conveyancing Cases, but do not fail to read the cases given (and the notes) in Indermaur's Epitome of Conveyancing Cases. A separate study of the Statutes, other than the Conveyancing and Settled Land Acts, may no doubt also be omitted. All should, however, strive to commit to memory the references or short titles of the most important of the Statutes.

Finally, we have to deal with those who will not, or cannot, even go through this modified course, meaning to do only what is actually essential. To such we can only say, omit also Williams' Real Property and Williams' Personal Property, and Prideaux, and that will leave for essential study Goodeve's Real Property, Goodeve's Personal Property, Elphinstone's Conveyancing, the Conveyancing and Settled Land Acts, Epitome of Cases, and something in the shape of a consideration of the Statutes. If time is very pressing we may also add that it *may* be sufficient as regards Goodeve's Personal Property to read only Chapters 6, 13, 16 and 20.

All classes of readers should, however, carefully study the Test Questions, and the Digest of Questions and Answers given in this work (see *post*, pages 48 and 59, *et seq*). As to the Test Questions, they should be considered and studied during, or directly after, a perusal of the text books, and it will be excellent practice to write out answers to the Test Questions, or, at any rate, to a number of the more important of them. These Test Questions are mainly founded on Mr. Williams' and Mr. Goodeve's works. The final study with every one, to conclude the course of reading, should be the Digest of Questions and Answers, for by means of those the student's knowledge is focussed and brought as it were to a point.

II.—EPITOME OF THE CONVEYANCING AND SETTLED LAND ACTS.

44 & 45 Vict., C. 41.

Conveyancing and Law of Property Act, 1881.

(Commencement of Act, 1st January, 1882.)

Part I.—is Preliminary and gives Definitions.

Part II.—Sales and other Transactions.

Sec. 3.—(1.) Under a contract to sell and assign a term of years derived out of a leasehold interest in land, the intended assign has no right to call for the title to the leasehold reversion.

(2.) A purchaser of enfranchised copyholds has no right to call for the title to make the enfranchisement.

(3.) A purchaser not to require any abstract or copy or production of any instrument affecting title prior to time prescribed (by law or agreement) for commencement of the title, even although the same creates a power subsequently exercised by an instrument abstracted in the abstract furnished to purchaser; and no prior enquiry to be allowed; and recitals in abstracted documents as to prior title to be presumed correct unless contrary appears.

(4.) Where land sold is held by lease (not including underlease), purchaser shall assume, unless the contrary appears, that the lease was duly granted; and on production of receipt for the last payment due for rent, shall assume, unless the contrary appears, that the rent and all covenants have been duly paid and performed up to completion.

(5.) Where land sold is held by underlease, the purchaser shall assume, unless the contrary appears, that the underlease and every superior lease were duly granted; and on production of receipt for the last payment due for rent, shall assume, unless the contrary appears, that the rent and covenants have been duly paid and performed up to completion of the purchase, and further that all rent due under every superior lease, and all covenants therein have been duly paid and performed up to that date.

(6.) On a sale of any property, the expenses of the production and inspection of all documents *not in the vendor's possession*, and the expenses of all journeys incidental to such production or inspection, and all other expenses relating thereto, and all attested, stamped, office or other copies thereof, shall be borne by the purchaser; and where the vendor retains possession of any document, the expenses of making any copy which a purchaser requires shall be borne by such purchaser.

(7.) On a sale of any property in lots, a purchaser of two or more lots, held wholly or partly under the same title, shall not have a right to more than one abstract of the common title, except at his own expense.

(10.) This section applies only to sales made after 1881.

Sec. 4.—Where any person dies after 1881, leaving a contract enforceable against his heir (or devisee) for the sale of the fee simple or other freehold interest descendible to his heirs general, his personal representatives shall have power to convey the same.

Sec. 5.—Where land subject to any incumbrance is sold, the Court may, on application of any party to the sale, allow payment into Court of a sum sufficient to meet such incumbrance, and any costs and interest (not usually exceeding one-tenth of original amount paid in), and thereupon Court may declare land to be freed from such incumbrance. The Court has power afterwards, on notice to persons interested in the fund paid in, to direct transfer thereof.

Sec. 6.—In conveyances made after 1881, the ordinary "general words" formerly inserted after the parcels are deemed to be included.

Sec. 7.—(1.) In conveyances, settlements, assignments, mortgages, &c., made after 1881, if grantor is expressed to convey *as beneficial owner*, the ordinary covenants for title (as heretofore inserted) shall be implied. (2.) Where a conveyance is made by a person *by direction of the beneficial owner*, such beneficial owner shall be deemed to convey as beneficial owner, and covenants on his part shall be implied accordingly. (3.) Where, in a settlement, the grantor conveys *as settlor*, a limited covenant for further assurance is implied. (4.) When any person conveys *as trustee*, or *as mortgagee*, or *as personal representative of a deceased person*, or *as committee of a lunatic*, or *under an order of Court*, a covenant is implied that such person has not incumbered. (5.) Where husband and wife convey *as beneficial owners*, the wife to be deemed to convey by direction of husband, and, in addition to the covenant implied on the part of the wife, there shall be implied (*a*) a covenant on the part of the husband as the person giving that direction, and (*b*) a covenant on the part of the husband in the same terms as the covenant implied on the part of the wife. (6.) Section not to extend to leases at a rent, or to any customary assurance except a deed conferring right to admittance.

Sec. 8.—In sales after 1881, purchaser not to be entitled to require that deed shall be executed in his solicitor's presence, but, *at his own cost*, can nominate a person (who may, if he thinks fit, be his solicitor) to attest vendor's execution.

Sec. 9.—Where a person retains possession of documents and gives to another an *acknowledgment* in writing of the right of that other to production of those documents and to delivery of copies thereof, or an *undertaking* in writing for safe custody thereof, such acknowledgment and undertaking respectively, shall have generally the same effect as the ordinary covenants for the purpose heretofore entered into, and shall satisfy any liability to give any such covenants.

Part III.—*Leases.*

Sec. 10.—In leases made after 1881, the rent and benefit of lessee's covenants and conditions of re-entry are to run with reversion, notwithstanding severance of reversionary estate, and are recoverable and enforceable accordingly.

Sec. 11.—Like provision with regard to the obligations imposed by lessor's covenants.

Sec. 12.—Also on any severance of reversion, every condition, right of re-entry, &c., shall be apportioned.

Sec. 13.—On a contract, made after 1881, to grant a lease for a term of years to be derived out of a leasehold interest with a leasehold reversion, the intended lessee shall not have the right to call for the title to that reversion.

Sec. 14.—(1 and 5.) Lessor cannot enforce a condition of re-entry or forfeiture in lease—except a condition (1) against assigning or underletting, or (2) for forfeiture on bankruptcy or execution,* or (3) on breach of the covenant for inspection in a mining lease, until he has served on lessee a notice specifying breach, and (if capable of remedy) requiring him to remedy same, and demanding compensation, and lessee fails within a reasonable time to comply therewith. (2.) Where lessor is proceeding to enforce any such condition, the Court has power in lessor's action, or in any action brought by lessee, to grant lessee relief on such terms as it shall think fit. (7.) 22 & 23 Vict., c. 35, secs. 4 to 9, and 23 & 24 Vict., c. 126, sec. 2, are repealed. (8.) This section does not affect law relating to re-entry or forfeiture or relief in case of non-payment of rent. (9.) This section applies to all leases whenever made, *and shall have effect notwithstanding any stipulation to the contrary.*

Part IV.—*Mortgages.*

Sec. 15.—In all mortgages (whenever made, and even if

---

* But see sec. 2 of Conveyancing Act 1892, *post* page 27.

expressly stipulated to the contrary) the mortgagee—not having been in possession—is bound (if required) on payment to assign the mortgage debt and transfer the mortgage property to any third person instead of reconveying. (See section 12 of Conveyancing Act 1882, *post*, page 26.)

Sec. 16.—Mortgagor, whilst he has right of redemption, under a mortgage made after 1881, to have right on payment of mortgagee's costs to inspect and make copies, &c., of title deeds.

Sec. 17.—The doctrine of consolidation shall not apply to a mortgage made after 1881, unless the mortgage says otherwise.

Sec. 18.—A mortgagor *in possession*, and a mortgagee *in possession* respectively can make absolutely binding leases as follows :—

An agricultural or occupation lease not exceeding 21 years, and a building lease not exceeding 99 years ; such lease to take effect within 12 months from date, to be at the best rent that can be obtained, without fine, to contain a covenant for payment of rent and condition of re-entry on non-payment for not exceeding 30 days, and a counterpart to be executed by lessee and delivered to lessor ; of which execution and delivery the execution of lease by lessor shall in favour of lessee be sufficient evidence. A building lease must be in consideration of houses or buildings erected or improved &c., or to be erected or improved &c., within 5 years from date ; and a nominal or less rent than that ultimately payable, may be reserved for first 5 years or any part thereof. A mortgagor leasing under this section must, within one month of making the lease, deliver to the mortgagee (or where more than one, to mortgagee first in priority) the counterpart duly executed by lessee ; but the lessee is not to be concerned to see that this provision is complied with. All this is subject to the express provisions of the mortgage deed ; and applies only to mortgages made after 1881, unless otherwise agreed in writing.

Sec. 19.—Mortgagee under deed executed after 1881 has following powers :—*When principal money due*, power of sale in the ordinary way, and also power to appoint a receiver ; and, *at any time after date of deed*, power to insure against fire ; and, *when in possession*, power to cut and sell ripe timber (not planted for shelter or ornament), such sale to be completed within 12 months from the contract. These powers may be varied or extended by the mortgage deed.

Sec. 20.—The said power of sale not to be exercised (1) until default in payment for *three* months after notice served on mortgagor, or one of the several mortgagors, *or* (2) unless interest in arrear for *two* months, *or* (3) there is breach of some other provision in the mortgage deed.

Secs. 21 and 22.—Mortgagee selling under above power can convey whatever interest in the property is the subject of the mortgage* to the purchaser, whose title is not to be impeached, though the sale was not under the circumstances authorised. Money received from sale to be applied in discharging prior incumbrances, then costs of sale, then the mortgage debt with interest and costs, and then any balance to mortgagor. Mortgagee not to be liable for any involuntary loss on sale. The sale may be by any person for the time being entitled to receive and give a discharge for the mortgage money. Mortgagee's receipt to be sufficient discharge to purchaser.

Sec. 23.—Insurance against fire by mortgagee under sec. 19 shall not exceed amount specified in mortgage deed ; or (if no amount specified) two-thirds of the amount required in case of total destruction to restore the property insured. The said power to insure is not to apply where there is a declaration in the mortgage that no insurance is required, *or* where mortgagor keeps up insurance in accordance with the mortgage deed, *or* where the mortgage deed contains no

---

* He cannot convey the legal estate if he has not got it. *Re* Hodson and Howe's Contract, 56 L. J., Ch., 755.

covenant as to insurance but mortgagor insures to the amount which the mortgagee is authorised to insure for. All money received under insurance shall, at the option of mortgagee (and without prejudice to any obligation imposed by law or special contract), be applied in rebuilding, or towards discharge of mortgage debt.

Sec. 24.—(1 to 5.) The power to appoint a receiver conferred by sec. 19 shall not be exercised until mortgagee has become entitled to exercise power of sale given by Act. Then he may be appointed by writing under mortgagee's hand, and in like manner he may be removed and a new receiver appointed. When appointed, receiver to have all full and necessary powers; and to be deemed the agent of the *mortgagor*, who is to be solely responsible for his acts and defaults, unless the mortgage deed otherwise provides. Any person to be safe in paying to receiver. (6.) Receiver may retain out of moneys received—by way of remuneration and in satisfaction of all costs, charges, and expenses incurred by him as receiver—a commission at such rate, not exceeding 5 per cent. on the gross amount received, as is specified in his appointment, and if no rate specified, then at the rate of 5 per cent. on that gross amount, or at such higher rate as the Court, on the receiver's application, thinks fit to allow. (8.) Receiver to apply moneys thus:—(*a*) In discharging rents, rates, outgoings, &c.; (*b*) In keeping down all annual or other payments, and the interest on any principal sums, having priority; (*c*) In payment of his commission, and any premiums on proper policies of insurance, and any necessary or proper repairs directed in writing by the mortgagee; (*d*) In payment of interest accruing due under the mortgage; and (*e*) The residue he shall pay to the person who, but for his possession, would have been entitled to receive the income of the mortgaged property.

Sec. 25.—Any person entitled to redeem can insist on a

judgment for sale, instead of for redemption, if he brings an action for redemption, or for sale, or for sale or redemption in alternative. In any action for foreclosure, sale or redemption, the Court may, on request of any person interested, direct a sale on such terms as it thinks fit, including if it thinks fit, the deposit in Court of a reasonable sum to meet expenses of sale and to secure performance of the terms. In an action brought by a person interested in the right of redemption and seeking a sale, the Court may direct the plaintiff to give security for costs, and may give the conduct of the sale to any defendant, and may give such directions as it thinks fit respecting the costs of the defendants. The Court may direct a sale without previously determining the priorities of any incumbrancers. 15 & 16 Vict., c. 86, sec. 48, is repealed.

Part V.—*Statutory Mortgage.*

Sec. 26.—A mortgage of *freeholds or leaseholds* may be by deed expressed to be made by way of statutory mortgage in the form given in Part I. of Schedule 3 to Act, with such variations as necessary. In such a deed there shall be implied—*(a)* covenants for repayment of principal, and for payment of interest half-yearly, and *(b)* proviso for redemption on payment.

Sec. 27.—(1 and 2.) A transfer of such a statutory mortgage may be by deed, by way of statutory transfer, in such one of the three forms, A, B, and C, given in Part II. of Schedule 3 to Act, as may be appropriate, with such variations as necessary; and such a transfer shall vest in transferee all powers and rights as if he had been original mortgagee. (3) If the transfer is in the form B—*i.e.*, mortgagor joining in transfer—a covenant shall be implied by him to pay the principal money on the next day fixed for payment of interest, and if not then paid to continue to pay interest.

Sec. 28.—On a statutory mortgage or statutory transfer—

if there are several mortgagors or covenantors, any implied covenants are to be deemed joint and several; and if there are several mortgagees or transferees, any implied covenants to be deemed with them jointly, unless mortgage money expressed to be secured in shares or distinct sums, when covenants to be deemed with each severally as regards the sum secured to him.

Sec. 29.—A reconveyance of a statutory mortgage may be by statutory reconveyance, in form given in Part III. of Schedule 3 to Act, with variations as necessary.

Part VI.—*Trust and Mortgage Estates on Death.*

Sec. 30.—If a sole trustee or mortgagee dies after 1881, the trust or mortgage estate* shall, notwithstanding any testamentary disposition, go to his personal representatives, who shall have all proper powers, and shall be deemed, for the purposes of this section, the heirs and assigns of the deceased within the meaning of all trusts and powers. 37 & 38 Vict., c. 78, s. 4, and 38 & 39 Vict., c. 87, s. 48, repealed.

Part VII.—*Trustees and Executors.*

Sec. 31.—When, in trusts created before or after 1881, any trustee is dead, or remains abroad for more than a year, or desires to be discharged, or refuses or is unfit to act, or is incapable of acting, then the person or persons (if any) nominated by the instrument creating the trust, and if none, or none able and willing to act, then the surviving or continuing trustees or trustee, or the personal representatives of the last surviving or continuing trustee, may appoint new trustees or trustee, and so that the original number of trustees may be increased or diminished, but, except when only one trustee was originally appointed, there must be always two

---

* By section 45 of the Copyhold Act 1887, this provision does not apply to trust or mortgage estates in copyholds of inheritance, which still go to the devisee or heir.

trustees to perform the trust. The provision as to a dead trustee includes the case of a trustee under a will predeceasing testator, and that relative to a continuing trustee includes a refusing or retiring trustee. This section is subject to any contrary intention, or any terms or provisions, in the trust instrument. (See also 1882 Act, sec. 5, and 1892 Act, sec. 6, *post*, pages 23 and 28.)

Sec. 32.—When, in trusts created before or after 1881, there are more than two trustees, if one by deed declares that he is desirous of being discharged, and if his co-trustees and any other person empowered to appoint trustees consent by deed to his discharge and to the vesting in the co-trustees alone of the trust property, then the trustee desirous of being discharged shall be deemed to have retired, and shall by the deed be discharged from the trust, without any new trustee being appointed in his place. This is subject to any contrary intention, or any terms or provisions, in the trust instrument.

Sec. 33.—When the Court appoints new trustees, any such new trustee shall *as well before* as after the trust property becomes properly vested in him, have all powers, &c., as if he had been originally trustee.

Sec. 34.—In deeds executed after 1881, either appointing a new trustee or discharging a retiring trustee, a mere declaration that the trust property shall vest in the new trustee or continuing trustee, as the case may be, shall have all the effect of a conveyance or assignment. But this does not apply to (1) copyholds, (2) mortgages, and (3) shares, stocks, &c.—all of which must still be separately conveyed.

Sec. 35.—In trusts created after 1881, and subject to any contrary provision or intention in the instrument, trustees having a power of sale may sell or concur with any other person in selling all or any part of the property, subject to prior charges or not, by public auction or private contract, and generally as they think fit.

Sec. 36.—Trustees' receipts for any money, securities, or other personal property, payable or deliverable to them under their trust, to be a sufficient discharge.

Sec. 37.—In all executorships and trusts existing either before or after 1881, and subject to the provisions or intentions of the trust instrument—executors may pay or allow any debt or claim on any evidence they think sufficient; and one executor, or two or more trustees acting together, or a sole acting trustee where authorised to act by himself, shall have full power to accept compositions, or take security for debts, or to allow time, or submit to arbitration, or release or settle debts, &c., provided any such act done in good faith. This section does not apply to an administrator. *In re* Clay and Tetley, 16 Ch. D., 3.]

Sec. 38.—In executorships and trusts constituted after or created by instruments coming into operation after 1881, powers given to two or more executors or trustees jointly, may, unless contrary expressed, be exercised by survivor or survivors.

Part VIII.—*Married Women.*

Sec. 39.— Notwithstanding a married woman is restrained from anticipation, the Court may, if it think fit, where it appears to be for her benefit, by judgment or order, with her consent, bind her property.

Sec. 40.—A married woman, whether an infant or not, shall have power to appoint an attorney to execute any deed or do any act which she herself might execute or do.

Part IX.—*Infants.*

Sec. 41.—Where an infant is entitled to a fee simple, or to any leasehold interest at a rent, the land to be deemed a settled estate within the Settled Estates Act 1877.

Sec. 42.—When under an instrument coming into operation after 1881, an infant is beneficially entitled to possession of any land, and, if a woman, unmarried, the trustees under settlement, or trustees appointed by the Court on the application of guardian or next friend of infant, may enter into and continue in possession of the land, and shall then have full powers to cut timber in usual course for sale or repairs, to pull down and rebuild houses, &c., and generally manage the property in the same way that infant might, if of full age, and may apply the income in keeping down expenses of management and (at their discretion) for maintenance of infant, and shall invest and accumulate the residue in trust for infant on attaining 21, or, if a woman, married whilst an infant, for her separate use, or if infant dies, in trust for the parties then entitled. These provisions only apply so far as no contrary intention in the instrument under which infant derives the property.

Sec. 43.—Trustee (under any instrument operating either before or after 1881) shall, unless instrument says otherwise, have absolute discretion to apply income for the maintenance, education, or benefit of any infant either absolutely or contingently entitled, and may for this purpose resort to accumulations of past years.

Part X.—Rent Charges, &c.

Sec. 44.—A person entitled to a rent charge, or other similar annual payment, *under some instrument coming into operation after* 1881 has the following powers to recover and enforce it :—(*a*) If in arrear for 21 days, power of distress; (*b*) If in arrear for 40 days, power to enter into possession and take income till satisfaction; (*c*) If in arrear for 40 days—instead of or in addition to (b)—power to demise the land to a trustee for a term of years on trust, by mortgage or sale or demise of the term, to raise the money to satisfy him. These powers are subject to any contrary provisions or intention in the instrument.

Sec. 45.—Any quit rent, chief rent, rent charge, or other annual sum issuing out of lands,—which is perpetual and is *not* tithe rent charge, or rent reserved on a sale or lease, or rent payable under a grant or licence for building purposes—can be redeemed by the landowner. He must obtain a certificate from the Land Department of the Board of Agriculture of the amount to be paid for redemption; and then, after one month's notice to the person entitled to the rent, pay or tender the amount certified; and the Department then give a conclusive certificate that rent is redeemed.

Part XI.—*Powers of Attorney.*

Sec. 46.—Person executing a deed under a power of attorney may execute either in his own name, or in the name of the donor of the power.

Sec. 47.—Attorney not to be liable for any payment made, or other act done by him, *bonâ fide*, under a power without notice of donor's death, lunacy, bankruptcy, or revocation. But this does not affect any right against the person to whom money has been paid.

Sec. 48.—Powers of attorney, on their execution being verified, may be deposited in the Central Office of Supreme Court of Judicature; and an office copy thereof is sufficient evidence of the contents of the instrument and its deposit there. (Rules of Court may be made for carrying out this section.)

Part XII.—*Construction and Effect of Deeds, &c.*

Sec. 49.—In conveyances, either before or after 1881, the word "Grant" is not necessary to convey any tenements or hereditaments.

Sec. 50.—After 1881, freehold land, or a chose in action may be conveyed by one person direct to himself and another; or by a husband to wife, or wife to husband, either alone or jointly with others.

Sec. 51.—After 1881, to pass a fee simple, the words " in fee simple" to be sufficient without word " heirs;" and to create an estate tail, the words "in tail" to be sufficient without the words "heirs of the body;" and to create an estate in tail male or female, the words "in tail male," or "in tail female," to be sufficient.

Sec. 52.—Any person entitled to a power, whether coupled with an interest or not, may, by deed, release or contract not to exercise it. (See also sec. 6 of 1882 Act, *post*, page 24.)

Sec. 53.—A deed expressed to be supplemental to another shall be read and have effect as if endorsed thereon, or as if it contained a full recital thereof.

Secs. 54, 55.—In deeds executed after 1881, receipt for consideration in the body of deed is sufficient without a receipt endorsed; and any receipt, whether in body or endorsed, shall be sufficient evidence of payment to satisfy any subsequent purchaser not having actual notice of non-payment.

Sec. 56.—A solicitor in completing a purchase, &c., need not produce an authority from his client to receive the money, but his production of the deed duly executed, with receipt thereon, shall be sufficient authority for payment to him."

Sec. 57.—Deeds in the form in Schedule 4, or in like form, or using like expressions, shall be sufficient.

Sec. 58.—Covenants made after 1881—(*a*) relating to lands of inheritance, shall be deemed to be made with the covenantee, his heirs and assigns, and (*b*) relating to other lands, shall be deemed to be made with the covenantee, his executors, administrators, and assigns.

Sec. 59.—A covenant and a contract under seal made after 1881 (including a covenant implied under Act) shall, unless otherwise stated, bind the heirs and real estate (without naming them) as well as the personal representatives and personal estate of the covenantor.

---

* This is extended to cases where the vendors are trustees, by sec. 2 of the Trustee Act 1888, as from 1st January, 1889.

Sec. 60.—A covenant made after 1881 with two or more jointly shall (unless otherwise stated) enure for the benefit of the survivor or survivors, and any other person on whom the right to sue devolves.

Sec. 61.—In a mortgage, transfer of mortgage, &c., made after 1881, and subject to any contrary intention expressed in the instrument, when money is expressed to be advanced on joint account, or when the instrument is made to more persons than one jointly and not in shares, the money shall be deemed to belong to the mortgagees or transferees, &c., on a joint account as between them and the mortgagor or obligor; and the receipt of the survivors or survivor or personal representative of the last survivor shall be a complete discharge, notwithstanding any notice to the payer of a severance of the joint account.

Sec. 62.—Where, after 1881, freeholds are conveyed to the use that any person shall have an easement thereout, it shall operate to vest such easement in that person.

Sec. 63.—In conveyances made after 1881, and subject to any contrary intention, "all the estate" clause is deemed to be included.

Sec. 64.—In construing any covenant or proviso implied under this Act, words importing singular or plural number, or the masculine gender, shall be read as also importing the plural or singular number, or as extending to females, as case may require.

Part XIII.—*Long Term.*

Sec. 65.—Where a residue unexpired of not less than 200 years of a term, which, as originally created, was for not less than 300 years, is subsisting in land without any trust or right of redemption, and without there being (either originally, or by release, or other means) any rent, or with merely a peppercorn rent or other rent having no money value, incident to the reversion, then the term may be enlarged into a fee simple (to be subject, however, to the same trusts, powers, &c., as the term) by the execution of a deed containing a declaration to that effect by *(a)* Any person beneficially entitled in right of the term, whether subject to any incumbrance or not, to possession of any land comprised in the term, but, in case of a married woman, with the concurrence of her husband, unless she is entitled for her separate use (whether with restraint on anticipation or not) and then without his concurrence ; *(b)* Any person being in receipt of income as trustee in right of the term, or having the term vested in him in trust for sale, whether subject to any incumbrance or not ; or *(c)* Any person in whom, as personal representative of a deceased person, the term is vested, whether subject to any incumbrance or not. (See sec. 11 of 1882 Act, *post*, page 26.)

Part XIV.—*Adoption of Act.*

Sec. 66.—All persons, whether solicitors, trustees, or the parties concerned themselves, adopting the provisions of the Act to be protected in doing so.

Part XV.—*Miscellaneous.*

Sec. 67.—All notices required by this Act must be in writing, and may be served by being left at a person's last known place of abode or business ; or, if to be served on a lessee or mortgagee, by being left for him on the land or at any house or building comprised in the lease or mortgage, or in case of a mining lease by being left at office or counting-house of the mine ; or by sending through the post a registered letter, directed to the party by name at aforesaid place of abode, business, or counting-house, provided letter is not returned through the post undelivered

Sec. 68.—5 & 6 Wm. IV., c. 62, may be cited by the short title of The Statutory Declarations Act 1835 in any declaration made under or by virtue of that Act, or in any other document, or in any Act of Parliament.

Part XVI.—Court, Procedure, Orders.

Sec. 69.—(1.) All matters within the jurisdiction of the Court under this Act shall be assigned to the Chancery Division. (3.) Every application under the Act, except where otherwise expressed, shall be by summons at chambers. (8.) Rules for purposes of Act to be deemed Rules of Court under sec. 17 of Appellate Jurisdiction Act 1876 (39 & 40 Vict., c. 59, sec. 17.)

Sec. 70.—(1.) An order of the Court under any statutory or other jurisdiction, shall not, as against a purchaser, be invalidated on the ground of want of jurisdiction, or want of any consent, notice, or service.

Part XVII.—Repeals.

Sec. 71.—8 & 9 Vict., c. 119, and 23 & 24 Vict., c. 145, secs. 11 to 30, are repealed; but this is not to affect the validity or invalidity, or any operation, effect, or consequence of any instrument executed or made, or of anything done or suffered, before the commencement of this Act, or any action, proceeding, or thing then pending or uncompleted; and every such action, proceeding, and thing may be carried on and completed as if there had been no such repeal in this Act.

Part XVIII.—Relates to Ireland.

(The Schedules containing Forms are omitted.)

---

45 & 46 VICT., C. 39.
The Conveyancing Act 1882.
(*Commencement of Act,* 1st *January,* 1883.)

Sec. 1.—*Purchaser* includes a lessee or mortgagee, or an

intending mortgagee, or other person, who for valuable con‐
sideration takes or deals for property; and *purchase* has a
meaning corresponding with that of purchaser.

Searches.

Sec. 2.—Searches for judgments, deeds, or other
documents, whereof entries are allowed or required to be
made in the Central Office, may be made by an official; and
certificate of result of search shall be conclusive in favour of
a purchaser; and a solicitor obtaining an office copy of any
such certificate shall not be answerable in respect of any loss
that may arise from error in the certificate.

Notice.

Sec. 3.—(1.) A purchaser shall not be prejudicially
affected by notice of any instrument, fact, or thing, unless—

(i.) It is within his own knowledge; or would have come
to his knowledge, if such inquiries and inspections
had been made, as ought reasonably to have been made
by him; or

(ii.) In the same transaction with respect to which a
question of notice to the purchaser arises—it has come
to the knowledge of his counsel, as such; or of his
solicitor, or other agent, as such; or would have come
to the knowledge of his solicitor, or other agent, as
such, if such inquiries and inspections had been made
as ought reasonably to have been made by the solicitor
or other agent.

This section applies to purchases before or after this Act.

Separate Trustees.

Sec. 5.—On an appointment of new trustees—no matter
when the trust was created—a separate set of trustees may
be appointed for any part of the trust property held on trusts
distinct from those relating to any other part or parts of the
trust property; or if only one trustee was originally appointed,

then one separate trustee may be so appointed for the first-mentioned part. (See sec. 6 of 1892 Act, *post*, page 28.)

Powers.

Sec. 6.—(1.) A person to whom any power (whether coupled with an interest or not) is given, may, by deed, disclaim the power; and, after disclaimer, shall not be capable of exercising or joining in the exercise of the power; and on such disclaimer, the power may be exercised by the other or others, or the survivors or survivor of the others, of the persons to whom the power is given, unless the contrary is expressed in the instrument creating the power. This section applies to powers created by instruments coming into operation either before or after this Act.

Married Women.

Sec. 7.—(1.) In section 79 of the Fines and Recoveries Act, there shall be substituted for the words, "two of the perpetual commissioners, or two special commissioners," the words, "one of the perpetual commissioners," or "one special commissioner;" and in sec. 83 of the Fines and Recoveries Act there shall be substituted for the word "persons" the word "person," and for the word "commissioners" the words "a commissioner;" and all other provisions of those Acts, and all other enactments having reference in any manner to the sections aforesaid, shall be read and have effect accordingly.

(2.) Where the memorandum of acknowledgment by a married woman of a deed purports to be signed by a person authorised to take the acknowledgment, the deed shall, as regards execution by the married woman, take effect at the time of acknowledgment, and shall be conclusively taken to have been duly acknowledged.

(3.) A deed acknowledged before or after this Act by a married woman, before a judge of the High Court of Justice in England, or before a judge of a county court in England, or before a perpetual commissioner or a special commissioner, shall not be impeached or impeachable by reason only that such judge or commissioner was interested or concerned either as a party, or as solicitor, or clerk to the solicitor, for one of the parties, or otherwise, in the transaction giving occasion for the acknowledgment.

(4.) 3 & 4 William IV., c. 74, sec. 84, from "and the same judge" to the end of the section and sections 85 to 88 inclusive, and 17 & 18 Vict., c. 75, are repealed.

(5.) This section applies only to the execution of deeds by married women after 1882.

Powers of Attorney.

Secs. 8, 9.—(*a*) If a power of attorney, given for valuable consideration, is in the instrument creating the power expressed to be irrevocable, or (*b*) if a power of attorney (whether given for valuable consideration or not) is in the instrument creating the power expressed to be irrevocable for a fixed time therein specified, not exceeding one year from the date of the instrument—then, in favour of a purchaser, the power shall not be revoked at any time, or during the fixed period as the case may be, either by anything done by the donor of the power without the concurrence of the donee of the power, or by the death, marriage, lunacy, unsoundness of mind, or bankruptcy of the donor of the power; and any act done at any time, or during the fixed time as the case may be, by the donee of the power, in pursuance of the power shall be as valid as if anything done by the donor of the power without the concurrence of the donee of the power, or the death, marriage, lunacy, unsoundness of mind, or bankruptcy of the donor of the power, had not been done or happened; and neither the donee of the power nor the purchaser shall at any time be prejudicially affected by notice of anything done by the donor of the power without the concurrence of the donee of the power, or of the death, marriage, lunacy, unsoundness of mind, or bankruptcy of the donor of the power. This section applies only to powers of attorney created by instruments executed after 1882.

Executory Limitations.

Sec. 10.—Where there is a person entitled—under an instrument coming into operation after 1882—to land for an estate in fee, or for a term of years absolute or determinable on life, or for term of life, with an executory limitation over on default or failure of all or any of his issue, whether within or at any specified period or time or not, that executory limitation shall become void and incapable of taking effect, as soon as there is living any issue who has attained the age of twenty-one years, of the class on default or failure whereof the limitation over was to take effect.

Long Terms.

Sec. 11.—Section 65 of the Conveyancing Act 1881 shall apply to and include every term in that section mentioned, whether having as the immediate reversion thereon the freehold or not; but not—

(i.) Any term liable to be determined by re-entry for condition broken; or

(ii.) Any term created by sub-demise out of a superior term, itself incapable of being enlarged into a fee simple.

Mortgages.

Sec. 12.—The right of the mortgagor, under section 15 of the Conveyancing Act 1881, to require a mortgagee, instead of re-conveying, to assign the mortgage debt and convey the mortgaged property to a third person, can be enforced by each incumbrancer, or by the mortgagor, notwithstanding any intermediate incumbrance; but a requisition of an incumbrancer shall prevail over a requisition of the mortgagor; and, as between incumbrancers, a requisition of a prior incumbrancer shall prevail over that of a subsequent incumbrancer.

Saving.

Sec. 13.—The repeal by this Act of any enactment shall not affect anything that has taken place before 1883.

---

55 & 56 Vict., C. 13.
Conveyancing and Law of Property Act 1892.
(Commencement of Act, 20th June, 1892.)

An Act of six sections to amend the Conveyancing Act 1881.

Sec. 2.—*Leases, underleases, forfeiture.*—(1.) A lessor can recover as a debt due from the lessee (in addition to any damages) his reasonable costs properly incurred to a solicitor and surveyor, or valuer, or otherwise, in reference to any breach giving a right of re-entry or forfeiture which at the lessee's request is waived by the lessor, or from which the lessee is relieved under the Conveyancing Act 1881, or this Act.

(2.) The provision in section 14 of the Conveyancing Act 1881, that there is to be no relief against a condition for forfeiture of a lease on bankruptcy of the lessee or on taking in execution of the lessee's interest, shall apply only after the end of a year from the bankruptcy or execution and provided the lessee's interest be not sold within such year [*i.e.*, you can get relief (1) always within the year, or (2) after the year, if the interest is sold during the year]; but this provision does not apply to a lease of a farm, or minerals, or a public-house or beershop, or a furnished dwelling-house, or any property as to which the personal qualifications of the tenant are important to preserve the value or character of the property, or because of the neighbourhood of the lessor or his tenants.

Sec. 3.—*No fine to be exacted for license to assign.*—A condition in a lease against assigning or under-letting without license shall (*unless the lease expressly says otherwise*) be deemed to include a proviso that no fine shall be payable for such license, but that reasonable legal or other expenses in relation to such license shall be paid.

Sec. 4.—*Court may protect underlessee on forfeiture of superior lease.*—Where a lessor *is proceeding* by action or otherwise to enforce a right of re-entry or forfeiture under the lease, the Court *may*, on application by any underlessee either in the lessor's action or a separate action, make an order vesting in such underlessee all or any part of the property leased for the residue of the lease or a shorter term on such terms as the Court thinks fit. The underlessee cannot require a lease for a term longer than his under-lease [but apparently he may ask for it and the Court may give it].

Sec. 5.—*Definitions.*—In this Act, and in section 14 of the Conveyancing Act 1881, *lease* shall include an agreement for a lease where the lessee has become entitled to have his lease granted, and *underlease* shall similarly include an agreement therefor. In this Act [*i.e.*, in section 4] *underlessee* includes any one deriving title under or from an underlessee.

Sec. 6.—*Trustees.*—A separate set of trustees (or a separate trustee) may be appointed, under section 5 of the Conveyancing Act 1882, of a part only of the trust property, *although no new trustees (or trustee) are to be appointed of other parts of the trust property;* and any existing trustee may be appointed or remain one of such separate set of trustees; and every appointment already made of a separate set of trustees shall be valid, although there was no retiring trustee of other parts of the trust property and no new trustees were appointed of such other parts.

45 & 46 Vict., C. 38.
The Settled Land Act 1882.
(Commencement of Act, 1st January, 1883.)

Sec. 2.—*Settlement* in this Act means any deed, will, agreement, Act of Parliament, instrument, or number of instruments whether made or passed before or after this Act, whereby land stands limited to persons by way of succession. *Settled land* is land, and any estate or interest therein, which is the subject of a settlement. *Tenant for life* is the person for the time being beneficially entitled to possession of settled land for life; and, if more than one, they together. *Trustees of settlement* are the persons who under the settlement are trustees with power of sale or of consenting to sale, *or* (if none) persons declared trustees by the settlement, *or* (if none) persons named in sec. 16 of 1890 Act, *post*, p. 44, *or* (if none) persons appointed by Court.

Secs. 3, 4.—A tenant for life is to have a general power to sell, enfranchise, exchange, or make partition of the settled estate at the best price or consideration that can reasonably be obtained. The sale may be by public auction or private contract, together or in lots, with power to fix reserved biddings, and buy in at auction. Settled land in England must not be exchanged for land out of England.

Sec. 5.—On a sale, exchange, or partition, the tenant for life may, *with consent of the incumbrancer*, transfer an incumbrance from the land sold, exchanged, or partitioned on to any other part of the settled land whether already charged therewith or not.

Secs. 6, 7.—A tenant for life can make a building lease not exceeding 99 years,* a mining lease not exceeding 60 years, and any other lease not exceeding 21 years. Such leases to be by deed, to take effect within 12 months from date, at the best

---

* Note that by the Settled Land Act 1889 (52 & 53 Vict., c. 36) such a lease may contain an option to the lessee to purchase the fee simple within a term not exceeding 10 years at a price named in the lease.

rent that can reasonably be obtained with power to take a fine (which by the 1884 Act is capital money), to contain a covenant for payment of rent, and condition of re-entry on non-payment within a time not exceeding 30 days, and a counterpart to be executed by lessee; but the execution of the lease by the tenant for life to be sufficient evidence of this last point.

Secs. 8-11.—Every building lease to be partly in consideration of the erection or improvement or putting into repair of buildings; a nominal rent may be reserved for first five years. On contracts for building leases in lots, the entire rent may be apportioned among the lots; but rent on each lease must not be less than 10s., and must not exceed one-fifth of annual value of land in such lease after erecting the buildings. In a mining lease, the rent may be made ascertainable, or to vary, according to acreage worked or minerals obtained. In both mining and building leases, on application to the Court, and showing that it is customary to do so, or that it is difficult to make leases otherwise, the Court may authorise the granting of leases for longer terms, or even in perpetuity, on conditions expressed in the order. Under a mining lease, there shall always be set aside, as capital money, part of the rent, viz., when the tenant for life is impeachable for waste, three-fourths, and otherwise, one-fourth thereof.

Sec. 12.—The tenant for life may grant a lease to carry out a binding contract made by his predecessor, or under a binding covenant for renewal, or to confirm a void or voidable lease.

Sec. 13.—The tenant for life may accept a surrender of any lease either as to all or part only of the property.

Sec. 14.—Tenant for life of a settled manor may grant licences to copyhold tenants to make any such leases as he might make of freeholds; such licence may fix the annual value whereon fines and other customary payments are to be assessed, and must be entered on the court rolls of the manor.

Sec. 15.—Replaced by sec. 10 of 1890 Act, *post*, p. 42.

Sec. 16.—On a sale or grant or lease for building purposes the tenant for life, for the general benefit of the residents on the settled land (or any part thereof), may appropriate portions thereof for streets, roads, paths, squares, gardens, or other open places, and may execute any deed necessary for vesting them in any trustees or any company or public body. Such deed must be enrolled in the central office.

Sec. 17.—A sale, exchange, partition, or mining lease may be of land without minerals, or *vice versâ*; or of all or any of the minerals, &c.

Sec. 18.—*Mortgage.*—The tenant for life may mortgage to raise money required for enfranchisement, or for equality of exchange or partition, and the sum raised shall be capital money. [Also to pay costs under secs. 36 & 47; also under sec. 11 of 1890 Act.]

Sec. 20.—On a sale, exchange, partition, lease, mortgage, or charge, the tenant for life may convey the land (including *copyholds*, and leaseholds vested in trustees, and easements) by deed. Such deed passes the land, subject to (1) interests having priority over the settlement, (2) interests created under the settlement for securing money already raised, and (3) rights previously granted for value under the settlement. As to copyholds, the deed is sufficient without surrender, and admittance must be made thereunder; but the steward may require production of so much of the settlement as shows the title of the tenant for life and enter that on the court rolls.

Secs. 21-23.—Capital money arising under this Act (in addition to any particular purpose for which it is raised) may be applied as follows: In investment on Government or other securities in which trustees may invest either by law or under the settlement, or in debenture stock of any railway company in Great Britain or Ireland, provided it has for the ten preceding years paid a dividend on its ordinary stock; in discharge of incumbrances, land-tax, &c., on the settled land; in payment for any improvement* authorised by this Act (see sec. 25), or for equality of exchange or partition; in purchase of the seignory, reversion, or freehold in fee of any part of the settled land; in purchase of lands or mines or minerals in fee or of customary or copyhold tenure, or of leaseholds having not less than 60 years to run (but capital money arising from land in England not to be applied in purchase of land out of England, unless specially allowed by the settlement—sec. 23); in payment to any person becoming absolutely entitled; in payment of any costs or expenses in connection with any of the powers under this Act; and in any other mode in which money produced by the exercise of a power of sale in the settlement is applicable thereunder.

Sec. 22.—For the purpose of being invested or applied as specified in last section, capital money is to be paid to the trustees of the settlement, or into Court, at option of tenant for life; and investment or application to be according to direction of tenant for life, or in default, at trustees' discretion, subject to any direction in the settlement. Capital money, before investment or application, to be deemed and treated as land; and the income of any capital money is to go as the income of the land would have gone under the settlement.

Sec. 25.—This section enumerates the improvements

---

* By the Settled Land Act 1887 (50 & 51 Vict., c. 30), when any improvement authorised by the 1882 Act has been made—before or after 23rd August, 1887—and a rent-charge (temporary or perpetual) created under any statute to pay for it, capital money may be used to redeem or pay such rent-charge, and shall then be deemed to be applied for an improvement authorised by the 1882 Act, and sec. 28 of 1882 Act shall apply accordingly.

authorised by the Act for application of capital money. No less than twenty different kinds are given of which may be mentioned the following : Draining, warping, irrigation, inclosing, reclaiming, building farmhouses, farm cottages or saw mills, or construction of reservoirs, tramways, railways, canals, docks, jetties, piers, market places, streets, roads, trial pits for mines, &c.

Sec. 26.—A tenant for life desirous of applying capital money in improvements is to submit a scheme for approval to the trustees of the settlement, or the Court, showing proposed expenditure. Where the capital money is in trustees' hands, they may pay it for such improvements on production of (*a*) a certificate of the land commissioners (see sec. 48) that the works are properly executed and what amount is properly payable thereunder, *or* (*b*) a like certificate of a competent engineer or practical surveyor, nominated by the trustees and approved by the commissioners, *or* (*c*) an order of the Court. Where the capital money is in Court, the scheme has first to be approved by the Court, and then money to be paid on an order of the Court, which will be granted on either of such certificates as already mentioned, or on such other evidence as the Court thinks fit.

Sec. 28.—Tenant for life must maintain, repair, and insure against fire, any such improvements, at his own cost ; and must not cut timber planted as an improvement, except for proper thinning.

Sec. 29.—In executing, maintaining, or repairing any improvement authorised by this Act, the tenant for life, or any other person, not to be liable for waste, and may cut down and use timber and other trees not planted or left standing for shelter or ornament.

Secs. 30, 32, 33.—The improvements allowed by this Act are to be also allowed and to be deemed included in the Improvement of Land Act 1864 (27 & 28 Vict., c. 114, sec. 9) : and in the Land Clauses Consolidation Acts 1845 (8 & 9 Vict.,

c. 18), 1860 (23 & 24 Vict., c. 106), and 1869 (32 & 33 Vict., c. 18); and in the Settled Estates Act 1877 (40 & 41 Vict., c. 18); and in all settlements in which money is in the hands of trustees to be laid out in the purchase of lands.

Sec. 31.—In the same way that the tenant for life may make leases and sales, so also he may contract therefor, and may revoke such contracts and enter into fresh ones, as if he were absolute owner, and every contract shall be enforceable in favour of, or against, successors.

Sec. 34.—Trustees or the Court may require and cause the purchase-money paid in respect of a lease, or of any estate less than a fee simple, or in respect of a reversion dependent on any such lease, to be laid out, invested, and accumulated in such manner as, in the judgment of the trustees or the Court, will give to the persons interested in that money the like benefit therefrom as they might lawfully have had from the lease, estate, or reversion in respect whereof the money was paid, or as near thereto as may be.

Sec. 35.—A tenant for life, though impeachable for waste, may, with the consent of the trustees of the settlement or an order of the Court, cut and sell timber ripe and fit for cutting; but three-fourths of the net proceeds to be set aside as capital moneys, and the residue only to go as rents or profits.

Sec. 36.—The Court may, if it thinks fit, approve of any action, defence, petition to Parliament, parliamentary opposition or other proceeding taken or proposed to be taken for protection of settled land, or of any action or proceedings for recovery of such land; and direct the costs in connection therewith to be paid out of the settled estate. (Note—This section is instead of sec. 17 of 40 & 41 Vict. c. 18, which is repealed. See *post*, sec. 64.)

Sec. 37.—Heirlooms—*i.e.*, personal chattels settled on trust to devolve with the land—may, by an order of the Court, be sold by tenant for life: but the proceeds to be capital moneys, and to be dealt with as before authorised, or to be invested in purchase of other heirlooms.

Secs. 38, 39.—In default of trustees under a settlement, the Court may, on application of tenant for life, appoint new trustees; and they, or the survivors, or the personal representatives of the survivor, shall be deemed the trustees of the settlement; but no capital money shall be paid to less than two trustees, unless the settlement specially authorises it being paid to one only.

Secs. 40-43.—Trustees' receipts to be full and sufficient discharges. Each trustee to be liable for his own acts only, and not where he has only joined for conformity. No trustee to be liable for giving consents, or for omitting to take action upon notices received, or for dealings with land. Trustees may reimburse themselves expenses.

Sec. 44.—In case of difference arising between tenant for life and trustees of settlement, respecting any powers or any matters under this Act, either party can apply to the Court to give directions respecting the matter in difference and the costs.

Sec. 45.—Tenant for life intending to exercise any of the powers conferred by this Act shall send by registered post, not less than one month before he acts, a notice thereof to each trustee at his usual place of abode, and, if he knows the trustees' solicitor, to such solicitor also at his usual place of business. There must not, at the time of this notice, be less than two trustees, unless allowed by the settlement. A person dealing in good faith with the tenant for life is not concerned to enquire as to whether such notice has been given. (See amendment of this section by sec. 5 of the Settled Land Act 1884, *post*, page 39.)

Sec. 46.—The section contains regulations respecting payments into Court, applications, &c., of which the following are the chief:—Matters under the Act are assigned to the Chancery Division; payment into Court to be an effectual exoneration; applications to be made to the Court by petition,* or by summons in chambers; on an application by trustees of settlement notice to be served in first instance on tenant for life, and then on such persons as the Court shall think fit; general rules under the Act may be made, and to be deemed rules of Court. The County Court of the district where the settled estate is situate, or from where the capital money arises, or in connection with which personal chattels are settled, is to have jurisdiction under this Act, where capital money, or securities in which it is invested, or the value of the settled estate does not exceed £500, and the annual rateable value of the settled estate does not exceed £30 per annum.

Sec. 47.—Any costs, charges, or expenses may be directed by the Court to be paid out of income, or out of capital money, or raised by means of sale or mortgage out of the settled estate.

Secs. 48, 49.—The Inclosure Commissioners for England and Wales, the Copyhold Commissioners, and the Tithe Commissioners for England and Wales, shall by virtue of this Act, become and be styled, the *Land Commissioners for England*.† Every certificate and report approved and made by the Land Commissioners under this Act shall be filed in their office, and office copies shall be delivered out on application, and shall be sufficient evidence thereof.

Secs. 50-52.—The powers under this Act of a tenant for life are not capable of assignment or release, by express act or by operation of law; but remain exerciseable by tenant for life, notwithstanding assignment of his estate—except that, if tenant for life has assigned his estate for

---

* The Settled Land Act Rules say that all applications may be made by summons in chambers, and if a petition is presented without direction of a judge, only the costs of a summons shall be allowed. (Rule 2.)

† Now the Land Department of the Board of Agriculture. 52 & 53 Vict., c. 30.

value, this section shall not operate to assignee's prejudice, and his rights shall not be affected without his consent, but, if the assignee is not in possession, tenant for life still to have the power of making leases without taking a fine. Any contract by tenant for life not to exercise his powers under this Act is void, and any prohibition in the settlement or provision for forfeiture on exercise of such powers also void.

Sec. 53.—Tenant for life in exercising powers under this Act, to have the duties and liabilities of a trustee for all parties entitled under the settlement.

Sec. 54.—On sale, exchange, partition, lease, mortgage, or charge, under this Act, persons dealing *bonâ fide* to be conclusively taken, as against all parties interested under settlement, to have given the best price, consideration or rent, and to have complied with all requisitions of this Act.

Sec. 56.—All other powers subsisting under any settlement or statute or otherwise, exerciseable by tenant for life, or his trustees, to be still existing, and the powers conferred by this Act to be cumulative, but, in case of any conflict, provisions of this Act to prevail; and, accordingly, the consent of tenant for life shall, by virtue of this Act, be necessary to the exercise by trustees, or other persons, of any power conferred by the settlement exerciseable for any purpose provided for in this Act. Should any doubts arise on matters within this section, the Court may, on application of the trustees, or the tenant for life, or other person interested give its decision, opinion, advice, or direction thereon. (See Settled Land Act 1884, sec. 6, *post*, page 40.)

Sec. 57.—A settlement may confer powers larger than, or additional to, those contained in Act.

Sec. 58.—Each person, as follows, shall, when his estate or interest is in possession, have the powers of, and be deemed (for the purpose of the Act) to be a tenant for life, viz.:—(1) Any tenant in tail—except a tenant in tail of land purchased by money provided by Parliament in consideration of public services, who is restrained by Act of Parliament from barring his entail, the reversion being in the Crown. (2) A tenant in fee simple with an executory limitation over. (3) The owner of a base fee. (4, 5 and 6) A tenant for years terminable on life, or a tenant *pur autre vie* not holding merely under a lease at rent. (7) A tenant in tail after possibility of issue extinct. (8) A tenant by curtesy. (9) A person entitled to income of land under a trust or direction to pay it to him for a life, whether subject to costs of management or not, or until sale of land, or until forfeiture of his interest on bankruptcy or any other event.

Secs. 59, 60.—When an infant is in his own right entitled to land, for the purposes of this Act, the land is to be deemed settled land, and the infant a tenant for life. When an infant is tenant for life, the powers may be exercised by the trustees of the settlement, and (if none) by such person and in such manner as the Court, on application of the guardian or next friend of the infant, either generally or in a particular instance, orders.

Sec. 61.—When a married woman is tenant for life and is entitled for her separate use, then she, without her husband, to have the powers of a tenant for life. If entitled not for her separate use, then she and her husband together to have the powers. A restraint on anticipation not to prevent married woman's exercise of the powers of this Act.

Sec. 62.—When tenant for life is a lunatic, so found by inquisition, his committee, under order of Chancellor or other person entrusted by Queen's Sign Manual with the care of the persons and estates of lunatics, may exercise the powers of this Act.

Sec. 63.—Land subject to a trust or direction for sale, and the application and disposal of the sale money, or the income thereof, or the income until sale, or any part of such money or income, for the benefit of one or more for life shall be deemed settled land; and the person beneficially entitled for the time being to the income shall be deemed tenant for life; and the persons (if any) who are under the settlement trustees for sale of the settled land, or have power to consent to the sale, or if no such trustees, then the persons (if any) who are by the settlement declared to be trustees thereof for purposes of this Act, are, for the purpose of this Act, trustees of the settlement. (See amendment to this section by the Settled Land Act 1884, secs. 6, 7, *post*, pages 40, 41.)

Sec. 64 repeals 23 & 24 Vict., c. 145, Parts I. and IV., being the residue of the Act which the Conveyancing Act 1881 did not repeal; 27 & 28 Vict., c. 114, secs. 17 and 18, and sec. 21, from "either by a party" to "benefice or" inclusive; and from "or, if the landowner" to "minor or minors" inclusive; and, "or circumstance," twice; and (except as regards Scotland) 40 & 41 Vict., c. 18, sec. 17.

---

47 & 48 Vict., C. 18.

The Settled Land Act 1884.

(Commencement of Act, 3rd July, 1884.)

Sec. 3.—This Act is to be construed as one with the Settled Land Act 1882.

Sec. 4.—A fine received on the grant of a lease under the Act of 1882, is to be deemed capital money under that Act.

Sec. 5.—(1.) The notice, required by sec. 45 of the 1882 Act, of intention to make a sale, exchange, partition, or lease, may be notice of a general intention.

(2.) On the request of the trustees, the tenant for life must furnish such particulars and information as may be reasonably required of him as to sales, exchanges, partitions, or leases effected, or in progress, or immediately intended.

(3.) A trustee may, by writing, waive notice or accept less than a month's notice.

Sec. 6.—(1.) In the case of a settlement within the meaning of sec. 63 of the 1882 Act, any consent not required by the terms of the settlement is not, by force of anything in the 1882 Act, to be deemed necessary to enable the trustees of the settlement, or any other person, to execute any trusts or powers created by the settlement.

(2.) In the case of every other settlement, not within sec. 63 of the 1882 Act, if two or more persons constitute the tenant for life, then, notwithstanding anything in sec. 56 of the 1882 Act requiring the consent of all those persons, the consent of one only of those persons is to be deemed necessary to the exercise by the trustees, or by any other person, of any power under the settlement for any purpose provided by the 1882 Act.

Sec. 7.—With respect to the powers conferred by sec. 63 of the 1882 Act, the following provisions are made:—

(1.) Those powers are not to be exercised without the leave of the Court.

(2.) The Court may by order give leave to exercise all or any of those powers, and the order is to name the person or persons to whom the leave is given.

(3.) The Court may from time to time rescind or vary any order or make any new order under this section.

(4.) So long as an order under this section is in force, neither the trustees of the settlement, nor any person other than the person having the leave, shall execute any trust or power created by the settlement, for any purpose for which leave has been given.

(5.) An order under the section may be registered and re-registered as a *lis pendens* against the trustees of the settlement, describing them as "Trustees for the purposes of the Settled Land Act 1882."

(6.) Any person dealing with the trustees is not to be affected by any order made under this section, unless registered and re-registered as a *lis pendens*.

(7.) An application to the Court under this section may be made by the tenant for life.

(8.) An application to rescind or vary an order may also be made by the trustees of the settlement, or any person beneficially interested.

(9.) The person or persons to whom leave is given shall be deemed the proper person or persons to exercise the powers conferred by sec. 63 of the 1882 Act.

(10.) This section is not to affect any dealings which took place before the passing of this Act.

Sec. 8.—For the purposes of the 1882 Act the estate of the tenant by the curtesy is to be deemed an estate arising under a settlement made by his wife.

53 & 54 Vict., C. 69.
Settled Land Act 1890.
(*Commencement of Act*, 18*th August*, 1890.)

Sec. 4.—Every instrument whereby a tenant for life (in consideration of marriage or by way of a family arrangement, not being a security for a loan) assigns or creates a charge on his interest under the settlement shall be deemed (whether made before or after this Act) one of the instruments creating the settlement, and not an instrument vesting in any person any right as assignee for value within sec. 50 of the 1882 Act.

Sec. 5.—On an exchange or partition (1) any easement, right, or privilege may be reserved or granted over or in relation to the settled land, or (2) other land or an easement, right, or privilege of any kind may be given or taken in exchange or on partition for land or for any other easement, right, or privilege.

Sec. 6.—A tenant for life may make any conveyance necessary or proper for giving effect to a contract entered into by a predecessor in title, and which if made by such predecessor would have been valid as against his successors in title.

Sec. 7.—A lease not exceeding 21 years at the best rent that can be reasonably obtained *without fine*, and whereby the lessee is not exempted from punishment for waste, may be made by a tenant for life—

(1) Without any notice of intention to make it being given under sec. 45 of the 1882 Act; and

(2) Although there are no trustees of the settlement for the purposes of the Settled Land Acts; and

(3) By signed writing containing an agreement by the lessee to pay rent, if the term does not exceed three years from the date of the writing.

Sec. 8.—*In a mining lease* (1) the rent may be made to vary according to the price of the substances gotten; (2) such price may be the saleable value, or the price or value appearing in any trade or market or other price list or return from time to time, or may be the marketable value as ascertained in manner prescribed by the lease (including arbitration), or may be an average of any such prices or values during a specified period.

Sec. 9.—Where, on a building grant by a tenant for life, the land is conveyed in fee simple with, or subject to, a reservation thereout of a perpetual rent or rentcharge, the reservation shall create a rentcharge in fee simple issuing out of the land, and having incident thereto all remedies for recovery thereof conferred by sec. 44 of the Conveyancing Act 1881, and the rentcharge so created shall go to the same uses and trusts as those upon which the land itself was held before such conveyance.

Sec. 10.—Repeals sec. 15 of the 1882 Act, and provides instead that the principal mansion house (if any), and the pleasure grounds and park and lands (if any) usually occupied therewith, shall not be sold, exchanged, or leased by the tenant for life without the consent of the trustees of the settlement or an order of Court, except (1) where the house is usually occupied as a farmhouse, or (2) where the site of the house and the pleasure grounds and park and lands usually occupied therewith do not together exceed 25 acres in extent.

Sec. 11.—Where money is required for discharging an incumbrance (which is not any annual sum payable only during a life or lives or during a term of years absolute or determinable) on the settled land, the tenant for life may raise such money, and the costs, on mortgage (1) by conveyance of the fee simple or other estate subject to the settlement, or (2) by creation of a term of years in the settled land, or otherwise, and the money so raised shall be capital money for that purpose.

Sec. 12.—Where a sale of settled land is to be made to the tenant for life, or a purchase is to be made from him of land to be made subject to the settlement, or an exchange is to be made with him of settled land for other land, or a partition is to be made with him of land, an undivided share whereof is subject to the settlement, the trustees of the settlement shall stand in the place of the tenant for life, and shall (in addition to their powers as trustees) have all his powers for negotiating and completing the transaction.

Sec. 13.—The improvements authorised by the 1882 Act shall include (1) bridges; (2) making any additions or alterations to buildings reasonably necessary or proper to enable the same to be let; (3) erection of buildings in substitution for buildings in an urban sanitary district taken by a local or other public authority, or for buildings taken under compulsory powers, provided the expenditure does not exceed the amount received for the buildings taken and their site; and (4) re-building the principal mansion house, provided the expenditure does not exceed half of the annual rental of the settled land.

Sec. 14.—Capital money paid into Court may be paid out

to the trustees of the settlement for the purposes of the Settled Land Acts.

Sec. 15.—The Court may order capital money to be applied in or towards payment for any improvement authorised by the Settled Land Acts, although a scheme was not, before execution of the improvement, submitted for approval to the trustees of the settlement or to the Court.

Sec. 16.—If there are, for the time being, no trustees of the settlement for the purposes of the 1882 Act, the following persons shall be such trustees :—

 (i.) Any persons for the time being under the settlement trustees, with power of or upon trust for sale of any other land comprised in the settlement and subject to the same limitations as the land to be sold, or with power of consent to or approval of the exercise of such a power of sale; or, if no such person, then

 (ii.) Any persons for the time being under the settlement trustees with future power of sale, or under a future trust for sale of the land to be sold, or with power of consent to or approval of the exercise of such a future power of sale, and whether the power or trust takes effect in all events or not.

Sec. 17.—All the provisions of the Conveyancing Act 1881 as to appointment of new trustees and discharge and retirement of trustees shall apply to trustees for the purposes of the Settled Land Acts, whether appointed by the Court or by the settlement or under provisions contained in the settlement.

Sec. 18.—The provisions of sec. 11 of the Housing of the Working Classes Act 1885, and of any enactment which may be substituted therefor—*i.e.*, *now* sec. 74 of the Housing of the Working Classes Act 1890—shall have effect as if " working classes " included all classes of persons who earn their livelihood by wages or salaries : but this section shall apply only to buildings of a rateable value not exceeding £100 per annum.

III.—LIST OF IMPORTANT STATUTES.

13 Edw. 1, c. 1	De Donis.
18 Edw. 1, c. 1	Quia Emptores.
27 Hen. 8, c. 10	Statute of Uses.
32 Hen. 8, c. 1	⎫
1 Vict., c. 26	⎬ Wills.
15 & 16 Vict., c. 24	⎭
13 Eliz., c. 5	Fraudulent Dispositions.
27 Eliz., c. 4	Voluntary Conveyances.
12 Car. 2, c. 24	Abolishing Feudal Tenures.
4 Geo. 2, c. 28	⎫ Landlord and Tenant.
11 Geo. 2, c. 19	⎭
39 & 40 Geo. 3, c. 98	Thellusson Act.
55 & 56 Vict., c. 58	Accumulations Act 1892.
9 Geo. 4, c. 94	Resignation Bonds.
1 Will. 4, c. 40	Undisposed of Residue.
1 Will. 4, c. 46	⎫ Illusory and Exclusive Appoint-
37 & 38 Vict., c. 37	⎭ ments.
2 & 3 Will. 4, c. 71	Prescription Act.
3 & 4 Will. 4, c. 74	Fines and Recoveries Act.
3 & 4 Will. 4, c. 104	⎫ Debts.
32 & 33 Vict., c. 46	⎭
3 & 4 Will. 4, c. 105	Dower.
3 & 4 Will. 4, c. 106	Descent.
1 & 2 Vict., c. 110	⎫ Judgments.
27 & 28 Vict., c. 112	⎭
8 & 9 Vict., c. 106	Real Property Amendment Act, 1845.
8 & 9 Vict., c. 112	Satisfied Terms.
12 & 13 Vict., c. 26	⎫ Defects in Leases under Powers.
13 & 14 Vict., c. 17	⎭

14 & 15 Vict., c. 25 - 46 & 47 Vict., c. 61 -	} Agricultural Fixtures and Agricultural Holdings generally.
17 & 18 Vict., c. 113- 30 & 31 Vict., c. 69 - 40 & 41 Vict., c. 34 -	} Real Estate Charges Acts.
18 & 19 Vict., c. 43 -	Infants' Settlements.
20 & 21 Vict., c. 57 -	Married Women's Reversionary Interests.
22 & 23 Vict., c. 35 - 23 & 24 Vict., c. 38 -	} Lord St. Leonard's Act, and Amendment thereof.
25 & 26 Vict., c. 108	Trustees' Powers as to selling Lands, reserving minerals.
30 & 31 Vict., c. 48 -	Sale of Land by Auction.
31 Vict., c. 4	Sales of Reversions.
33 Vict., c. 14 -	Naturalization Act 1870.
33 & 34 Vict., c. 23 -	Abolition of forfeitures for treason and felony.
33 & 34 Vict., c. 35 -	Apportionment Act.
33 & 34 Vict., c. 93 - 37 & 38 Vict., c. 50 - 45 & 46 Vict., c. 75 - 47 & 48 Vict., c. 14 -	} Married Women. (The first two of these Acts are repealed, but should still be considered on account of matters occurring before 1st January, 1883.)
37 & 38 Vict., c. 57 -	Real Property Limitation Act 1874.
37 & 38 Vict., c. 78 -	Vendor and Purchaser Act 1874.
40 & 41 Vict., c. 33 -	Contingent Remainders.
44 & 45 Vict., c. 41 - 45 & 46 Vict., c. 39 - 55 & 56 Vict., c. 13 -	} The Conveyancing Acts 1881, 1882, and 1892.
45 & 46 Vict., c. 38 - 47 & 48 Vict., c. 18 - 50 & 51 Vict., c. 30 - 52 & 53 Vict., c. 30 - 53 & 54 Vict., c. 69 -	} Settled Land Acts 1882, 1884, 1887, 1889, and 1890.

47 & 48 Vict., c. 71 -	⎫ Intestates Estates Acts 1884
53 & 54 Vict., c. 29 -	⎭ and 1890.
50 & 51 Vict., c. 73 -	Copyhold Act 1887, particularly sections 1, 4, and 45.
51 & 52 Vict., c. 42 -	⎫ Mortmain and Charitable Uses
54 & 55 Vict., c. 73 -	⎭ Acts 1888 and 1891.
51 & 52 Vict., c. 51 -	Land Charges Registration and Searches Act 1888.
51 & 52 Vict., c. 59 -	Trustee Act 1888.
52 & 53 Vict., c. 32 -	Trust Investment Act 1889.
53 & 54 Vict., c. 70, secs. 74, 75 -	⎫⎭ Housing of Working Classes Act 1890.

IV.—TEST QUESTIONS ON THE LAW OF REAL AND PERSONAL PROPERTY.

1. Explain the origin of the terms "Real" and "Personal" property respectively, stating some essential differences between the two.

2. What are the different freehold estates in land, and the estates less than freehold respectively?

3. How is it that, notwithstanding 12 Car. 2, c. 24, the following special and peculiar tenures still exist:—(*a*) Gavelkind; (*b*) Borough English; (*c*) Grand Serjeanty; (*d*) Petit Serjeanty; (*e*) Frankalmoign?

4. How do you account for the origin of copyholds? Point out the main distinctions between freeholds and copyholds.

5. Explain the relative rights of the lord and his tenant in copyholds.

6. What is the object of enfranchising copyholds, and state how an enfranchisement may be effected, pointing out any differences that occur when the enfranchisement takes place at the instance of the lord or the tenant respectively?

7. On an enfranchisement of copyholds, who has the right to the mines and minerals?

8. To whom do enfranchised copyholds escheat, when the owner dies intestate and without an heir?

9. What differences are there between ordinary copyholds and customary freeholds?

10. An estate may be the same as another in quality, and yet different to it in quantity. What do you understand by this?

11. What difference (if any) is there in the case of freeholds between a grant or devise to A, and a grant or devise to A and his heirs?

12. Can personalty be limited by way of estates to one and then to another? What would be the effect of a grant or devise of personalty to A for life, and then to B absolutely?

13. It is desired that personalty shall be so settled that A may enjoy it for his own life, then B, if he survives, for his life, and then that it shall go absolutely to a certain person. In what way may this object be accomplished?

14. Give an instance of the application of the maxim: *Cujus est solum ejus est usque ad cœlum.*

15. Explain the position of a tenant for life with regard to the following three particulars: (*a*) waste; (*b*) granting leases; (*c*) selling the estate.

16. Explain practically the effect of the Apportionment Act 1870 (33 & 34 Vict., c. 35).

17. What was originally, and what is now, the effect of a grant of freeholds to A, and the heirs of his body? Refer to the statute on the subject, and explain how you account for its having been passed.

18. By what words can you create an estate tail (*a*) in a deed (*b*) in a will?

19. How was the object of the statute *De Donis* frustrated? How is this frustration, originally accomplished in a circuitous way, now effected? Name the present authority.

20. What is the effect of a limitation of copyholds to A and the heirs of his body?

21. Explain the position of a tenant in tail with regard to waste, showing in what respects his position is different if he is a tenant in tail after possibility of issue extinct.

22. When is there a protector to a settlement, and what are his powers and position? How do you account for the existence of such an office?

23. What is a base fee, how may it be created, and how may it be enlarged into an estate in fee simple absolute?

24. Lands are limited unto and to the use of A and his

heirs, in trust for B for life, and then to C and the heirs of his body. During B's life who would be the person to join in the disentailing assurance; and with regard to the parties to so join in barring the entail, what difference, if any, would there have been prior to the 3 & 4 Wm. 4, c. 74?

25. If A, having a remainder in fee after a life estate, grants out of his remainder an estate to B in tail, is there any protectorship here?

26. What is the effect of a grant and devise respectively to A and his heirs male?

27. What difference is there, and why, in the case of either of the following paying off an incumbrance upon the inheritance :—(*a*) A tenant for life. (*b*) A tenant in tail in remainder. (*c*) A tenant in tail in possession?

28. What is an estate in fee simple? How many kinds of fee simple are there? Is it correct to say that the owner of a fee simple estate has an absolute property in it?

29. Explain the object and effect of the statute of *Quia Emptores* (18 Edw. 1, c. 1).

30. What was, and is, the position of an alien with regard to holding property?

31. What is necessary at the present day to constitute a good gift of lands to a charity? Can such a gift ever, and if so, when, be made by will?

32. Give a short history of the past and present law as to judgments affecting land.

33. What circumstances led to the passing of the Statute of Uses? State its chief enactment, and show how its object was frustrated.

34. What is the effect of a grant simply to A without consideration, and why? What difference would it make if it were unto and to the use of A?

35. Grant to A to the use of B in trust for C. Explain the rights and position of each, with reasons.

36. A *cestui que* trust of real and personal property

respectively, dies intestate, and without heirs, or next of kin, to whom does the property go?

37. What were formerly, and what are now, the rights of a husband in the following properties of his wife—(*a*) Her freeholds; (*b*) Her leaseholds; (*c*) Her choses in possession; (*d*) Her choses in action?

38. Define curtesy. What are the essentials to curtesy? What peculiarities are there with regard to it in copyholds and in gavelkind land respectively?

39. Define dower, and show the difference with regard to it if the parties were married prior to or since the 1st January, 1834, both with regard to the right to it and the mode of barring it.

40. Detail and explain the modern method of barring dower when the persons were married prior to 1st January, 1834.

41. Distinguish between (*a*) a reversion and a remainder; and (*b*) a vested and a contingent remainder, giving an instance of each.

42. How is it that although the Common Law rule was different, yet at the present day an assignee of a reversion is able to take advantage of the conditions of re-entry inserted in the original lease?

43. Explain the following:—Attornment, rent service, rent charge, rent seck, quit rent, fee farm rent, rack rent.

44. What was formerly, and what is now, the effect upon an underlease of the merger or surrender of its reversion?

45. Explain the rule in Shelley's Case. Does it have any application to personal property?

46. Give the rules for the creation of contingent remainders. With regard to one of such rules, what was the object of inserting in settlements a limitation to trustees to preserve contingent remainders?

47. With regard to the same rule, what was the effect of 8 & 9 Vict., c. 106, sec. 8, and 40 & 41 Vict., c. 33, respectively?

48. Grant to A for life, and after his decease to the heirs of B. A dies during B's lifetime. What becomes of the estate?

49. Explain and illustrate the doctrine of *cy près*—(*a*) as regards contingent remainders, (*b*) as regards charitable bequests.

50. Define an executory interest. In what two ways may an executory interest arise? Why is it that it can only arise in a deed by means of the Statute of Uses?

51. Distinguish between a shifting and a springing use respectively, giving an instance of each.

52. Within what time must an executory interest arise? What is the leading case on the subject?

53. Give the provisions of the Thellusson Act (39 & 40 Geo. 3, c. 98), limiting the period for accumulation of income. State particularly the exceptions in the Act.

54. What is the effect of a direction to accumulate income exceeding the period allowed by the Thellusson Act? Refer to the leading case on the point.

55. Define a power of appointment, showing how it operates, and explaining why it properly comes under the denomination of an executory interest.

56. Does an appointee, taking under a power, take simply from the person *exercising* the power, or from the person *creating* the power? Explain your answer by illustrations.

57. What difference is there as regards the rule against perpetuities between a general and a special power respectively?

58. What is the effect under 12 & 13 Vict., c. 26, of a lease made by a limited owner under a power, but not strictly in conformity with the terms of that power? What would have been the position in such a case prior to the Act?

59. A tenant for life mortgages his life interest. Does this mortgage affect the power of leasing conferred on him by the Settled Land Act 1882?

60. Powers may be classified as (1) general and special, (2) appendant, in gross, and collateral. Explain and instance each of these.

61. With regard to powers, explain the effect of 1 Wm. 4, c. 46, and 37 & 38 Vict., c. 37, respectively.

62. Define incorporeal property, and compare the mode of conveying it with the original mode of conveying corporeal property. Why can either property be now conveyed by deed of grant?

63. Define and compare rights of common and easements respectively.

64. What do you understand by a *profit à prendre*? Give an instance. What do you understand by a *profit à prendre* being claimed as a *que estate*?

65. What rights cannot be claimed by custom?

66. Give an instance of an easement arising by necessity.

67. How many kinds of rights of common are there? Explain each kind.

68. With regard to an easement, explain what is meant by the dominant and servient tenements respectively.

69. What are the chief ways in which an easement may be extinguished? What is the one case in which unity of possession will not extinguish an easement?

70. With regard to the length of time of enjoyment that will give a title either to a right of common, or an easement, state the provisions of the Prescription Act (2 & 3 Wm. 4, c. 71). What was the law on this point prior to that Act?

71. What is an advowson? How many kinds of advowsons are there? Distinguish between each.

72. Are advowsons and next presentations respectively, real or personal property?

73. What is the proper length of title to be shown to an advowson?

74. What are tithes? Distinguish between tithes, a tithe

rent charge, and a modus. Explain how it was that tithes came into lay hands.

75. If a person having a right to tithes bought the land out of which the tithes issued and subsequently resold that land, would his right to tithes revive? Does merger occur of a tithe rent charge?

76. What is a Resignation Bond, and when is it valid?

77. Define simony, and refer to the point decided in the case of Fox v. Bishop of Chester. What purchase of a living by a clergyman would be simoniacal, although not so on the part of a layman?

78. On the death of an incumbent explain the rights and liabilities as to dilapidations as between his representatives and the successor to the living.

79. What bearing respectively did the Statute of Frauds (29 Car. 2, c. 3, secs. 1, 2, & 3), and the Real Property Amendment Act 1845 (8 & 9 Vict., c. 106, sec. 3), have upon leases?

80. What is the effect of a parol lease for four years?

81. A, having a lease for seven years, holds over after the expiration of that lease. Explain his position directly the lease expires, and how and why that position becomes altered by the acceptance of rent by the landlord.

82. What is the effect of a yearly tenant not quitting in pursuance of notice (*a*) when the notice is given by the landlord, and (*b*) when the notice is given by the tenant?

83. What is the difference between privity of contract and privity of estate? Give an instance of liability in respect of privity of estate.

84. A, having but an interest consisting of a term of seven years in land, professes to make a lease for twenty-one years. In another case, having no interest at all, he professes to make a like lease. In both cases he immediately afterwards becomes possessed of the fee simple. State fully in each case the position and rights of the lessee.

85. State shortly the provision of the Conveyancing Act 1881 with regard to forfeitures of leases for breaches of covenant.

86. State the three most prominent alterations in the law of descent introduced by the Inheritance Act, 3 & 4 Wm. 4, c. 106.

87. How has the first rule of descent been amended by 22 & 23 Vict., c. 35, secs. 19, 20?

88. Explain the rule as to the admission of the half blood, and compare the position of the half blood with regard to realty and personalty respectively.

89. An estate descends to two daughters as co-parceners. One of them dies leaving a son. To whom does her share go, and why?

90. Distinguish on an intestacy between persons taking *per stirpes* and *per capita*, giving an instance of each.

91. A person dies intestate, leaving (*a*) a wife and two children, (*b*) two children and no wife or other relative, and (*c*) a wife and no other relative. In what way in each case will his personal property go?

92. A person dies intestate, leaving a wife, a father, and a brother. How does his personalty go?

93. A person dies intestate, leaving a mother, a brother, and a sister. How does his personalty go?

94. A person dies intestate, leaving a mother, a brother, and two nephews, children of a deceased sister. How does his personalty go?

95. A person dies intestate leaving six nephews, five of them being children of a deceased brother, and one the child of a deceased sister. How does his personalty go?

96. A person dies intestate leaving a nephew and two grand nephews, the children of a deceased nephew. How does his personalty go?

97. A person dies intestate leaving one child of a deceased

son, five children of a deceased daughter, a wife, and a father. How does his personalty go?

98. What do you understand by hotchpot? Illustrate your answer.

99. Give the outline of an ordinary settlement of real estate upon marriage, particularly pointing out how the pin money, jointure, and portions respectively are provided for.

100. Give the outline of an ordinary settlement of personal estate upon a marriage. It is desired to settle personalty upon marriage in the same way as if it were realty, viz., in strict settlement. Can this be done?

101. When, and in what way, and to what extent, can infants make valid marriage settlements?

102. On the death of a trustee under a settlement, in what different ways may a new trustee be appointed? On whom does the trust property now devolve on death of a trustee?

103. What leases may, under the Settled Land Act 1882, be made by the tenant for life? Is any consent or notice necessary prior to leasing?

104. The like question as regards a sale by the tenant for life.

105. How may satisfied terms arise? With regard to them, what is now the provision contained in 8 & 9 Vict., c. 112?

106. Are any special formalities necessary to be observed in either an ante-nuptial or a post-nuptial settlement of furniture?

107. What do you understand by uses in strict settlement?

108. Can a settlement of leaseholds ever be construed as a voluntary settlement so as to be bad in the case of a subsequent sale of the property? Give reasons, pointing out in what respects a settlement of such property is different from a settlement of freeholds.

109. Give a short history of the chief different instruments which have from time to time been used to convey lands *inter vivos*.

110. What is the proper mode of conveying copyholds on a sale and on a mortgage respectively?

111. What powers are, by the Conveyancing Act 1881, conferred on mortgagees, and when do they respectively arise? Is it safe to rely on this Act, or should express powers be inserted in the mortgage?

112. What are the differences between the position of a lessee and assignee of a lease respectively?

113. Explain an *interesse termini*.

114. On a lease of a house is there any implied contract by the landlord that it is reasonably fit for habitation? Refer to the Housing of the Working Classes Act 1890.

115. What is the title to be shown on an open contract for the sale of a freehold and leasehold estate respectively?

116. What is the title to be shown to lands which have been the subject of an exchange? Distinguish between the cases of the exchange having been made prior to and since 1845.

117. Trace the position with regard to the making of a will of lands from the earliest down to the present time.

118. The like, with regard to a will of personalty.

119. Are the following competent witnesses to a will:— The executor, a creditor of the testator, a legatee under the will, the husband or wife of any legatee, the child of any legatee?

120. State the different ways in which a will may be revoked.

121. A makes a will devising Whiteacre to B, and subsequently contracts to sell Whiteacre, and then dies. What is the position of B?

122. When, under a general devise, did trust and mortgaged estates pass? What do the Conveyancing Act

1881 and the Copyhold Act 1887 now provide on the point?

123. Explain the following: general legacy, specific legacy, demonstrative legacy, ademption, abatement.

124. What is a lapse? What alterations did the Wills Act (1 Vict., c. 26) make in the law of lapse?

125. When does a legacy carry interest?

126. Give two instances of a construction being placed on words in a will different to what would be put on the same words in a deed.

127. Devise to X after the death of Y. Does Y take any, and what, estate, and why?

128. What estate do trustees take under a devise to them without words of limitation? What difference was there before 1 Vict., c. 26?

129. Where a testator by his will has charged his real estate with payment of his debts, but has made no express provision as to who is to have the power of sale to raise the necessary money, in whom is the power of sale vested under the provisions of 22 & 23 Vict., c. 35?

130. Limitation to A, and if he shall die without issue to B. What was the effect of this at Common Law, and how has it been affected by 1 Vict., c. 26, and the Conveyancing Act 1882 respectively?

V.—DIGEST OF QUESTIONS AND ANSWERS ON THE LAW OF REAL AND PERSONAL PROPERTY.

(The Answers, except where other references are given, are composed mainly from Williams' Real Property, Goodeve's Real Property, Williams' Personal Property, and Goodeve's Personal Property, and all due acknowledgment is here made to the Authors and Editors of those works.)

1.—INTRODUCTORY.

Q. Explain the origin and meaning of the distinction between "real" and "personal" property.

A. After 12 Charles 2, c. 24, lands, tenements, and hereditaments were classified as real property, and goods and chattels as personal property. The expressions originated in the legal remedy for the deprivation of possession. When the possession of land was withheld from its rightful owner, his remedy was by a real action (*actio in rem*) to recover it; but for a wrongful withholding of goods, the remedy was by a personal action (*actio in personam*) against the wrongdoer to recover damages, since the goods might have been destroyed.

Q. In what essential respects do personal property and real property differ from each other in nature, title, and ownership respectively?

A. Personal property is not affected by the feudal rules of tenure which affect real estate; is essentially the subject of absolute ownership; consists of goods and chattels, and includes interests less than freehold in real property; the remedy for its deprivation has always been by personal action for damages against the wrong doer; it is transferred by delivery, or bill of sale, or will; and on the death of the owner always devolves on his legal personal representative in trust to pay debts and then divide amongst the legatees or next-of-kin; the descent is governed by the law of the owner's domicile, for *mobilia sequuntur personam*. Real property consists of lands, tenements and hereditaments; is practically indestructible, and, therefore, not the subject of absolute ownership, estates only being held in it; is governed by the feudal rules of tenure; the remedy for its deprivation has always been by real action to recover the *res ipsa* (action for the recovery of land); it is transferred by deed or will; on the death of the owner it devolves on his devisee or heir-at-law, subject, however, to debts if the personalty is insufficient; and its descent and alienation are governed by the *lex loci rei sitæ*.

Q. *Give the principal exceptions, or apparent exceptions, to the rule that personal property is essentially the subject of absolute ownership and cannot be held for any estate.*

A. (*a*) Chattels so closely connected with land that they partake of its nature, pass with it when disposed of, and descend with it to the heir of the deceased owner. These are (1) title deeds; (2) heirlooms, which are strictly chattels that go to the heir by special custom, *e.g.*, crown jewels, coat armour, deed boxes, but popularly (and under the Settled Land Act 1882) are personalty settled to devolve along with real estate in strict settlement; (3) fixtures; (4) chattels vegetable, not being emblements; and (5) animals *feræ naturæ*, unless a special property has been acquired in them. (*b*) At law, a term of years might be given to one person for life and then to another absolutely, but not any other property; in equity, however, all kinds of personalty, except articles *quæ ipso usu consumuntur*, might be given to one for life and then to another; and now under the Judicature Acts, the equity rule prevails.

Q. *What are fixtures? Can a tenant remove them?*

A. Personal chattels annexed to the freehold. The common law maxim is *Quicquid plantatur solo, solo cedit;* so they were irremovable. But exceptions have always been permitted allowing tenants to remove, during the term, fixtures erected for purposes of trade, ornament, or domestic use. And by 14 & 15 Vict., c. 25, and the Agricultural Holdings Act 1883, the like privilege is accorded to agricultural fixtures on certain conditions being complied with. (See Elwes v. Mawe, and Notes in Indermaur's Common Law Cases, 7th edition, 75.)

Q. (a) *On the death of a tenant in fee simple of a house, who is entitled to the fixtures set up by him in it?* (b) *On the death of the tenant for life of a house who would be entitled to the fixtures set up by him?* (c) *When houses or buildings are let for a term of years, and the tenants set up fixtures for the purposes of trade, or of ornament, or domestic convenience, who is entitled to them on the expiration of the term?* (d) *When fixtures are demised with the buildings in which they are, in whom does the property in the fixtures remain?*

A. (a) If he devised the house, all the fixtures go to the devisee, but if he died intestate, the legal personal representative takes the fixtures put up for the purposes of trade, ornament, and domestic convenience. (Williams on Executors, 738-745.) (b) The rules as to the right of a tenant for life to fixtures put up by him are not clear, but his executor appears to have the right to all fixtures put up for trade, ornament, or domestic convenience. (*Ibid*, 747-751.) (c) The tenant is entitled to the fixtures, but he must remove them before the expiration of his tenancy. There are special rules, however, applicable to agricultural tenants. (See previous answer.) (d) The property in the fixtures remains in the landlord.

Q. *Explain the following maxims:*—(1) *The father to the bough, the son to the plough.* (2) *Mobilia sequuntur personam.*

A. (1) This is a maxim having reference to the tenure of

gavelkind, and signifies that here there was never an escheat on attainder or conviction for murder. (2) This expression means that moveables follow the person and are governed by the law of the domicile of the owner, unlike lands which are governed by the *lex loci rei sitæ*.

Q. *Explain fully the following terms: Emblements, Estate pur autre vie, Springing Use.*

A. *Emblements* are the fruits of the earth produced by labour and manurance, and brought to perfection within the year, *e.g.*, corn, but not clover. The executors of a tenant for life have a right to them unless the tenancy ends by the act of the tenant for life. *An estate pur autre vie* is a freehold estate held by one man for the life of another. Formerly, if the tenant *pur autre vie* died during the life of the *cestui que vie*, the first person who entered on the lands could hold them as *general occupant* until the *cestui que vie* died; unless, indeed, the grant had been to the tenant and his heirs, or the heirs of his body, in which event the heir took as *special occupant* during the remainder of the life of the *cestui que vie* by virtue of his being named in the grant. But by 1 Vict., c. 26, secs. 3 and 6, the owner of an estate *pur autre vie* may dispose of it by will; and if he does not, and there is no special occupant, the lands go to the legal personal representative of the dead tenant *pur autre vie* as part of his personal estate. *A springing use* is an executory interest arising by deed under the Statute of Uses, *e.g.*, a power of appointment over freehold land.

Q. *What is meant by Escheat?*

A. *Escheat* is the resulting of freehold estate to the lord of whom it is held, where the tenant dies without disposing of it and without heirs. It is (1) *propter defectum sanguinis* —*i.e.*, where the tenant dies literally without issue; or (2) *propter delictum tenentis*—*i.e.*, where the tenant was attainted for treason or convicted for felony, which corrupted his blood and interrupted the succession. This second kind can only happen now on outlawry in criminal proceedings, 33 & 34 Vict., c. 23. The Intestates Estates Act 1884 extended the law of escheat to incorporeal hereditaments, and to equitable estates in corporeal hereditaments. The Copyhold Act 1887 enacts that escheat of enfranchised copyholds shall be to the lord of the manor if the enfranchisement takes place since 16th September, 1887.

Q. Explain the following terms:—advowson, chief rent, feoffment, shifting use, enfranchisement.

A. *An advowson* is the perpetual right of presentation to an ecclesiastical benefice; it is an incorporeal hereditament, and real property; it is presentative, collative, donative, or elective; it is either appendant to a manor, or in gross, *i.e.*, a separate property; and it is either an advowson of a vicarage or a rectory. *A chief rent*, or quit rent, is the small fixed rent paid by the freehold tenants of a manor, by payment of which they are free from all other service in respect of their tenure. *A feoffment* was a conveyance at common law used to convey a freehold estate in possession in corporeal hereditaments; its requisites are competent parties, words of pure donation, ascertained property, proper words of limitation, livery of seisin in deed or in law subsequently perfected by entry during the lives of feoffer and feoffee; and since 8 & 9 Vict., c. 106, a deed, except in conveyances by an infant under the custom of gavelkind. *A shifting use* is an executory interest created under the Statute of Uses, by which the legal seisin of freeholds is moved from one person to another, *e.g.*, the name and arms clause in a will by which lands are given to A., but if within a given time he does not take the testator's name and arms, then to B. *Enfranchisement* is the conversion of copyholds into freeholds; and it is either voluntary by the lord conveying the freehold to the tenant, or compulsory under the Copyhold Acts 1852-1887; if voluntary, the lord loses all his rights, but if compulsory the lord retains his right of escheat and (unless otherwise expressed) his minerals and rights of sporting.

Q. Explain heir-at-law, customary heir, heir-apparent, heir presumptive.

A. A man's heir-at-law is the person upon whom, on the man's death intestate, his real estates devolve by the rules of law. A customary heir is one who inherits under any special custom, *e.g.*, Borough English. A man cannot have an heir until he is dead, for *nemo est hæres viventis;* neither can he make his heir, for *solus deus hæredem facere potest, non homo;* but he may have an heir-apparent, *i.e.*, some person living who must be the heir if he survive, *e.g.*, an eldest son, or an heir-presumptive, *i.e.*, a person who if the man were to die now would be his heir but is liable to be cut out by the birth of a nearer relative, *e.g.*, a daughter whose claim would be ousted by birth of a son.

Q. State the principal provisions and date of the Statute of Frauds.

A. The statute was passed in 1677 (29 Chas. 2, c. 3) to prevent fraudulent practices, enacts (1) leases and interests of freehold, &c., not put in signed writing shall only have the force of estates at will, except leases not exceeding three years at two-thirds of a rack rent; (2) freehold and leasehold estates must be surrendered by deed or signed writing; (3) no action can be brought against a personal representative on a promise to answer damages out of his own estate, *or* on a guarantee, *or* on an agreement upon consideration of marriage, *or* on any contract or sale of lands, tenements or hereditaments, or any interest in or concerning them, *or* on an agreement not to be performed within one year from its making, unless made in writing signed; (4) trusts of land must be evidenced by signed writing, except those created, transferred or extinguished by implication of law; (5) assignments of any trust must be in signed writing; (6) an equitable fee simple shall be assets by descent, but the heir is not personally liable; (7) writs of execution to bind the debtor's goods from delivery to the sheriff; (8) a contract to sell goods for £10 or more not to be good unless the buyer accepts and receives part of the goods, or gives earnest, or partly pays, or put in writing signed by the party to be charged, or his agent; and (9) husband to take administration to wife's personalty as her next-of-kin.

2.—TENURES, ESTATES, &c.

Q. Distinguish between allodial lands and feudal lands. Who were tenants in capite, who lord paramount, who mesne lords?

A. Allodial lands were enjoyed as free and independent property, held of no one and charged with no service; the owners could dispose of them at pleasure. Feudal lands were lands held of a superior, subject to the performance of services, generally military; instead of being the absolute owner, the holder of the feud had merely the usufruct, and could not even dispose of that at his pleasure. Tenants *in capite* were those who held feudal lands from the sovereign direct. The king was lord paramount, all lands being in theory held of him. Mesne lords were tenants *in capite*, who had granted out all or part of their lands to be held of them in subinfeudation.

Q. Trace the causes which led to the decline of the feudal system in England, mentioning any special enactments which tended to that result.

A. The system of subinfeudation, which was an essential element, was found prejudicial to the interests of the chief lords by exposing them to the frequent loss of their escheats, wardships, and marriages. The statute of Quia Emptores (18 Edw. 1, c. 1) was the first great blow struck against the feudal system by abolishing subinfeudation. The nation began more to cultivate the arts of peace, and

F

in a variety of ways the old feudal system became inconvenient, the services often being commuted for a money payment called scutage. The final blow to the system was given by 12 Car. 2, c. 24, which abolished the old feudal tenures, and converted them into free and common socage.

Q. What was subinfeudation? When, why, and how was it abolished?

A. Subinfeudation was the method by which a feudal owner conveyed those parts of his feud not required by himself, so that the grantee held of him, subject to the performance of services, and by a tenure similar to his own. Subinfeudation of the fee simple was abolished in 1290, by the Statute of Quia Emptores, 18 Edw. 1, c. 1, at the instigation of the barons who perceived that their privileges as superior lords were gradually being encroached upon. The statute enacts that every free man may sell his fee simple at his pleasure, but that the purchaser shall hold of the same chief lord of the fee and subject to the same services and customs as the vendor held.

Q. Describe and distinguish the various kinds of conditional estates.

A. Estates upon condition are those, the existence of which depends on the happening, or not happening, of some uncertain event, whereby the estate may be originally created, or enlarged or finally defeated. They are on condition *implied*—e.g., a grant of an office or franchise, or *expressed*. In the latter case the condition is either precedent—*i.e.*, where unless and until the condition is performed the estate cannot vest; or subsequent—*i.e.*, where the estate vests at once, but is liable to be defeated by the grantor re-entering if the subsequent condition is not performed. There is also a conditional limitation—*i.e.*, an estate so limited that it must determine when the contingency on which it is granted fails—*e.g.*, grant to A and his heirs tenants of Dale. Where an estate is granted with a condition which is illegal or impossible or repugnant to the nature of the estate—if the condition is precedent, the estate never vests; if subsequent, the grantee gets the estate free from the condition.

Q. Mention the different kinds of estates which may exist in land.

A. Freehold estates and estates less than freehold. The latter of these are estates for years, estates at will, and estates at sufferance. The former are (1) Freeholds of inheritance—viz., estates in fee simple and estates tail; and (2) Freeholds not of inheritance—viz., all life estates; and these may be conventional—*i.e.*, created by the act of the parties, or legal—*i.e.*, arising by operation of law, viz.: curtesy, dower, and estate tail after possibility of issue extinct.

Q. Define, (a) estate in fee simple, (b) in fee tail, (c) in base fee, (d) after possibility of issue extinct, (e) at sufferance, and (f) chattels real and personal.

A. (*a*) An estate to a person and his heirs; (*b*) an estate to a person and the heirs of his body, either general or special, male or female; (*c*) an estate created by the barring of an estate tail by a tenant in tail in remainder without the consent of the protector; (*d*) an estate in special tail when the person from whose body the issue are to come dies without issue; (*e*) the estate of a person who, having come lawfully into possession, holds over after the expiration of his lawful title; (*f*) chattels real and personal are personal property, the first though personal yet being connected with realty, and the latter purely personal.

Q. Enumerate and classify the various kinds of estates for life which may subsist in freehold and copyhold lands.

A. They are either conventional (*i.e.*, created by the act of the party by deed or will), or legal (*i.e.*, created by operation of law). Conventional life estates are either for the holder's own life or *pur autre vie*. Legal life estates are

F 2

those in dower, curtesy, and tenancy in tail after possibility of issue extinct.

Q. By what words may an estate for years, for life, in tail, and in fee be created by deed and will respectively?

A. No precise words are needed to create an estate for years, but the words used must indicate that the tenant is to hold for a fixed period of time, *i.e.*, for years, months, weeks, or days. An estate for life is created in a deed by a grant to A for his own life or for the life of another, or by a grant to A simply; but in a will, the intention must be expressed that the devisee shall not take more than a life estate, because a devise to A simply will give him all the testator's interest unless a contrary intention is expressed (1 Vict., c. 26, sec. 28). An estate tail is created in a deed by a grant to A and the heirs of his body, or to A in fee tail (Conveyancing Act 1881, sec. 51); but in a will, it may be created by any words of procreation evincing the intention, *e.g.*, to A and his seed, to A and his offspring. To create a fee simple in a deed the words of limitation must be clear and precise, viz.: "to A and his heirs," or by the Conveyancing Act 1881, "to A in fee simple"; but in a will a mere devise "to A" without further words of limitation will pass the fee simple or other the testator's whole interest, unless it clearly appears on the face of the will that such was not the testator's intention. (1 Vict., c. 26, sec. 28.) In a conveyance by deed to a corporation, the words used would be "to the corporation and their successors."

Q. Mention the various cases in which an estate in lands may be made to vest by virtue of a statute or statutory authority.

A. This would happen by virtue of the Statute of Uses in the following cases :—(1) By means of a bargain and sale. (2) By means of a lease and release. (3) By means of a covenant to stand seised to uses. (These three modes of conveying property are, however, now obsolete.) (4) By means of an appointment under a power. (5) By means of a grant to uses. Also under the Trustee Act 1850, where the Court makes a vesting order; also by declaration in a deed appointing new trustees under the Conveyancing Act 1881; also under sec. 5 of that Act on paying the amount of an incumbrance into Court; also by a tenant for life under the provisions of the Settled Land Act 1882; also by order of the County Court for cost of improvements under the Agricultural Holdings Act 1883; also under the Judicature Act 1884, when the Court nominates a person to execute a conveyance, when one ordered by the Court to do so neglects or refuses; also by award of the Land Commissioners (now the Board of Agriculture) made under the Copyhold Acts, or the General Inclosure Acts, or for redemption of tithe rent charge, or of quit rents, &c.; also under the Land Transfer Act 1875.

3.—LIFE ESTATES, SETTLED LAND ACTS, &c.

Q. What estate or interests may be created in land with regard to their quantity and quality respectively? What difference is there in the quality of an estate limited to A for life, and of an estate limited to A for 1000 years if he shall so long live?

A. The quantity of an estate means the time of its continuance. The quality of an estate has reference to the mode of its enjoyment; from this point of view estates may be (1) legal or equitable; (2) in possession or expectancy; (3) in severalty, in joint tenancy, in tenancy in common, or in coparcenary. In the case put there is no difference in quality; the difference is in quantity, the life estate being freehold and real estate, and the term of years less than freehold and personal property.

Q. Define legal waste and equitable waste.

A. Legal waste is such waste as a Court of Law took cognizance of; but if a life estate were granted without impeachment for waste, although at law the tenant could commit any kind of waste, a Court of Equity would not allow the tenant to do such unconscionable acts of waste as pulling down or destroying the mansion house or cutting ornamental timber, and so these acts were called equitable waste. Under the Judicature Act the rules of equity prevail.

Q. (a) *What is meant by voluntary waste and by permissive waste?* (b) *Is the estate of a legal tenant for life liable after his death to the remainderman for permissive waste suffered in his lifetime?* (c) *Will the Court interfere at the instance of a remainderman to restrain an equitable tenant for life from suffering permissive waste upon the trust property?*

A. (a) Waste is any spoil, injury, or destruction to, or alteration of, the inheritance. Voluntary waste is waste committed by actually pulling down, altering, or injuring the property; permissive waste is allowing the property to deteriorate for want of repairs. (b) A tenant for life is liable for all acts of voluntary waste, but not for permissive waste (*Re* Cartwright, Avis v. Newman, 41 Ch. D., 532) unless the instrument creating his estate expressly makes him so (Woodhouse v. Walker, 5 Q. B. Div., 404); and his estate would be answerable or not accordingly. (c) Not unless the tenant was expressly bound not to commit such waste (Woodhouse v. Walker, *supra*).

Q. *A freeholder, having granted a lease for years at a rent payable quarterly, dies during the last quarter of a year intestate. The rent was three-quarters of a year in arrear at his death, and the fourth quarter's rent has become payable. To what person, or persons, does the whole year's rent belong, and by what person, or persons, must it be received?*

A. The three-quarters' arrears of rent, being actually due at the death, belong to the legal personal representative of the dead landlord, who may sue and distrain for them. The proportion of the fourth quarter's rent up to the death also belongs to them, and the balance belongs to the remainderman, reversioner, heir, or devisee (as the case may be); and the whole quarter's rent may be sued and distrained for by the remainderman, etc., who is personally liable to the representatives in an action by them for the apportionment. (See 33 & 34 Vict., c. 35.)

Q. State briefly the effect of the regulations under which the powers given to the tenant for life under the Settled Land Act 1882 are to be exercised.

A. Under the 1882 Act, sec. 45, a month's notice must first be sent by registered post to the trustees and their solicitors, if known; but, under the 1884 Act (sec. 5), this may (as regards a sale, exchange, partition, or lease) be a general notice, and be waived or shortened. Under the 1890 Act (sec. 10) no sale, exchange, or lease of the principal mansion-house can be made without consent of trustees or an order of Court, unless the house is a farmhouse, or the house and park do not exceed 25 acres. Under the 1882 Act (sec. 37), a sale of heirlooms cannot be made without an order of Court. Under secs. 3 and 4, a sale is to be at the best price that can be obtained, either by public auction or private contract, together, or in lots. Under sec. 7, the lease must be at the best rent that can be obtained, to take effect in possession not later than twelve months after its date, and is to contain a covenant for payment of rent, and a condition of re-entry on non-payment within a time not exceeding 30 days. Secs. 8-11 also contain further regulations specially relating to building and mining leases.

Q. State the effect of the general regulations under which a tenant for life may lease settled lands for building and mining purposes.

A. The term may not exceed 99 years for a building lease, and 60 years for a mining lease. The lease must be by deed; to take effect in possession within 12 months; must reserve the best rent, regard being had to any fine (which by the 1884 Act is capital money) and to any money laid out for the benefit of the settled land and to the circumstances; must contain a covenant to pay rent, and a right of re-entry if the rent is not paid within a time named, not exceeding 30 days; a counterpart must be executed by the lessee and delivered to the tenant for life. The building lease must be made partly in consideration of the erection, or improvement, or repair, of buildings or improvements; a peppercorn rent may be reserved for the first five years; if the land is to be leased in lots, the entire rent may be apportioned, but the rent on each lot must not be less than ten shillings, nor greater than a fifth of the annual value of the land with the buildings. The 1889 Act allows an option to be given to the lessee to buy the fee simple within a time not exceeding ten years at a price named in the building lease. In the mining lease, the rent may be an acreage or a tonnage rent; and a minimum rent may be reserved, with power to make up back-workings or not; and the tenant for life gets three-quarters, or (if impeachable for waste) only a quarter of the rent, the rest being capital. The tenant for life must give one month's notice to the trustees, which (by the Act of 1884) may be a general notice and may be waived or shortened. (Settled Land Act 1882, secs. 6-11, 45.)

Q. By whom are the powers conferred by the Settled Land Acts exercisable when the tenant for life is (a) an infant, (b) a married woman, (c) a lunatic?

A. (*a*) By the trustees of the settlement, and if there are none then by such person and in such manner as the Court, on the application of a testamentary or other guardian or next friend of the infant, either generally or in a particular instance, orders (sec. 60). (*b*) Where the married woman is entitled for her separate use, or under any statute for her separate property, or as a *feme sole*, by the married woman; and where she is entitled in any other way, then by her and her husband together (sec. 61). (c) By the committee of his estate, under an order from the Lord Chancellor, obtained on petition by the committee or any person interested in the settled land (sec. 62).

Q. What are the provisions of the Settled Land Act 1882 with reference to the assignment or release of, or the restriction of the exercise of, the tenant for life's powers? and what is the effect of a conflict between those powers and any other powers given by the settlement?

A. Sec. 50 provides that the powers do not pass to an assignee but remain exercisable by the tenant for life; though if he has assigned his estate he cannot exercise his powers to the prejudice of the assignee, except that if the assignee has not gone into possession he may still exercise his power of leasing without the assignee's consent if no fine is taken. By secs. 50, 51 and 52 any contract by the tenant for life not to exercise his powers is void, and any prohibition or forfeiture on exercise of such powers is also void. By sec. 57 a settlement may confer larger or additional powers than those contained in the Act. By sec. 56, in case of conflict between the provisions of the Act and those of the settlement, the provisions of the Act are to prevail.

Q. For what purposes of the Conveyancing Act 1881 and the Settled Land Act 1882, respectively, are trustees of a settlement needed, and who would be trustees for those purposes if none were appointed by the settlement?

A. Under sec. 42 of the Conveyancing Act 1881, trustees are needed where the beneficial owner of land is an infant, and, if a female, is unmarried, for the purpose of managing the property, and applying the income as directed by that section. Under the Settled Land Act 1882, trustees are needed—(1) to receive notice of the tenant for life's intention to exercise his powers under the Act; (2) to consent to a sale or lease of the mansion and demesne; (3) to consent to a sale of ripe timber where the tenant for life is impeachable for waste; (4) to approve a scheme for improvements; (5) to receive and pay money; (6) to make investments under the direction of the tenant for life; and (7) to exercise the powers of the life tenant, where such tenant is an infant. Under both Acts, if there are no trustees under the settlement, the Court will appoint trustees, on application by or on behalf of the tenant for life.

Q. What are the provisions of the Settled Land Act 1882 with reference to the cutting and sale of timber by a tenant for life?

A. By sec. 35 a tenant for life—who is impeachable for waste with respect to any timber—may cut and sell that timber provided it is ripe and fit for cutting, and he gets the consent of the trustees or an order of Court, but three-fourths of the net proceeds are capital and the balance only income. By sec. 29 the tenant for life may cut and use timber which is not ornamental in order to execute, maintain, or repair any improvements under the Act.

Q. Explain the operation of a conveyance by a tenant for life under the Settled Land Act 1882. What estates and charges are, and what are not, capable of being over-reached by such conveyance?

A. It operates by virtue of the Act to pass at once by the deed the estate subject to the settlement in whatever manner is requisite for giving effect to the sale, exchange, partition, lease, mortgage, or charge. It can over-reach all the limitations, powers and provisions of the settlement, and all estates, interests and charges subsisting or to arise thereunder; but subject to and except (1) estates, interests, and charges which (*a*) have priority to the settlement, or (*b*) are created for securing money actually raised at the date of the deed, and (2) grants at fee farm rents and grants of easements or commons or other rights granted for value before the date of the deed. (Sec. 20 of 1882 Act.)

Q. What power is given by the Settled Land Acts for the protection or recovery of settled land?

A. By sec. 36 of the 1882 Act, the Court may approve (1) of any action, defence, petition to Parliament, parliamentary opposition, or other proceeding for protection of settled land; or (2) of any action or proceeding for recovery of such land; and may direct payment of the costs out of the settled property.

* *Q. Thomas Styles, who died in 1884, by his will, made in 1870, devised his real estate in Kent and Lancashire to his married daughter Mary Smith for her life, for her separate use, without power of anticipation; remainder to her husband John Smith for his life; remainder to the first and other sons of John and Mary Smith successively, according to seniority, in tail male; and he declared that he intentionally omitted from his will any power of sale. Mr. and Mrs. Smith, whose eldest son is an infant, desire to sell a farm, part of the settled land in Kent. Advise them how they should proceed, and by whom a conveyance to a purchaser can be made.*

A. I should advise that the declaration is inoperative (Settled Land Act 1882, sec. 51); and Mrs. Smith as tenant for life can sell and convey the farm alone without her husband (secs. 61–63). The wife should obtain the sanction of the trustees, or an order of Court, if the farm forms part of the lands usually occupied with the mansion-house (sec. 10 of 1890 Act); and in any case sell the property, paying regard to the provisions of the Act as to mode of sale and disposal of the net proceeds, which will be capital. Notice must be given to the trustees of the settlement and their solicitor (unless waived), and, if there are no trustees, the tenant for life can be restrained from selling until two have

---

* This question and the three subsequent ones, were all asked in one paper, and form a series.

been appointed (sec. 38). But a person dealing in good faith with the tenant for life is not concerned to inquire respecting the giving of the notice.

Q. By the will referred to in the preceding question, a collection of pictures was settled as heirlooms annexed to the principal mansion on the Kent Estate. How can any of the pictures be sold; to whom must the proceeds be paid; and how may they be applied?

A. Mrs. Smith as present tenant for life under the settlement, can sell the (so-called) heirlooms; but she must obtain an order of Court, on application by summons at chambers. The proceeds of sale are capital money, and must be paid either to the trustees of the settlement or into Court, at the option of the tenant for life; but may not be paid to fewer than two persons as trustees, unless the settlement gives express authority for receipt of capital by one trustee. The proceeds may be applied (1) in the purchase of other chattels, to be settled and held on the same trusts as and devolve like the chattels sold, and (2) in any way in which capital money is directed to be applied by the Settled Land Act 1882. (See secs. 37, 22, 21, 25.)

Q. Mr. and Mrs. Smith believe that coal may be found in part of the settled land in Lancashire, and they wish to spend £1,000 out of the sale money of the heirlooms, in borings and trial pits to ascertain if coal exists capable of being worked to a profit. Can they do so, and how?

A. Yes, under sub-sec. 19 of sec. 26 of the Settled Land Act 1882. They should submit a scheme for the execution of the works, showing the proposed expenditure, to the trustees of the settlement or to the Court. If the money is in the hands of trustees, the application for approval may be to them (sec. 26), and they may pay the money over on a certificate of the Land Department of the Board of Agriculture, or a competent engineer or able practical surveyor, or an order of Court. There is an appeal from the decision of the trustees to the Court (sec. 44); and where the money is in Court the application must be made to the Court (sec. 26). The trustees are not justified in paying the money until the work has been done.

Q. If they discover good coal, who can grant a lease of it to a colliery company; and what must be done with the rent?

A. Mrs. Smith, as tenant for life, may lease for not longer than 60 years (Settled Land Act 1882, secs. 2 (10) and 6); or if the settlement gives power to the trustees to grant mining leases they may do so with the consent of the tenant for life (sec. 56). If Mrs. Smith is tenant for life without impeachment of waste, she is entitled to three-fourths of the rent as rents and profits, and the remaining one-fourth is capital money under the Settled Land Act 1882, and must be set aside and applied accordingly; but if she is liable for waste, then one-fourth comes to her as income and three-fourths go as capital money (sec. 11).

Q. A father devised freehold land to trustees (whom he appointed trustees of the settlement) in fee, upon trust to receive the rents, and thereout pay annuities which at present absorb the entire rents, and to pay any surplus to his son till he shall become bankrupt, or assign or encumber his life estate, or die; with an executory trust for the remaindermen on the happening of any such event. No such event has happened. Who can sell the land and convey the fee simple to the purchaser, and who must be parties to the conveyance?

A. Under secs. 2 and 58 of the Settled Land Act 1882, the son is tenant for life; and can therefore sell (under secs. 3 and 4), and convey the estate to the purchaser (under sec. 20). He must, of course, give notice to the trustees, and it is their duty to bring the matter before the Court if they have reason to think that the sale will not be *bonâ fide* in the interest of all interested. The annuitants would have a *locus standi* on the hearing.

Q. State the general nature of the provisions of the Settled

Land Act 1882, sec. 34, relative to the application of the purchase-money arising from a sale, under the Act, of a lease for years, or of a reversion expectant on such a lease.

A. This section provides that the trustees or the Court may, notwithstanding anything in the Act, require and cause the same to be laid out, invested, and accumulated in such a manner as in the judgment of the trustees, or the Court, as the case may be, will give to the parties interested in that money the like benefit therefrom as they might lawfully have had from the lease, estate, interest or reversion in respect whereof the money was paid, or as near thereto as may be. The object of this section is to prevent a sale, made under the Act, of a limited interest, or an interest not in possession, from operating to the prejudice of any person interested under the settlement, whether tenant for life or remainder-man. (Hood and Challis' Conveyancing and Settled Land Acts, notes to sec. 24.)

Q. Trustees having a power of sale over a settled estate with the consent of the life tenant in possession, are asked by him to sell the coal under part of the estate separately from the surface. You are requested to advise them if they can, under any circumstances, comply with his wish.

A. Yes, they may under the Confirmation of Sales Act 1862, obtain leave to do so on applying to the Chancery Division in a summary way (25 & 26 Vict., c. 108). Or the tenant for life may himself, without any leave of the Court, sell under the Settled Land Act 1882 (sec. 17).

Q. State briefly the provisions contained in the Settled Land Acts relating to settlements by way of trust for sale.

A. By sec. 63 of the Settled Land Act 1882, any land which under any instrument, whenever made, is subject to a trust or direction for sale, and for application of the purchase-money or income for the benefit of any person for life or any other limited period, shall be deemed settled land, and the instrument a settlement; and the beneficial owner for the time being of the income shall be deemed tenant for life, and shall have all the powers given by the Act to a tenant for life; and the persons who are trustees for sale or have power to consent to or approve or control a sale, are trustees for the purpose of the Act. By sec. 56 the consent of the tenant for life was needed to enable the trustees to exercise any powers under the settlement, which embraced any objects which are within the powers given by the Act to the tenant for life. It was decided that the tenant for life's consent to a sale by the trustees was not needed where it was the positive duty of the trustees to sell, but was needed where the trustees had a discretion (Taylor v. Poncia, 25 Ch. D., 646). By sec. 6 of 47 & 48 Vict., c. 18, no consent, which is not required by the settlement, is now necessary to enable the powers given by it to be exercised; and by sec. 7 the powers conferred by sec. 63 are not to be exercised by the tenant for life without the leave of the Court. If the Court makes such an order (and as to when it will do so, *see Re Harding's Settled Estates*, 60 L. J., Ch., 277) then whilst it is in force the powers of the trustees are taken away from them. Such an order should be registered as a *lis pendens*, otherwise a purchaser from the trustees is protected.

Q. Enumerate the limited owners to whom powers of alienation are given by the Settled Land Act 1882.

A. The person for the time being beneficially entitled under a settlement to possession of settled land for his life, sec. 2 (4). Also a tenant in tail; a tenant in fee simple with an executory limitation over; the owner of a base fee; a tenant for years determinable on life, or a tenant *pur autre vie*—not holding merely under a lease at a rent; a tenant for life or years determinable on life, whose estate is liable to cease on any event during the life, or to be defeated by an executory gift over, or is subject to a trust for accumulation; a tenant in tail after possibility of issue extinct; a tenant by curtesy; and a person entitled to income of land under a trust or direction for any life, or until sale of the land, or until forfeiture of his interest (Sec. 58).

Q. State concisely the purposes to which capital money arising under the Settled Land Acts may be applied.

A. (1) Investment on Government securities *or* other securities on which the trustees are, by the settlement, or by law, authorised to invest, *or* in bonds, mortgages, or debentures, or debenture stock of a railway company in Great Britain or Ireland, incorporated by special statute, and having for ten years previous paid a dividend on its ordinary stock or shares; with power to vary. (2) In discharge, purchase, or redemption of incumbrances affecting the inheritance of the settled estate, or in land tax, tithe rent charge, crown rents, chief rents or quit rents affecting the settled land. (3) In improvements under the Act. (4) In payment for equality of exchange or partition. (5) In buying the seignory of freeholds or the fee simple of copyholds, or (6) the reversion or freehold in fee of leaseholds—subject to the settlement. (7) In buying any fee simple or copyhold lands or leaseholds having 60 years unexpired, with or without minerals. (8) In buying minerals or mining privileges in fee simple, or for at least 60 years. (9) In payment to any absolute owner. (10) In paying costs. (11) In any other way authorised by the settlement. (Sec. 21 ; see also secs. 34, 36 and 37.)

Q. Who are trustees for the purposes of the Settled Land Acts?

A. Original trustees may be appointed by the settlor or by the Court, and, if there are no trustees at any time, the Court may appoint trustees. Further, under the Settled Land Act 1890 (sec. 16), if there are, for the time being, no trustees of the settlement for the purposes of the Act, the following persons shall be trustees : (*a*) Any persons for the time being under the settlement trustees with power of sale of other land comprised in the settlement and subject to the same limitation as to the land to be sold or with power of consent to or approval of the exercise of such a power of sale, or if no such persons then (*b*) any persons for the time being under the settlement trustees with future power of sale or under future trust for sale of the land to be sold or with power to consent to or approval of the exercise of such a future power of sale, and whether the power or trust takes effect in all events or not.

4.—Estates Tail.

Q. Explain the meaning of an estate tail. By virtue of what statute is it created? In what cases and how can a tenant in tail create a base fee, and convey an estate in fee simple?

A. An estate tail is an estate given to a man and the heirs of his body; it may be general or special, male or female; and it is created by virtue of the statute *De Donis Conditionalibus*. Where a tenant in tail in remainder bars the entail without the consent of the protector, he creates a base fee—which may subsequently be enlarged into a fee simple by a new disentailing deed executed with the consent of the protector, or after the protector's death, or by merger in the reversion in fee, or by 12 years' possession after the protector's death. A tenant in tail in possession (or one in remainder with the protector's consent) can convey an estate in fee simple by deed, enrolled in the central office within six months. Every tenant in tail can convey a fee simple under the Settled Land Acts, but the entail would attach to the purchase-money.

Q. What were the provisions of the statute "De Donis Conditionalibus"? State the reasons which led to the enactment, and show how its effects were counteracted.

A. This statute (13 Edw. 1, c. 1) provided that the will of the donor should be observed *secundam formam in cartâ doni expressam*, and that an estate given to a man and the heirs of his body, should strictly so descend, notwithstanding any alienation by the donee. The reason for this enactment was that a grant to a man and the heirs of his body was construed as creating a conditional fee, that the donee could alienate absolutely on the birth of issue. Its effects were counteracted by the system that grew up of suffering fines and recoveries, the first instance of one being allowed being found in Taltarum's Case, which was decided about 200 years after the statute.

Q. *State shortly the effect of the Fines and Recoveries Act as to barring estates tail.*

A. It abolished the methods of barring an estate tail by fine and by common recovery, and substituted a deed executed by the tenant in tail and enrolled in the Central Office of the High Court within six months afterwards. As regards an estate tail in remainder, if the consent of the protector of the settlement is not obtained, a base fee only is acquired.

Q. *Show the different effect of a gift to a man and the heirs of his body of freeholds, copyholds and leaseholds.*

A. In freeholds, the man takes an estate tail by the statute *De Donis*, which he can bar under 3 & 4 Wm. 4, c. 74. In copyholds—if the custom of the manor allows entails, he takes an estate tail which he can bar under 3 & 4 Wm. 4, c. 74; but if not, he has a fee simple conditional which he cannot alienate until the birth of living issue. In leaseholds, he gets the absolute ownership, because there can be no estates in personalty, and words which give an estate tail in realty give absolute ownership of personalty.

Q. *Under a devise of freehold land to two persons and the heirs of their bodies, what estates are created where (a) such persons can intermarry, and (b) where they cannot?*

A. (*a*) An estate in special tail which will descend only to the heirs of their two bodies. As long as A and B live they share the rents and profits equally; on the death of either the survivor is entitled to the whole for life, and on the death of the survivor the heir of their body (if they have intermarried) will succeed by descent. (*b*) A and B are ordinary joint tenants for life; on the death of one the survivor takes the whole for life, but on the death of the survivor the inheritance is severed, and the heir of the body of A, and the heir of the body B, become tenants in common in tail without further survivorship.

Q. Who is a tenant in tail after possibility of issue extinct? Can he bar the estate tail? Give your reason.

A. He is the owner of an estate in tail special (*i.e.*, to him and the heirs of his body by a particular wife) where the particular wife is dead without issue. He is expressly restricted from barring the entail by 3 & 4 Wm. 4, c. 74, sec. 18. But he has the powers of a tenant for life under the Settled Land Act 1882.

Q. What difference is there in the effect of a limitation to a man and his heirs male when contained in a deed, and when contained in a will? Explain the reason.

A. In a deed, a fee simple will be created, for there are no words of procreation; in a will, however, such words will create an estate in tail male, on account of the guiding rule that the intention shall be observed.

Q. Land was limited to A and his heirs by B, his wife. B having died without issue, can A sell the fee simple?

A. In a deed, this limitation would be construed as passing a fee simple, so that A would always have full power of disposition. In a will, however, the intention of the testator is to be observed, and it would be construed as an estate in special tail, and after B's death without issue, A being tenant in tail after possibility of issue extinct, could not bar the entail if it still subsisted, and therefore could not sell the fee simple —except under the Settled Land Act 1882, under which he is a tenant for life.

G 2

Q. What analogy to the office of "protector" of a settlement existed previously to the Fines and Recoveries Act? Show in what respects the establishment of the office was a new departure.

A. Before the Act, it was absolutely necessary that the first tenant for life who had possession of the land should concur in the proceedings, for no recovery could be suffered unless on a feigned action brought against the feudal holder of the possession. Now, the office of protector is established when the estate tail is in remainder, but, although the protector is usually the first tenant for life, not more than three persons may be specially appointed by the settlement. Where a previous life estate does exist, it does not confer the office of protector unless it is created by the same settlement which created the estate tail. (Williams' Real Property, 97, 98.)

Q. A being tenant for life with remainder to B in tail, under one instrument, what power has B over the estate, first, with A's consent; and, secondly, without it?

A. During the continuance of A's life estate, B can only completely bar the entail with his consent as protector. If B does not get A's consent, though B can bar his own issue, he cannot bar the remainders over, and will create what is known as a base fee.

Q. By marriage settlement freehold lands were limited to A for life, remainder to his first and other sons successively in tail male, remainders over; and copyholds were surrendered to trustees, their heirs and assigns, and leaseholds were assigned to trustees, their executors, administrators, and assigns, upon trusts corresponding with the uses of the freeholds. A is dead, and his first son B, having attained majority, wishes to acquire absolute interests in the whole property. How can this be done?

A. As to the freeholds, B must execute a disentailing deed, and enroll it in the Chancery Division within six months after execution; he will thereby acquire the absolute fee simple in possession. As to the copyholds—(1) if the custom of the manor permits entails, B can bar the equitable entail by surrender or deed enrolled, and so acquire the absolute estate; (2) otherwise, he has an estate analogous to the old fee simple conditional, and can only acquire the absolute ownership by alienation during the life of his issue. As to the leaseholds, he is absolute equitable owner of them, for words which create an estate tail in freehold give the absolute ownership of personalty.

Q. What is a base fee, and how may it be enlarged into a fee simple absolute?

A. A base fee is one to exist only whilst a certain qualification is attached to it, and the term is particularly applied to the estate which a tenant in tail in remainder creates who bars the entail without the consent of the protector. Such an estate may be enlarged into a fee simple absolute (1) by the execution of a new disentailing assurance, with the consent of the protector; (2) by the execution of a new disentailing assurance when the estate tail becomes an estate in possession; (3) by the base fee and the ultimate limitation in fee simple becoming vested in the same person; and (4) by lapse of time under the Statute of Limitations (37 & 38 Vict., c. 57, sec. 6).

Q. What powers of sale and leasing belong to a tenant in tail in possession and a person entitled in possession to a base fee?

A. Under sec. 58 of the Settled Land Act 1882, both of these parties have the powers of a tenant for life under that Act, viz., full power of sale, and a power of leasing, 99 years for a building lease, 60 years for a mining lease, and 21 years for any other lease. Also under the 3 & 4 Wm. 4, c. 74, there is a power of leasing for 21 years. These powers may be exercised without barring the entail.

5.—DEVOLUTION ON DEATH.

Q. State the rules of descent of an estate in fee simple

where the last purchaser leaves issue, and define last purchaser. When does land, of which a man died seised, descend on his father, and when does it descend on his eldest brother?

A. See the rules set out in Williams' Real Property. The rules specially asked for are 1, 2, 3, 4, and 7, but rules 5, 6, 8, and 9 should be considered also to make the answer complete. The last purchaser is the person who last acquired the lands otherwise than by descent, or by escheat, partition or enclosure (3 & 4 Wm. 4, c. 106, sec. 1). When the issue of the purchaser fail, the lands descend upon his father; and if the father is dead, or if he succeeds and then dies without disposing of the lands, they go to the purchaser's eldest brother.

Q. State the alterations introduced by the Act for the amendment of the Law of Inheritance as to tracing descent from the purchaser and the admission of the half-blood.

A. Under this Act (3 & 4 Wm. 4, c. 106), instead of the old rule *seisina facit stipitem*, the rule now is that the descent is to be traced from the last " purchaser," *i.e.*, the last person entitled otherwise than by descent, escheat, partition, or enclosure. The half-blood formerly could not inherit, whereas, under this Act, they now inherit (*a*) next after a kinsman of the same degree of the whole blood and the issue of such kinsman, when the common ancestor is a male, and (*b*) next after the common ancestor, when the common ancestor is a female.

Q. A bought freehold land, and died intestate, leaving a widow and an only child, a daughter. The widow married again and had a son by her second marriage. The daughter has died an infant and without having married, leaving her mother, her half-brother, and a paternal first cousin surviving her. To whom does the land belong, and for what estates?

A. The descent is to be traced from A as "the purchaser" (rule 1); the daughter took by descent and did not break the line of descent; A's issue being extinct, recourse must be had to his lineal ancestor (rule 5), who was his father (rule 6), and who is represented by his lineal descendant, the child of A's brother or sister and first cousin to A's daughter (rule 4). The first cousin, therefore, takes the land, subject to the widow's right to dower, unless that is barred.

Q. Land descended on A from his mother; he settled it upon himself for life, with remainder to his first and other sons successively in tail, with remainder to his own right heirs. He died a bachelor, and intestate. Is his heir to be traced through his father, or through his mother, and why?

A. Through his father, because the settlement broke the line of descent, and constituted A "the purchaser" (3 & 4 Wm. 4, c. 106, sec. 3), and as A has no issue, the descent is traced through A's nearest lineal ancestor, who is his father. (Rules 5 and 6.)

Q. What are the different modes of descent of lands held in gavelkind, and borough English respectively?

A. The descent of gavelkind and borough English lands follows the rules which apply to ordinary freeholds so far as those rules are consistent with the peculiar customs of either tenure; *e.g.*, in both tenures, the descent goes to males before females, to lineal heirs before collateral heirs. In gavelkind, by special custom, all the sons inherit equally, and this applies to collaterals. In borough English the younger son inherits, but this does not apply to collaterals.

Q. A (a bastard) dies intestate, seised in fee simple of land, and leaving a widow, B, and an only child, C. C dies intestate, an infant. Could B at common law, and can she now, inherit?

A. B at Common Law could not inherit, as a bastard can have no heirs except those of his body; but since Lord St. Leonard's Act (22 & 23 Vict., c. 35), she will inherit, as the heir of C, who was the person last entitled.

Q. Tenant in fee of some, and in tail male in possession of other, common socage and gavelkind lands, died in 1878 intestate, leaving a widow and the following issue: two daughters of his deceased eldest son, two sons, and a son of his deceased daughter. Who are entitled to the lands, and for what estates and interests?

A. The fee simple socage lands descend to the two daughters of the deceased eldest son, as coparceners (rules 1, 2, 3, and 4); the fee simple gavelkind lands descend to the two living sons and to the two daughters of the deceased son taking *per stirpes*, as coparceners (the same rules varied by the custom of gavelkind); the entailed socage lands descend to the elder of the two living sons, the daughters of the deceased son being excluded by the limitation in tail male (the same rules); the entailed gavelkind lands descend on the two living sons as coparceners in tail male (the same rules varied by custom and limitation).

Q. Tenant in tail general died in 1880, leaving issue only three daughters—Mary, Eliza and Jane. Mary died in 1883, leaving a husband and an only son. Eliza died in 1884, a spinster. There has been no disentail. Who are now entitled to the land, and in what shares, and for what estates?

A. Mary, Eliza and Jane took as coparceners in tail general (rules 1, 2, 3). On Mary's death, her share descended to her son in tail general (rule 4), subject to her husband's life estate by curtesy. On Eliza's death, her share descended on her sisters Mary and Jane as coparceners in tail general (rules 1, 2, 3), but Mary being then dead, her share went to her son in tail general (rule 4) freed from curtesy.

Q. A married woman, tenant in tail in possession, dies leaving a husband and an only son; what estates in the land do the husband and son respectively take, and what estates can either of them convey to the other, and by what means?

A. The husband takes a life estate as tenant by curtesy, and the son takes an estate tail subject to that life estate.

The husband can by deed surrender his life estate to the son, so as to merge it and accelerate the estate tail into possession. The son can (if 21) bar the entail, and so acquire a fee simple absolute; and he can then convey that estate by a deed of release to his father, and so merge the life estate in the fee. The father also has the powers of a tenant for life under sec. 58 of the Settled Land Act 1882, and can sell and convey the fee simple to the son under that Act, the result being that the life estate of the father and the estate tail in remainder of the son would attach to the purchase-money and the lands be freed.

Q. *What is meant by " next of kin " and " statutory next of kin "? A dies leaving a father, a mother, a wife, a son, and two grand-daughters, the children of a deceased child. Who are A's next of kin, who are his statutory next of kin, and who are beneficially entitled to the personalty of which he dies intestate?*

A. *Next of kin* means those who literally are the nearest of kin in the strict sense of the word; while *statutory next of kin* means those persnos who under the Statutes of Distribution are entitled to share in the personal estate of an intestate, and thus includes persons who, not being themselves next of kin, take as representing deceased next of kin, A's next of kin are his father, mother and son. A's statutory next of kin are his wife, son, and two grand-daughters; and the wife takes one-third of the personalty, the son another third, and the two grand-daughters the remaining third equally, because issue of the intestate always take *per stirpes.*

Q. *State the general effect of the rules by which the succession to the residue of an intestate's personal estate is regulated.*

A. The widow takes a third if the intestate left a child or children; and, subject to her share, the children take the whole equally between them, and if any child has died leaving issue such issue always take the parent's share *per stirpes (In re* Natt, 57 L. J., Ch., 797). If there is no issue, the widow gets £500 charged rateably on the realty and personalty (Intestates Estates Act 1890) and also half the residue, and the other half goes to the next of kin, who would be the father, if living. Failing a father, the mother and brothers and sisters of the deceased take equally, and if any brother or sister is dead leaving issue, the issue take the parent's share *per stirpes* if any of the prior class (*i.e.*, a brother or a sister or the mother) are living. No representation is allowed after brothers' and sisters' children. Beyond the above details it is simply a question for enquiry as to who are the nearest next of kin.

Q. A died intestate and childless, and without leaving father or mother, but leaving a widow, a half-brother, and two nephews, the children of his only sister of the whole blood deceased. He never had any other brother or sister. Who are entitled to his real and personal estate respectively, and for what interests, and in what shares?

A. The widow first gets £500 rateably out of the realty and personalty (Intestates Estates Act 1890). Then the widow gets dower (if not barred) out of the real property, and (subject to the dower) the real property goes to the elder of the two nephews absolutely (rule 7). And the personalty goes as to one moiety to the widow, and as to the other moiety half goes to the brother of the half-blood, and the other half equally between the nephews, taking *per stirpes*.

Q. A died intestate, leaving his father, a widow, and a child. B died intestate, leaving several children, but no father, mother or widow. C died intestate leaving no child or representative of one, but a widow and a father. D died intestate leaving no child or representative of one, no father or mother, but a widow and several brothers and sisters. State between whom, and in what shares, the several personal estates of A, B, C, and D are divisible.

A. (1) One-third of A's personalty goes to his widow and

the remainder to his child. (2) B's personalty is divided equally amongst his children. (3) C's personalty is divided equally between his widow and father *after* the widow has first got her £500 under the Intestates Estates Act 1890. (4) After D's widow has had £500, half of D's personalty goes to his widow and the other half equally between his brothers and sisters. (22 & 23 Chas. 2, c. 10; 1 Jas. 2, c. 17, sec. 7.)

Q. *A man dies intestate leaving real and personal estate, a widow, and no relative by blood. To whom, and in what shares, does his property belong?*

A. The widow first gets £500 rateably out of realty and personalty (1890 Act). Then subject to his widow's dower (if not barred) his real estate escheats to the Crown, whether it is legal or equitable, corporeal or incorporeal (47 & 48 Vict., c. 71, sec. 4); and the widow takes half the personalty, whilst the other half goes to the Crown as *bona vacantia*.

Q. *A man died intestate without child or father, but leaving his wife, his mother, two brothers, three sisters, and ten nephews and nieces him surviving. Who are entitled, and in what shares to his personal estate?*

A. The wife takes £500 and a moiety of the balance; and the remaining moiety is divided equally between the mother, brothers, and sisters, the ten nephews and nieces taking *per stirpes* the share to which their deceased parent would have been entitled.

Q. *Freehold land was limited to the use of A in tail male, remainder to B in fee. B by his will devised all his real estate to A.* (1) *If, under these circumstances, A dies intestate leaving issue only a son, what estate will the son take?* (2) *If A dies intestate leaving only a daughter, what estate will the daughter take?* (3) *In either case will A's widow be dowable?*

A. The estate tail does not merge in the remainder in fee because of the statute *De Donis*. (1) The son, therefore, takes an estate in tail male, with a remainder in fee simple, as heir-at-law of his father the purchaser. (2) The estate tail is extinct, as A the purchaser has no male issue; the daughter, therefore, takes a fee simple absolute in possession by descent from A. (3) In both cases A's widow is entitled to dower, if it is not barred.

Q. A purchases land and dies intestate, leaving a wife, son and daughter. His property comprises lands held in fee simple, in tail general, pur autre vie, and for terms of years. In whom do these properties vest?

A. The fee simple lands go absolutely to the son, subject to dower (if not barred); the tail general lands go to the son as tenant in tail by descent, subject to dower (if not barred); the estate *pur autre vie*, if granted to the deceased and his heirs, will go to the son as special occupant, but if merely granted to the deceased will go to the deceased's administrator as part of his personal estate (1 Vict., c. 26, secs. 3 & 6); and the terms of years pass to the deceased's administrator as part of his personalty. Until an administrator is appointed, the personalty vests in the President of the Probate Division.

Q. A testator died in 1883 having by his will, dated in the same year, bequeathed a share in his residuary estate to trustees, upon trust to pay the income to his daughter for life, and after her death for her children equally. The daughter died in 1885, having had three children only—namely, John, who died in the testator's lifetime leaving issue; Henry, who survived the testator and died in his mother's lifetime leaving issue; and Jane, who is living, an infant, and married. Advise the trustees as to the distribution of the fund.

A. I should advise the trustees that neither John nor his issue took anything, for though 1 Vict., c. 26, sec. 33, provides that there shall be no lapse in the case of a gift to a child or other issue of the testator who dies leaving issue, yet it has been held that this provision does not apply to a bequest to children as a class (Brown v. Hammond,

1 Johns, 210.) I should advise them that Henry took half, and to enquire whether he had left a will, and if not as far as it is personalty letters of administration must be taken out, and as far as realty it will go to his heir. I should also advise them that Jane took the other half, but she being an infant it cannot be paid over to her, and a guardian should be appointed. (See Viner v. Francis, Indermaur's Conveyancing and Equity Cases, 38.)

Q. Explain the meaning of the term Hotchpot.

A. Hotchpot appears to have originally meant a pudding, as being composed of things mixed or placed together. It was applied, as regards lands held in the obsolete tenure of frankmarriage, to prevent the owner of such lands taking any share as a coparcener on the death of the ancestor from whom the lands were derived, without bringing those lands into the common lot. Under the statute for the distribution of the personalty of intestates, it is used to prevent any child taking a larger share than he or she would be entitled to if the advances made during the deceased's life were taken into account. And it is commonly incorporated into a settlement of personalty to prevent any child, to whom a share is appointed, claiming to share in the unappointed part without bringing the appointed share into account.

6.—OWNERSHIP.

Q. Define an estate in severalty, joint tenancy, and tenancy in common.

A. An estate in severalty is held by a man in his own right only without any other person being joined with him in interest during his estate. A joint tenancy is where an estate is acquired by two or more persons in the same property, by the same title (not being descent), at the same time, and without words importing that they are to take distinct shares. A tenancy in common is where two or more persons hold the same land with interests accruing under different titles, or under the same title (not being descent) but at different periods, or conferred by words of limitation importing that they are to take in distinct share. (1 Stephen's Commentaries.)

Q. How did a tenancy by entireties arise, and what were its incidents? Can it arise now?

A. It arose by a gift to two persons, who were husband and wife, and their heirs. The husband took the rents and profits during his life, but could not dispose of the inheritance without his wife's concurrence. Unless they both agreed in making a disposition, each of them ran the risk of gaining the whole by survivorship, or losing it by dying first. Such a tenancy cannot now arise in consequence of the provisions of the Married Women's Property Act 1882.

Q. If freehold land be limited to A and B (husband and wife) and C and their heirs, what shares, estates, and interests do A, B and C respectively acquire in the land?

A. If the limitations are in an instrument coming into operation before 1883, A and B as one legal personage and C as another legal personage are joint tenants in fee, and with regard to A and B's rights between themselves they possess a tenancy by entireties. If the limitations are in an instrument coming into operation on or after 1st January, 1883, the result is the same; except as regards the rights of A and B between themselves as to their moiety, which are those of any strangers and not those of tenants by entireties (*In re March, Mander v. Harris*, 27 Ch. Div., 166; *In re Jupp, Jupp v. Buckwell*, 57 L. J., Ch., 774).

Q. What is coparcenary? Can men be coparceners?

A. Coparcenary is where two or more form a joint heir. Females always inherit as coparceners; but males do so only under the custom of gavelkind tenure.

Q. By which modes may joint tenancy, tenancy in common, and coparcenary, be converted into estates in severalty?

A. A joint tenancy may be severed by partition (voluntary,

or compulsory under the Partition Acts 1868 and 1876); by alienation *inter vivos* of his share by any joint tenant by absolute conveyance (which includes a mortgage) without partition, which makes the alienee a tenant in common with the remaining joint tenants; by a deed of release to one joint tenant by the others, which gives him an estate in severalty; by the *jus accrescendi;* and by accession of interest, as if there be two joint tenants for life and one obtains the inheritance this severs the jointure. A tenancy in common may be severed by partition (as above stated); or by all the titles and shares being united in one person, either by conveyance or descent. Coparcenary may be severed in the same two ways as tenancy in common, and also by one coparcener alienating her share because that destroys the essential unity of title.

Q. By what words may joint tenancy and tenancy in common respectively be created amongst children? (a) *A father having four children bequeaths his residuary personalty to all his children " equally." One son dies in his lifetime.* (b) *An uncle bequeaths £2,000 to his nephews, A, B and C. A dies in his lifetime. How are the residue and the legacy respectively divisible? Does it in either case make any difference whether the deceased person left issue living at the testator's death?*

A. No technical words are needed, but a gift to children as a class will create a joint tenancy, unless words are used showing that the testator intended each child to take a separate and distinct share. (*a*) This creates a tenancy in common, because of the word "equally," but only the children living at the testator's death will take. (See Brown v. Hammond, *ante,* page 92.) (*b*) The £2,000 legacy creates a joint tenancy, and must be divided between B and C, A's share failing. It makes no difference in either case that the deceased person left issue living at the testator's death.

Q. Residue consisting of freeholds and leaseholds was

devised to trustees upon trust to allow A to receive the rents for her life, and after her death to sell and divide the proceeds equally between the testator's nephews, B, C, D, and E, and their respective executors, administrators and assigns. B died in the testator's lifetime. C died in A's lifetime. A is dead, and all the property has been sold in one lot for £8,000. Who are entitled to the money and in what proportions?

A. This is a gift to B, C, D, and E as tenants in common. B's share lapses and goes to the heir and next-of-kin of testator according to proportion of realty and personalty. C's interest, however, was vested immediately on testator's death, and will go to his representatives, or according as he has dealt with it. D and E take their shares.

Q. How should a limitation to three persons as tenants in common in fee, and another to three persons as joint tenants in fee, be framed? State the course of descent in each case.

A. Some words must be used to indicate the intention that the grantees are to take distinct shares, otherwise the limitation will be treated as creating a joint tenancy. The limitations should be to X, Y and Z, as tenants in common in fee; and to X, Y and Z as joint tenants in fee, or simply to X, Y and Z and their heirs. Under the tenancy in common, the descent of each tenant's undivided share is traced from him as purchaser by the ordinary rules of descent; but so long as the joint tenancy exists, the *jus accrescendi* determines the descent, so that the ultimate survivor will take the whole, and the descent will then be traced from him as purchaser.

Q. What is the proper form of assurance between joint tenants, and why? And between tenants in common, and why?

A. Between joint tenants, a deed of release which operates to extinguish a right, for each joint tenant of a freehold estate is already seised of the whole land; but between tenants in common a conveyance is necessary, for each tenant in common has a separate title, is seised of an undivided and certain share, and therefore has to convey that share.

Q. It being a rule of the Common Law that the estate of joint tenants must arise at the same time, state what exceptions have been established to this rule.

A. The exceptions are: (1) Where the estates take effect under the Statute of Uses, *e.g.*, if A limits lands to the use of himself and his future wife for life, and afterwards marries, they are joint tenants for life; (2) devises, which stand on the same footing as uses; and (3) bequests.

Q. How can a partition be obtained between joint tenants or tenants in common, when they cannot agree?

A. By any of the tenants bringing an action for partition in the Chancery Division, or, if the property does not exceed £500 in value, in the local County Court; or by application to the Land Department of the Board of Agriculture to make an order for partition under their seal. In a partition action— the Court (1) may direct a sale and division of the proceeds at its discretion, (2) may direct a sale on application by any interested party unless the other parties will agree to buy his share, and (3) must direct a sale if parties interested to the extent of a moiety request it, unless it sees good reason to the contrary (31 & 32 Vict., c. 40; 39 & 40 Vict., c. 17).

Q. What is the general rule as to survivorship in—(a) estates, (b) the benefit and burden of covenants, (c) the exercise of powers vested in, or entered into by or with, two or more persons? Show what exceptions have been introduced by modern legislation in any of the above-mentioned cases.

A. (*a*) Survivorship of estates is applicable to joint tenants only as distinguished from co-parceners and from tenants in common. (Edwards, 156.) (*b*) In the case of covenants for title *by* joint tenants, each covenants s
as to his own acts, for otherwise all would be liable
acts of each, and the whole burden of the covenant

devolve on the survivor; but if the conveyance is *to* joint tenants, the covenants should be entered into with them jointly, so that the survivors may get the full benefit. (Goodeve's Realty, 251.) The benefit and the burden of covenants creating a debt entered into by or with two or more persons jointly will pass to the survivor. By the Bankruptcy Act 1883, the discharge of a bankrupt shall not release any person who was jointly liable with him. After the decease of one joint debtor the survivor may be sued for the whole debt as though the deceased had no share in it, and the estate of the deceased will be discharged from all liability both at law and in equity. (Williams' Personalty, 399.) Partnership debts are joint only, but the estate of a dead partner may be separately sued (1890 Act). (c) A power given to two or more persons by name, and not expressly made exerciseable by all or any of them, must be exercised by all the donees, and if one dies the survivor cannot exercise it. But the Conveyancing Act 1881, says a power given to two or more executors or trustees jointly may be exercised by the survivor (sec. 38), and the Conveyancing Act 1882, says that where a joint power has been disclaimed by one of the persons to whom it is given, the others, or other, or survivor, may still exercise it (sec. 6). In both cases a contrary intention expressed in the instruments will prevent the Act applying. (Edwards, 211.)

7.—FUTURE ESTATES AND INTERESTS.

Q. What is the difference between a reversion and a remainder?

A. A reversion is the residue of an estate left in the owner of property after he has granted out a smaller (particular) estate than he himself possesses; whilst a remainder is where, by the same instrument that creates the particular estate, the whole or part of the reversion is granted out to take effect in possession after the particular estate. A reversion arises by act of the law, a remainder by the act of the parties. Tenure exists between the owner of the particular estate and the owner of the reversion, but not between the owner of the particular estate and the remainderman.

Q. Define a vested remainder, a contingent remainder, and an executory interest.

A. A vested remainder is one which is necessarily capable of taking effect whenever the particular estate on which it is dependent comes to a termination, *e.g.*, grant to A for life, remainder to B and his heirs. A contingent remainder is one where, from some uncertainty affecting itself, either as to the person intended to take or the happening of the event on which it is to take effect, the remainder itself is in a state of contingency, *e.g.*, a grant to A for life with remainder to the son of B, a bachelor, or a grant to A for life, remainder to B for life, remainder in case B dies before A to C for life. An executory interest is a future estate, arising of its own inherent strength when the time comes, and not depending for protection on, or waiting for the determination of, a prior estate, but on the contrary, often putting an end to a prior estate: it is created (1) by deed under the Statute of Uses, when it is called a springing or shifting use, or (2) by will, when it is termed an executory devise.

Q. In what respects do executory interests created by will correspond in their incidents with springing and shifting uses?

A. In that by their means a future estate may be made to spring into existence after a limitation in fee simple, arising of its own inherent strength, and being in its nature indestructible. Generally the rules as to executory interests apply to all limitations coming in under that denomination, including for instance the rule against perpetuities.

Q. State the rules as to the creation and failure of contingent remainders, and the changes in the law made by 8 & 9 Vict., c. 106, and 40 & 41 Vict., c. 33.

A. (1) There must be a particular estate to support the remainder. (2) The particular estate and the remainder must be created by the same instrument. (3) The remainder must be limited to take effect directly the particular estate ends. (4) If the contingent remainder is freehold, the particular estate must be freehold. (5) The contingent remainder must vest before or at the determination of the particular estate. (6) If there is a remainder to an unborn person for life followed by a remainder to the issue of such unborn person, the remainder to such issue is void—except where the limitations are in a will and the remainder to the issue is an estate tail, in which case, by the *cy-près* doctrine, the unborn person himself takes an estate tail. (7) If one contingent remainder is limited after another contingent remainder which is not an estate tail, the second one is void if it can transgress the rule against perpetuities, *Re* Frost, 43 Ch. D., 246. The three first rules apply to vested remainders as well. The two statutes have in most cases, but not in all, done away with the rule by which the contingent remainder fails unless the contingency has been complied with before the particular estate determines. 8 & 9 Vict., c. 106, sec. 8, enacts that where the particular estate determines by forfeiture, surrender, or merger, before the contingent remainder is ready to vest, such contingent remainder shall not fail; and this rendered trusts to preserve contingent remainders unnecessary. 40 & 41 Vict., c. 33, enacts that where a contingent remainder, created by instrument executed since 2nd August, 1877, fails because it is not ready to vest when the particular estate determines, such remainder shall still be capable of taking effect, provided it would have been good originally as an executory interest (*i.e.*, could not infringe the rule against perpetuities) if there had been no particular estate to support it as a remainder. (See illustrations in four next answers.)

Q. Lands were limited unto and to the use of trustees

in fee, in trust for A for life, with remainder to his first and other sons who should attain the age of 21 years successively in tail male. A died leaving several infant sons, but no son who had attained 21. Would the contingent remainder to his sons fail, and if not, why not?

A. It would not fail; because the legal estate in fee is given to the trustees and the limitations are of equitable estates only, to which the Common Law rule 5 in the preceding answer never applied, and the limitations to the sons will take effect quite irrespective of 40 & 41 Vict., c. 33, in favour of the sons who live to attain 21. (*Re* Finch, Abbiss v. Burney, 17 Ch. D., 211; 50 L. J., Ch., 348.)

Q. *What is the effect of a limitation to A, a bachelor, for life, and after A's death to his eldest son for life, and after the son's death to A's eldest daughter then alive?*

A. The second contingent remainder to the daughter is void, because A might have a son who would live more than 21 years after A's death, and thus the daughter who is to take may not be ascertained within the rule against perpetuities. (See Rule 7, *ante*, page 100.)

Q. *If freehold hereditaments be limited to A in tail, and if A shall have no child who attains the age of 25 years to B in fee, is the limitation to B good? Give reasons.*

A. This a good limitation, for it is a contingent remainder, and does not transgress the rule as to contingent remainders, which is a distinct rule from that as to executory interests. (Whitby v. Mitchell, 44 Ch. D., 85.) But even if it might be considered as tending to perpetuity (see Frost v. Frost, 43 Ch. D., 246), yet it is perfectly good, being after an estate tail, for here as the entail might be barred, the remoteness of the event is of no consequence. (Williams' Realty, 360.)

Q. *A testator wishes to devise his freehold farm to his nephew, a bachelor, for life, with remainder to the nephew's first son who shall attain 25. What danger is there of the gift to the son failing?*

A. The nephew being a bachelor, this is a contingent remainder, and liable to fail by the nephew dying before he has a son of that age. The limitation would be void as an executory interest for exceeding the rule against perpetuities, and 40 & 41 Vict., c. 33, would not here assist. (See Brackenbury v. Gibbons, 2 Ch. D., 417.)

Q. *Land is conveyed to A for a term of 20 years, with remainder, if B shall survive the term, to B in fee. Is the remainder good, or bad, and why ?*

A. The limitation to B is a contingent remainder of an estate of freehold ; it, therefore, requires a particular estate of freehold to support it, and as there is no such estate, the contingent remainder is void.

Q. (a) *Upon the marriage of A, a bachelor, lands were settled upon him for life, with remainder to his eldest son for life, with remainder to the first son of such eldest son in fee. Which of the above limitations would be valid, and which void, and why ?* (b) *Lands were devised to A, a bachelor, for life, with remainder to his eldest son for life, with remainder to the first and other sons of such eldest son successively in tail. What would be the effect of that limitation, and why?*

A. (*a*) The limitations to A for life and to his eldest son for life are good ; but the further limitation to the son of the eldest son in fee is void, because it infringes rule 6 (see page 100) for the creation of contingent remainders. (*b*) The limitation to A for life is good, and the remaining limitations are construed by the *cy-près* doctrine as giving an estate tail to A's eldest son. (See further *ante*, page 100.)

Q. *Explain the necessity which formerly existed for trusts to preserve contingent remainders.*

A. Because in the absence of such trusts, if the particular estate ended by forfeiture, surrender, or merger, before the contingent remainder was ready to vest, such contingent remainder failed, as it had no particular estate to support it. 8 & 9 Vict., c. 106, did away with the necessity for such trusts.

Q. What restriction existed at Common Law with regard to the alienation of contingent remainders? By what statute was this restriction removed?

A. At law, when the person in whom the contingent remainder must vest (if it ever does vest) was once ascertained, he could release it to a person having a vested interest in the land, or could devise it to anybody; but in equity, any conveyance of it for value was enforced. By 8 & 9 Vict., c. 106, a contingent interest is made alienable by deed, whether the object of the limitation of such interest is or is not ascertained; and the Wills Act 1837 makes all contingent interests devisable. (Edwards, 142.)

Q. What is meant by a vested estate subject to being divested?

A. An estate vested in any person, but liable to be overreached and brought to an end by means of an executory limitation, *e.g.*, where lands are given to A and his heirs to such uses as B shall appoint, and in default of and until appointment to the use of C and his heirs, here C has a vested estate in fee simple in possession, of which, however, he may be divested (in all or in part) by B exercising his overriding power of appointment.

Q. Explain the meaning of the following terms:—"Possibility of reverter." "Contingency with a double aspect."

A. *Possibility of reverter* signifies the chance of the lord of the fee getting back the lands granted either by forfeiture or by escheat. A *contingency with a double aspect* is the alternative limitation of two interests, *e.g.*, a limitation to A for life, and, if A leave a son, to that son in fee, but, if A leave no son, to A's daughter in fee; and is valid despite the rule that there can be no remainder limited after a fee simple, for the second contingent remainder is not limited after, but is in substitution for, the former.

Q. A testator bequeathed a legacy to B, to be paid when he attained the age of 21 years; a legacy to C, payable three years after his (the testator's) death ; a legacy to D, if he attained 21 ; *a legacy to E, at the age of* 21 ; *a legacy to F when he attained* 21, *with a direction that interest at* 5 *per cent. on the last-mentioned legacy should in the meantime be applied for the benefit of F; and, lastly, a legacy to G at the death of the testator's wife; and made his wife residuary legatee.* B, D, E, *and* F *respectively died under the age of* 21 *years;* C *died three months after the testator; and* G *died in the lifetime of the testator's widow. Which of the legatees took vested interests in their legacies, and which did not?*

A. The legacy to B vested at testator's death, for the time of payment only was postponed, the gift being a present one, and B's next-of-kin will get the legacy. C's legacy also vested and goes to his personal representative for the same reason. The legacies to D and E did not vest, but were given contingently on their respectively attaining 21 ; both legacies, therefore, pass to the testator's widow as residuary legatee. F's legacy is saved from the fate of those to D and E by the gift of interest until the contingency happens, which makes the legacy a vested one, and consequently it passes to F's legal personal representative in trust for his next-of-kin. G's legacy vested at testator's death, the time of payment only being postponed. (Hanson v. Graham, Indermaur's Conveyancing and Equity Cases, 50.)

Q. *A fund was bequeathed to A for life, and after his decease to the children of B in equal shares.* B *had five children, three born in A's lifetime, and two after A's death: but one of the children born in A's lifetime died an infant before A's death. Who, upon A's death, would be entitled to the fund, and why?*

A. The fund is divided equally amongst the three children born in A's lifetime, the deceased child's share passing to his next-of-kin. One of the rules for construing testamentary gifts to children is that where a particular interest is carved out (here, A's life interest), with a gift over to the children of any person, such gift over embraces all the children who come into existence before the period of distribution (A's death). (See notes to Viner v. Francis in Indermaur's Conveyancing and Equity Cases, 38.)

Q. State the rule in Shelley's case. Do you know the reasons for the rule? Does it apply to wills as well as to deeds?

A. If a person by any conveyance has an estate of freehold, and, by the same conveyance, an estate is limited (mediately or immediately) to his heirs in fee or in tail, the word "heirs" is a word of limitation and not of purchase, *i.e.*, it marks out the estate taken by the person himself and gives nothing directly to the heirs—*e.g.*, limitation to A for life with remainder to the heirs of his body, A takes an estate tail. The reasons for the rule appear to be three—(1) The two limitations virtually accomplished the same purposes as a gift of the inheritance to the ancestor, and therefore the law construed them as such a gift, so as to avoid the injury sustained by the claims of the lord and the specialty creditors of the ancestor being fraudulently evaded; (2) a desire to facilitate alienation, by vesting the inheritance in the ancestor instead of keeping it in abeyance till his death; (3) the carrying out of the primary intention that the ancestor should enjoy the estate for his life and, subject thereto, it should descend to his heirs, by sacrificing the secondary intention that the ancestor should have a life estate only, and that his heirs should take by purchase. (Smith's Compendium, 6th edition, page 181.) The rule is applied to limitations in wills, except where its application would clearly have a result contrary to the intention of the testator as expressed in the will itself.

Q. What difference is there between a limitation to A for life, with remainder to the heirs male of his body, and a limitation to A for life with remainder to his first and other sons successively, and the heirs male of their respective bodies?

A. In the first case A takes an estate tail male under the

rule in Shelley's case; in the second case only a life estate, and his son an estate tail male.

Q. *Define a "perpetuity," and state the rules governing the limitations of estates in land in reference to the law of perpetuities.*

A. A perpetuity means any limitation of a future estate or interest whereby the vesting of the absolute ownership or of an indefeasible estate in fee simple may be postponed for a longer period than the law permits. As to remainders, the rules are that an estate cannot be limited to the child of an unborn person in remainder after a particular estate limited to its parent, and that a contingent remainder must (unless within the Contingent Remainders Act 1877) vest not later than the ending of the particular estate (see page 100). Executory interests, and equitable contingent remainders, and contingent remainders of copyholds, and future interests in personalty, are governed by the Rule against Perpetuities which makes them void if, at the time when the limitation comes into force, there is a possibility that the estate or interest limited will not vest within the period of a life or lives then in being, and 21 years longer; but this rule does not vitiate (1) limitations following an estate tail, (2) charitable trusts, (3) powers of sale in a settlement of land, (4) a trust to accumulate for payment of debts, and (5) restrictive covenants binding land. (Edwards, 323—329.)

Q. *State the rule of law as to perpetuities. A, by his will, gives personal property on trust for his daughter, B, for life, remainder in trust for any man whom she may marry for life, with remainder as to both capital and income, to such of B's children as attain 21. He makes a similar gift in favour of his daughter, C, and her husband, with remainder, as to both capital and income, to such of C's children as shall be living at the death of the survivor of C and her husband, and attain 21. Are any of these gifts void for remoteness?*

A. All executory interests must commence within the

period of any fixed number of existing lives and 21 years afterwards, with a further period for gestation where it actually exists. The rule against perpetuities is reckoned from the date when the instrument comes into operation—here, the death of A. All these gifts are good. In B's case the limitations must vest within 21 years after B's death; and in C's case it is the same, as C is actually married when A dies. (Cadell v. Palmer, and Notes, in Tudor's Real Property Cases.)

Q. Mention the various periods during which accumulations are allowed by the Thellusson Act (39 & 40 Geo. 3, c. 98), and the cases to which the Act does not apply.

A. Income may not be accumulated for a longer period than (1) the life of the grantor, settlor, devisor, or testator; or (2) 21 years after his death; or (3) the minority of any person living or *en ventre sa mère* at such death; or (4) the minority of any person who, if living, and of full age, would be entitled to the accumulations. Where a direction for accumulation exceeds those limits, the excess only is void (Griffiths v. Vere, Indermaur's Conveyancing and Equity Cases, 23); unless the period may transgress the rule against perpetuities, when it is void altogether (Cadell v. Palmer, Indermaur's Conveyancing and Equity Cases, 23). Income directed to be accumulated contrary to the Act goes to the person who would have been entitled in the absence of such direction (sec 1). The Act does not apply to provisions (1) for payment of debts; (2) for raising portions for children; and (3) as to the disposal of the produce of timber or wood—and in these three cases the accumulation may be for the full rule against perpetuities. The Accumulations Act 1892, forbids accumulations *for investment in land only* being valid beyond the minority of the next owner.

Q. A testator, who died in 1837, directed his trustees, out of the income of his real and personal estate, to pay an annuity to his wife during her life, and to accumulate the rest of the income during her life, and at her death to pay the accumulations to such of his brothers as should then be living. His wife died in 1870, and two brothers of the testator were then living. How far, if at all, was the direction valid, and to whom did the surplus income from the death of the testator to that of the wife belong?

A. The direction is good for twenty-one years after the testator's death, and the accumulations during that period will go to the two brothers living at the wife's death in 1870; but the direction is void after the twenty-one years, and the excess income from 1858 to 1870 goes to the persons entitled in the absence of any such direction, *i.e.*, so far as it comes from realty, to the residuary devisee under the will, or the heir-at-law, as the case may be, and so far as it comes from personalty, to the residuary legatee or next-of-kin. (See last answer.)

Q. What restriction has been placed on executory limitations by the Conveyancing Act 1882, sec. 10?

A. That where, under any instrument coming into operation after 1882, any person is entitled to "land" in fee, or for years (absolute or determinable on life), or for life, with an executory limitation over on default or failure of his issue, such executory limitation shall not take effect if any issue capable of inheriting attains twenty-one. (See also next question, and *post*, page 139.)

Q. A testator, who died in 1883, devised a freehold farm to A in fee simple; but if A should die without leaving issue living at his death, then over to persons who cannot now be ascertained. A, who has adult children, has sold the farm as absolute owner. The purchaser objects that the title is bad, A's estate being defeasible by his death without leaving issue. Is the objection sustainable, and is the date of the testator's death important?

A. The objection is not sustainable, because the executory limitation over in default of issue is in an instrument which came into operation after 1882, and A, on whose death without issue the property is to go over, actually has issue who has lived to attain twenty-one. (Conveyancing Act 1882, sec. 10.) If the testator had died before 1st January, 1883, the objection would have been fatal.

Q. (a) *What is a power?* (b) *How do the estates created under a power take effect with respect to the settlement which contains the power?*

A. (*a*) A power in its widest sense is an authority. With regard to freeholds, a power may be defined as the means of causing a use, with its accompanying estate, to spring into existence at the will of a given person. Powers may be either common law powers, equitable powers, statutory powers, or powers operating under the Statute of Uses. There are also general powers and special powers; powers appendant, in gross, and collateral; and special powers may be either exclusive or non-exclusive. (*b*) As if such estates had been actually limited in the settlement itself.

Q. *Give an example of a power* (a) *operating at law,* (b) *in equity only,* (c) *under the Statute of Uses.* (d) *Under which class of power does the power of sale formerly inserted in a mortgage fall? And state shortly how it operates when exercised.*

A. (*a*) Power of attorney to collect a debt; or where a fee simple owner by will simply directs B to sell his land. (*b*) Any power of appointing the equitable interest in property given to an equitable life tenant, or a mortgagee's power of sale. (*c*) Grant of freeholds to A and his heirs to such uses as B shall by deed or will appoint, and in default of and subject to such appointment to the use of C and his heirs. (*d*) Equitable powers, for the mortgagee as legal owner could dispose of the property if he were not prevented by the rules of equity, and the effect of the power is to partially remove the restraint imposed by equity. A mortgagee selling in the absence of such a power could convey the legal estate, but the purchaser's rights would be subject to the mortgagor's equity of redemption ; a sale under the power extinguishes the equity of redemption. (Goodeve's Realty, cap XI.; Elphinstone's Conveyancing, 8.)

Q. You are instructed to draw a conveyance of freehold land to A in fee simple, and to insert in the conveyance provisions authorising B to convey the land to any other person without A's consent. What is the proper method of framing these provisions? If B conveys under these provisions can he deal with the legal estate? State reasons for your opinion.

A. Convey the freehold land (1) to such uses as B shall by deed or will appoint, and (2) subject thereto to the use of A in fee simple. The power is an authority to cause a use with its accompanying legal estate under the Statute of Uses to spring up at the pleasure of B; so that if B appoints to C, the legal estate for life at once vests in C for life, and A is pushed aside, because all estates created under powers take effect as if they had been inserted in the instrument creating the power instead of the power itself.

Q. Define a general and a limited power of appointment. How are appointments thereunder affected by the rule against perpetuities?

A. A general power is one that may be exercised in favour of any one without restriction on the choice of the donee, and the rule against perpetuities applies as from the time when the power is exercised, *e.g.*, if exercised by deed from its execution, or if by will from the appointor's death. A special power is where the donee is restricted to exercise it in favour of specified persons or classes ; and here, as the property is really tied up to those special objects from the creation of the power, the donee cannot create any estate which could not have been created by the instrument conferring the power.

Q. Two funds of personalty are settled, one upon such trusts as A shall by will appoint, the other upon trust for A's children as he shall by will appoint. A bequeaths both funds to such of his children as shall attain 23 years. State the effect of the rule against perpetuities upon each of these appointments.

A. Under the first settlement, A has a general power, the rule against perpetuities is applied from its exercise, and as all his children must attain 23 within the period fixed by the rule, the appointment is good. But as to the second fund, A has a special power, the rule is applied from its creation, and, as the appointment may transgress the rule, it is void.

Q. *What are the legal requisites for the valid creation of a power?*

A. There are three requisites to the valid creation of a power, namely, (1) sufficient words to denote the intention; (2) an apt instrument; and (3) a proper object. (Sugden, 102.) No technical or express words are necessary to create a power, provided the intention be clear. A power may be created by a deed or will. In powers operating under the Statute of Uses, the land must be conveyed to uses, and the power is only over the use, though by force of the statute the appointee takes the legal estate. The objects may be of any nature provided the rules of law or equity are not thereby transgressed. Care must therefore be taken in creating a power not to exceed by possibility the limits of the rule against perpetuities. (See Farwell on Powers.)

Q. *Explain the distinction between powers and estates, and between powers collateral and those which relate to the land.*

A. A power is a bare authority, which confers no ownership but may give an interest to the donee; whilst an estate is actual ownership of property, which, if accompanied by the legal seisin, entitles the owner to possession, and, if an equitable estate, entitles the owner to compel the legal holder to account for the profits. Powers collateral are powers, operating under the Statute of Uses, given to mere strangers who take no interest in the land; whilst powers relating to the land are, also, powers operating under the Statute, but are given to persons having an estate in the land, and are either appendant, that is, may be exercised during the continuance of that estate, or in gross, that is, can only be exercised after the determination of the estate.

Q. State, giving examples, the rules governing the operation of excessive appointments under powers, and show in what cases the cy-près doctrine is applied to such appointments.

A. Where there is a complete execution of the power and something *ex abundanti* added, which is improper, the execution is good and the excess only void; but where there is not a complete execution of the power, where the boundaries between the excess and the execution are not distinguishable, it will be bad. The leading case of Alexander v. Alexander furnishes a good instance of an excessive execution of a power. The *cy-près* doctrine is applied in some cases of appointments by will, so as to give effect, as nearly as may be, to the testator's intention; thus, it has been decided that where a power of appointing land, or money to be laid out in land, is given in favour of children, and the power is exercised by will in favour of a child, with remainder to the children of such child in tail—here the Court will give an estate tail to the child to whom a life estate only is given by will. (Indermaur's Conveyancing and Equity Cases, 18, 19.)

Q. Give a summary of the legislation of the present century with reference to illusory and exclusive appointments.

A. Originally an illusory appointment was good at law though bad in equity. By 1 Wm. 4, c. 46, an illusory appointment is valid in equity as well as at law. An exclusive appointment was always void as not being a proper exercise of a special power of appointment. Now, by 37 & 38 Vict., c. 37, an exclusive appointment is good.

Q. Distinguish a common law power from a power operating under the Statute of Uses? Explain the operation of the power of sale formerly inserted in strict settlements.

A. A common law power is one recognised and given effect to by the courts of law, *e.g.*, a power of attorney to receive a debt; or a direction in a will that the executors, to whom no estate is given in the land, should sell testator's real estate. A power which operates under the Statute of Uses is an authority to create a use in freehold land, which is at once changed into the legal estate by the Statute, *e.g.*, if land be limited to A and his heirs to such uses as B appoints, and subject thereto to the use of C in fee. The trustees frequently took no estate in the land, and their power of sale was an equitable power, and it was necessary to insert in the settlement a further power to convey to the purchaser, and this latter power operated as the declaration of a use or by way of appointment. (Elphinstone, 9, 22.)

Q. Explain the difference in operation of the exercise of a power of sale by (a) a legal mortgagee, (b) a trustee under an ordinary settlement of real estate, (c) a tenant for life selling under the Settled Land Act 1882.

A. (*a*) This power depends either on contract or on the provisions of the Conveyancing Act 1881, and the mortgagee is by the power able to convey the estate to the purchaser free from the rule of equity that the mortgagor has an equity of redemption. (*b*) This depends on the settlement, and the trustee must keep strictly to its terms, and is only able under its powers to sell, and he conveys to the purchaser the estate vested in him by the settlement. (*c*) This depends on the statute, and is a purely statutory power, the tenant for life being able to pass a greater estate than he himself possesses.

Q. Enumerate and classify the different kinds of powers of sale.

I

A. (1) Common Law Powers, which take effect apart from the Statute of Uses. Thus, a direction in a will that X, who takes no estate in lands, should have a power of sale over them, would be a Common Law power, to be carried out by bargain and sale in exercise of a Common Law authority. The power given by the Settled Land Act 1882, to a tenant for life to sell and convey, is an analogous power. All powers over personalty come under this head, as the Statute of Uses has no application to personalty. (2) Equitable powers, *e.g.*, the power of sale in a mortgage deed. (3) Powers operating under 27 Hen. 8, c. 10, which may be either collateral or relating to the land (appendant or in gross).

Q. What is a power of attorney? How should a deed, executed under such a power, be signed? Is a deed so executed necessarily, or in any and what cases, invalidated by the previous death of the principal?

A. A power of attorney is an authority under seal given by one person to another to do a certain thing or to act generally for him, *e.g.*, where one goes abroad. A deed executed under such a power had formerly to be executed in the name of the giver of the power; but now the attorney may execute the deed in his own name (44 & 45 Vict., c. 41, sec. 46). Formerly, a deed executed under such a power would be of no effect if the principal were already dead or the power revoked; but if the power of attorney was created after 1882, and was (1) given for value and expressed to be irrevocable, or (2) in any case expressed to be irrevocable for a period not exceeding a year, which period had not expired at the time of execution, the death or revocation of the principal makes no difference to the power. (45 & 46 Vict., c. 39, secs. 8 and 9.)

Q. Explain the doctrine of " Cy-près," and state the classes of cases and properties to which it is applicable.

A. The principle of the doctrine is that where a testator has two objects, one primary or general, and the other secondary or particular, and the latter cannot take effect, the Court will carry out the general object *as near as may be (cy-près)* to the testator's intention according to the law. (Wharton's Law Lexicon.) It is applied (1) to real property *devised* to an unborn person for life with remainder to his eldest son and the heirs of his body, by giving an estate tail to such unborn person; (2) to charitable bequests, by carrying out a *general* intention where the particular gift fails; and (3) to personal legacies accompanied by a condition precedent or subsequent, by holding that a substantial compliance with the condition is sufficient where a literal compliance is impossible from unavoidable circumstances without the fault of the legatee.

Q. Explain surrender and merger.

A. *A surrender* is the restoring or yielding up of an estate. It is usually applied to giving up a lease before the term expires, and its effect is to merge the estate of the surrenderor into that of the surrenderee. It may be (1) express, in which case it must be in writing, and if of more than a three years' term, by deed (29 Chas. 2, c. 3, sec. 3; 8 & 9 Vict., c. 106, sec. 3); or, (2) implied by act and operation of law, which is anything that amounts to an agreement by the tenant to abandon, and by the landlord to resume, possession of the demised premises, *e.g.*, delivery and acceptance of keys or creating a new tenancy. A surrender of copyholds is the giving up of the legal tenancy by an admitted tenant to the lord of the manor, either as a relinquishment of his estate, or as a means of conveying it to another. *Merger* is the annihilation by act of law of a particular estate in an expectant estate, consequent upon their meeting in the same person, in the same right, and without any intermediate estate (or where the estates so meeting are both freehold, subject only to an intervening term of years). An estate tail will not merge in the fee simple, because of the Statute De Donis; and any interest which is not an actual estate (*e.g.*, an *interesse termini*, or a contingent interest) does not merge in an immediate estate. Where tithe rent-charge, and the land out of which the same is payable, belong to the same owner, he is empowered by statute to merge the tithe rent-charge in the land by deed with consent of the Land Department of the Board of Agriculture. (6 & 7 Wm. 4, c. 71.)

8.—USES AND TRUSTS.

Q. State the effect of the first section of the Statute of Uses. Does it apply to leaseholds for years?

A. Where one person is seised to the use, confidence, or trust of another, the section (1) turns the use, confidence, or trust into an estate, *i.e.*, says the legal estate shall be in the *cestui que use*, and (2) vests the estate of the person seised in the *cestui que use* for the same estate that the latter had in the use. The section enables a freeholder to create a term of years which requires no entry by the lessee to perfect it, and upon this depended the efficacy of the conveyance by lease and release under the statute; but it does not enable a lessee for years to transfer his leasehold interest or create a sub-lease. (Elphinstone, 20.)

Q. When was the Statute of Uses passed? What was its object, and what has been its effect in conveyancing? In what case is it necessary, and in what case is it unnecessary to limit a use in conveyance of freeholds?

A. In the reign of Henry 8 (27 Hen. 8, c. 10). Its object was to put an end to the practice of conveying land to uses. Its direct effect in conveyancing has substantially been only to add the words "to the use of" to conveyances; but, beyond this, it enables various limitations of the use, with its accompanying estate, to be made which could not be made directly of the estate. It is necessary to limit a use where there is no consideration; or there is more than one person named, and it is desired that one shall take the legal estate, and another the equitable estate ; also where, in a deed, limitations by way of executory interest are desired.

Q Distinguish a use from a trust, and trace the history of the distinction.

A. By a use is meant the first use declared, being one which the Statute of Uses converts into the legal estate; whilst by a trust is meant a second or subsequent use on which the statute does not operate, but which confers, nevertheless, an equitable or beneficial estate. After the Statute of Uses, it was held in Tyrrell's Case that there could not be a use upon a use ; and upon this the Court of Chancery held that an equitable or beneficial estate was created by the subsequent use which is called a trust.

Q. What is meant by saying that a conveyance operates by transmutation of possession? Does a conveyance in fee simple made (a) by a tenant for life under the powers of the Settled Land Act, (b) by trustees under the power of sale formerly inserted in a strict settlement, operate in this manner?

A. That the legal estate or seisin passes at common law or by the operation of some statute other than the Statute of Uses—in contradistinction to a conveyance which operates as the declaration of a use only, so that the grantee gets the legal estate by virtue of the Statute of Uses. In the former class, if uses are declared on the seisin of the purchaser, such uses give the legal estate ; in the latter class, the uses merely give an equitable estate, as the Statute of Uses is already exhausted. (*a*) Apparently this conveyance may operate either by transmutation of possession or as a declaration of uses ; in practice, it is always framed to operate by transmutation of possession. (*b*) This operates as a declaration of a use, and not by way of transmutation of possession. (Goodeve's Realty, 363, 365.)

*Q. A grants freeholds to B "to hold to B and his heirs."
State what becomes of the legal estate when the conveyance is
made (a) for good (b) for valuable (c) without any consideration. Give reasons for your statement.*

A. In cases (*a*) and (*c*) there is a resulting use to the
grantor which gives him the legal estate under the Statute
of Uses; but in case (*b*) the valuable consideration implies a
use in favour of B, who therefore becomes the legal owner.

*Q. A grants freeholds to B "to hold to B and his heirs"
to the use of C for life, with remainder to the use of D and his
heirs. What estates, if any, do B, C and D respectively take?
Give reasons for your answer.*

A. The habendum may explain or enlarge the premises
but not lessen or contradict them. So that a fee simple is
passed through the grantee to uses (B), and by the Statute
of Uses C gets a legal estate for life with a legal remainder in
fee simple to D.

*Q. What methods of conveyance of land capable of being
now adopted operate partially, and what entirely, under the
Statute of Uses?*

A. Those operating partly under the Statute of Uses are
—(1) a feoffment to uses, which is a Common Law conveyance accompanied by a declaration of use of the estate
limited in fee or for life, and (2) a deed of grant to uses. A
bargain and sale and a covenant to stand seised operate
entirely under the Statute of Uses. A lease and release
consists of a limitation of a use under the Statute with a
Common Law limitation added. (Edwards, 356, 360.)

*Q. Distinguish the technical mode of operation of the
following assurances:— "Lease," "release," "surrender,"
"bargain and sale," "grant."*

A. *Lease* of land at common law is made by a grant of
the land for the term of years intended to be created,
followed by actual entry of the lessee, the grant merely
passing an *interesse termini;* but a lease of an interest lying

in grant (*e.g.*, advowson, right of common) takes effect by virtue of the grant merely. *Release* is a deed conveying a further interest in land to a person already in possession, such further interest passing by the deed without further ceremony. *Surrender* is a conveyance of an estate for life or years in possession to one who has an immediate remainder or reversion in which the estate conveyed is capable of being merged; the deed expresses that the surrenderor yields up his interest to the surrenderee, and the estate surrendered merges at once without any actual delivery of possession. *Bargain and sale* is a contract to sell an estate accompanied by payment of the price; this gives rise to an implied use in the purchaser and the Statute of Uses at once gives the purchaser the legal estate without entry; it must now be by deed enrolled under 27 Hen. 8, c. 16. *Grant* is a deed by the execution of which any interest in real property (except an estate in possession in a corporeal hereditament) can be passed at common law, and since 8 & 9 Vict., c. 106, such exception may also be passed. (Edwards, 315, 317, 318, 325, 314, 328.)

Q. In a conveyance on sale of freehold land the ordinary form of the habendum is " To hold the said premises unto the purchaser and his heirs to the use of the purchaser, his heirs, and assigns, for ever." Which of those words are, and which of them are not essential, and why?

A. The words "to the use," &c., are not required, for the purchaser pays a valuable consideration and the preceding part of the habendum is all that is needed. If the conveyance had been voluntary, all the words given above are needed, otherwise there would be a resulting use to the grantor which would revest the legal estate in him.

Q. What difference in effect is there between a limitation in a deed unto and to the use of A and his heirs, and a limitation to A and his heirs to the use of B and his heirs?

A. In the first case A takes the legal and beneficial estate, not by force of the Statute of Uses, for there is no one seised to the use of another, but he is in by Common Law. In the second case A has nothing, being merely a conduit pipe for passing the estate to B, and B will have a legal and beneficial estate ; but B is here possessed of his estate not by the Common Law, but by force of the Statute of Uses.

Q. If land is conveyed by deed to A to the use of B, his heirs and assigns, and A dies, what happens?

A. The estate granted to B determines, as only an estate for A's life is passed through A, and the person to whom the use is granted cannot have a larger estate than is passed through the grantee to uses or conduit pipe.

Q. What were the objects and advantages of using the conveyances called a bargain and sale, and a lease and release?

A. A bargain and sale was used to convey freeholds without the inconvenience and publicity of a feoffment with livery of seisin. A lease and release was used to avoid the necessity of inrolment under 27 Hen. 8, c. 16. A bargain and sale prior to 27 Hen. 8, c. 10, created a use enforced by a Court of Equity though disregarded by Common Law Courts; the statute turned this use into possession; 27 Hen. 8, c. 16, required a bargain and sale of freehold to be by deed, enrolled at Westminster within six months. But as the last-named statute did not apply to a bargain and sale for a term of years, whilst the Statute of Uses did (if created by a freeholder), the practice was adopted of making a bargain and sale for a year, which gave the lessee the feudal possession without entry, and then executing a deed of release dated the following day, by which the entire fee simple was passed to the bargainee.

Q. Explain the operation of the common conveyance called lease and release. Did either of the deeds by which this conveyance was effected operate by transmutation of possession?

A. The lease operated under the Statute of Uses and the release at Common Law. The lease had to be made by the freeholder, and took the form of a bargain and sale for value for a year; this operated as a declaration of a use, but did not fall within the Statute of Inrolments, and the lessee immediately on the execution of the lease became seised in possession without actual entry under the Statute of Uses; and being in possession he could by the Common Law take a release of the reversion in fee. The lease (or bargain and sale for a year) operated under the Statute; the release operated by transmutation of possession.

Q. Explain and illustrate—"*Even now a common purchase deed of a piece of freehold land cannot be explained without going back to the reign of Henry 8, or an ordinary settlement of land without having recourse to the laws of Edward 1.*"

A. (1) In a purchase deed the land is conveyed unto and *to the use of* the purchaser. The words in italics were rendered necessary by the Statute of Uses in voluntary conveyances to prevent a resulting use of the legal estate to the grantor; and although the valuable consideration renders them unnecessary in the purchase deed, they are always inserted. The Statute of Uses does not really apply to such a limitation, as it only relates to cases where land is conveyed to X to the use of Y; and where the conveyance is unto and to the use of X, X is said to be in by the Common Law. (2) In an ordinary settlement of land, uses are always inserted, which can only be explained by reference to the Statute of Uses; and estates tail are limited to the first and other sons of the marriage, and they can only be explained by reference to the Statute De Donis which created them.

Q. Explain the doctrine of Scintilla juris.

A. *Scintilla juris* was a doctrine by which it was contended that, where lands are conveyed to B and his heirs to the use of A and his heirs until some event (*e.g.*, a marriage) and then to the use of C and his heirs, a possibility of seisin remained in B until the event sufficient to enable C's use to be transmuted into the legal estate when the event happened; it was abolished by 23 & 24 Vict., c. 38, sec. 7, enacting that every use limited by a conveyance shall take effect by force of the seisin originally vested in the grantee to uses, *i.e.*, B.

9.—ALIENATION INTER VIVOS.

Q. Describe a feoffment and its necessary incidents. Has it any peculiar efficacy at the present day? If a feoffment be made to A and his heirs in trust for B and his heirs, what estates do A and B respectively take?

A. A feoffment was the Common Law conveyance used to pass a freehold estate in possession in a corporeal hereditament, and was perfected by livery of seisin (*i.e.*, delivery of the feudal possession) which was either (1) livery in deed, which took place on the lands, and could be performed by a deputy, or (2) livery in law, which took place within sight of the lands; writing was unnecessary until 29 Car. 2, c. 3, made it so by sec. 1 as to creation, and sec. 3 as to assignment of estates in land: by 8 & 9 Vict., c. 106, it must be by deed after 1st October, 1845, except when made by an infant under the custom of gavelkind; the word "give" was the technical term used in enfeoffing another. The publicity of delivery made a feoffment operate by wrong where the owner in possession of an estate granted out a larger interest than he possessed, so as to disseise the lawful owner until he re-asserted his estate by exercising his rights of entry; since 1845 no feoffment can operate by wrong, 8 & 9 Vict., c. 106. The word "give" in a feoffment implied a warranty of title; but since 8 & 9 Vict., c. 106, this is no longer so. A feoffment may still be used, but has now no practical advantage. It is the basis on which modern deeds have been formed. By the Statute of Uses, 27 Hen. 8, c. 10, A takes nothing, but is a mere conduit pipe to pass an estate to B, who gets the fee.

Q. How far is it correct to say that a man cannot legally convey to himself?

A. At Common Law a man could not occupy the position of grantor and grantee, and thus two conveyances were needed—(1) a conveyance to a third person, and (2) a conveyance from such third person to the original grantor, or to him and another. But under the Statute of Uses, one conveyance only is needed, as the interposition of a grantee to uses enables the grantor to settle his own fee simple on himself for life or in tail, or to convey it to himself and another. And since 1881, freehold land can be conveyed by a man to himself jointly with another without the interposition of a grantee to uses (44 & 45 Vict., c. 41, sec. 50.)

Q. Explain the different effects of executing a contract for sale in the case of real estate and personal chattels respectively.

A. As regards real estate, the legal ownership remains in the vendor until a proper deed of conveyance is executed; and although *in equity* the lands belong to the purchaser and the purchase-money to the vendor, *at law* each party merely acquires the right to sue the other for damages on breach of the contract. But as regards personal chattels, the legal ownership is transferred from the vendor to the purchaser without the necessity of anything further, provided the contract contains the legal requisites for a sale.

Q. State the different modes of alienation of personal chattels.

A. (1) By a mere gift accompanied by delivery—and the words of gift and the delivery may be contemporaneous, or either may precede the other; (2) by deed; (3) by sale; and (4) by will.

Q. What is meant by delivery of a deed? What is an escrow? A, by deed, duly executed in the presence of his solicitor, assigned his equitable interest in a fund comprised in his father's marriage settlement to B, but retained possession of the deed and destroyed it without either the trustees of the settlement or B having notice of the deed. Can B claim the benefit of the assignment on proving the delivery and contents of the deed?

A. Any words or signs showing an intention to deliver the document as a deed, *e.g.*, touching the seal and saying you deliver it as your act and deed, or handing the document to the grantee; what is a sufficient delivery is a question of fact to be ascertained from all the surrounding circumstances. An escrow is a deed delivered to some person who is *not* a party to it to take effect on a specified event. If the assignment was voluntary it was complete, and B can claim the benefit of it, for the destruction of a perfect deed does not vitiate it; if the assignment was for value, then B can only claim the benefit on giving the value. (Elphinstone, 54-56.)

Q. What is the use of "narrative" and "introductory" recitals? What is the effect of discrepancy between the recitals and the operative part of a deed? By an indenture made between A and B reciting that "B had agreed to lend £10,000 to A on mortgage of Blackacre, payable with interest at the rate and on the day hereinafter mentioned": the operative parts of the deed consist of the usual covenants for payment of principal and interest, and of the conveyance of Blackacre to B in fee simple, "subject to redemption as hereinafter expressed," but the proviso for redemption is omitted. What interest does B take in Blackacre?

A. *Narrative* recitals show the nature of the property that is to be dealt with by the deed; *introductory* recitals explain what is intended to be done by the deed. If both recitals and operative words are clear but inconsistent, the operative words govern; if one is ambiguous and the other clear, the one which is clear governs. B takes the fee simple as mortgagee subject to redemption. (Elphinstone, 67-70.)

Q. What is the object of the habendum? Draw the habendum in a conveyance of freeholds to a purchaser by mortgagee selling under the statutory power of sale?

A. To mark out the quantity of interest taken by the grantee. To hold the same unto and to the use of the purchaser in fee simple free from all equity of redemption or claims or demands under the mortgage. (Elphinstone, 100, 121.)

Q. What are the usual covenants in purchase deeds and mortgage deeds of freeholds, copyholds, and leaseholds respectively? Is there any difference between such covenants in purchase deeds and those in mortgage deeds?

A. In a purchase deed of freeholds, the usual covenants are that the vendor has good right to convey, for quiet enjoyment, free from incumbrances, and for further assurance. In a mortgage of freeholds the same covenants are inserted, with another for payment of the mortgage money. In a deed of covenant to surrender copyholds on a sale, the usual covenants are by the vendor to surrender to the use of the purchaser, for good right to surrender, for quiet enjoyment, free from incumbrances, and for further assurance. In a similar deed on a mortgage, the usual covenants are to surrender to the use of the mortgagee conditionally, and the same four other covenants as on a sale, and a covenant to repay the mortgage money. In a purchase deed of leaseholds, the usual covenants are (1) by the vendor that the lease is valid, and the rent and covenants have been paid and performed up to date, for good right to assign, for quiet enjoyment during the term, free from incumbrances, and for further assurance; and (2) by the purchaser, to pay rent and perform covenants during the term and to indemnify the vendor therefrom. In a mortgage deed of leaseholds by underlease, the usual covenants are by the mortgagor for right to demise, quiet enjoyment after default, free from incumbrances, for further assurance, to insure against fire, and to pay the rent and perform the covenants in the original lease and indemnify the mortgagee therefrom ; if the mortgage is by deed of assignment then the covenants are the same, except that the first covenant is for right to assign. The practical difference between covenants for title in a purchase deed and a mortgage deed is that in the latter the mortgagor covenants absolutely against all the world, whilst in the former the vendor only covenants for himself and those claiming through him and those through whom he claims since the last conveyance for value, not being a marriage settlement. (See Prideaux, Vol. I.)

Q. Under sec. 7 of the Conveyancing Act 1881, what covenants are implied by conveying "as beneficial owner," in a conveyance for valuable consideration of freeholds and leaseholds on a sale, and by way of mortgage respectively; and what covenants are implied by conveying "as settlor" in a conveyance by way of settlement?

A. On a sale of freeholds, the same four qualified covenants for title stated in the preceding answer; and on a mortgage, the same four absolute covenants for title. On a sale of leaseholds, the same five qualified covenants for title by the vendor that are set out in the preceding answer; and on a mortgage, the same five absolute covenants, and one to pay rent and perform covenants and indemnify the mortgagee are implied. In the settlement, the only covenant implied is one (limited to the settlor and those claiming through him) for further assurance.

Q. A buys a plot of building land from B and covenants that he will lay out £1,000 in building on the land, and also that he will not use any building on the land for a manufactory. A sells the land to C. Can the covenants, or either of them, be enforced by B against C?

A. By the rules of Common Law, the burden of a covenant relating to freehold land does not run with the land, and neither covenant could be enforced against C. But in equity, the burden of a restrictive covenant runs with the land to any one who takes with actual or constructive notice of it, so that an injunction can be obtained by B against C as regards the manufactory. (Tulk v. Moxhay, 2 Phil., 774.) And since the Judicature Acts, the rule of equity prevails.

Q. Give an analysis of a conveyance by a vendor seised in fee simple to a purchaser on sale, stating the names of the different parts of the conveyance.

A. Date; parties—(1) vendor, (2) purchaser; recitals, if any; witnessing part, consideration, receipt, operative words, vendor *as beneficial owner* hereby conveys to purchaser and his heirs; parcels; habendum and tenendum—unto and to the use of the purchaser in fee simple; testimonium. (Prideaux, Vol. I.)

Q. Sketch, in outline, a conveyance of freeholds on a sale by mortgagor and mortgagee.

A. Date; Parties—(1) mortgagee, (2) mortgagor as vendor, (3) purchaser; Recitals.—(1) of mortgage, (2) of agreement for sale, (3) of sum now due on mortgage, and (4) agreement to pay off mortgage out of purchase money; Testatum that in consideration of £   paid to mortgagee by direction of mortgagor (receipt acknowledged) and of the balance of purchase-money paid to mortgagor (payment and receipt acknowledged). The mortgagee *as mortgagee by direction of the mortgagor as beneficial owner* conveys and the mortgagor *as beneficial owner* conveys to purchaser; Parcels; Habendum to purchaser in fee freed from said mortgage; Testimonium. (Prideaux, Vol. I.)

Q. Conveyance to the purchaser of freehold land contracted to be sold to him by a testator who died in 1883, having by his will devised the land to his son John in fee, and appointed his wife his executrix; state who is entitled to the purchase-money, and who can convey the estate.

A. The contract for sale operates as a conversion, and the wife, as executrix, is entitled to the purchase-money. If the contract were binding on, and enforceable by, both vendor and purchaser at the death, the vendor was a trustee, and the legal estate passed to the widow, as executrix, by sec. 30 of the Conveyancing Act 1881, and she only can convey; but if the contract were not so binding on, and enforceable by, both parties, then either the widow, as executrix, can convey under sec. 4 of the Conveyancing Act 1881, or the devisee can convey.

Q. What is meant by a vendor's lien for unpaid purchase-money, and how can it be enforced? How is the actual receipt of the purchase-money usually acknowledged in a conveyance on sale?

A. The right of a vendor to have his unpaid purchase-money satisfied. *As regard goods*, this lien is a mere passive right to retain possession until the purchase-money is paid, and is lost by parting with the possession to the purchaser. *As regards lands*, the lien is an equitable right to have the unpaid purchase-money with interest at 4 per cent.; it commences only when the vendor parts with possession of the lands to the purchaser; and it may be enforced as a constructive trust by an action in the Chancery Division. Where the purchase deed was executed before 1882, both by a receipt in the body of the deed and a signed receipt indorsed on the back; but since 1881, a receipt in the body of the deed is sufficient. (44 & 45 Vict., c. 41, sec. 54.)

Q. What restrictions are placed on constructive notice by the Conveyancing Act 1882, sec. 3?

A. In every purchase, lease, mortgage, or taking or dealing for valuable consideration, of or with real and personal property, debts, choses in action, and any right or interest in the nature of property, whether in possession or not, the "purchaser" is not to be prejudicially affected by notice of any instrument or fact or thing, unless (1) it is within his own knowledge, or (2) would have been if he had made such inquiries and inspections as he reasonably ought to have made, or (3) in the same transaction with respect to which the question of notice arises, it has come to the knowledge of his counsel, solicitor, or other agent, as such, or (4) would have come to the knowledge of his solicitor or other agent, as such, if he had made such reasonable inquiries and inspections as he ought. But the "purchaser" is not relieved from any covenant, condition, proviso, or restriction in any instrument under which his title is derived; and he is not to be affected by notice where he would not have been affected if the section had not been enacted.

Q. What is "goodwill"? On a sale of it, what covenant should the buyer require from the seller, and why?

A. Goodwill is the benefit arising from connection and reputation, or the probability of the old customers going to the new firm which has acquired the business. A covenant that the vendor will not set up business in the same line within so many miles of the old place of business, and that he shall in no way solicit the former customers to deal with him. In the absence of this covenant, there is nothing to prevent the vendor setting up business next door to his old place of business, and soliciting his old customers in any way he likes; the only restriction being that he must not hold himself out as the old firm. (Pearson v. Pearson, 54 L. J., Ch., 32.)

Q. What are choses in action; and what practical difference has been made in the mode of assignment of them by the Judicature Act?

A. A chose in action is the right to bring an action to recover some debt or other thing resting in action. Formerly it was not assignable at law, and the plan adopted was to give the assignee a power of attorney to sue in the assignor's name. But now, under the Judicature Act 1873,

K

sec. 25 (6), a legal chose in action may be assigned absolutely by writing under the hand of the assignor, notice in writing being given to the holder of the chose, and the assignee can then sue in his own name.

Q. State briefly the principal rules regulating the transfer and mortgage of British ships.

A. The transfer is by bill of sale under the Merchant Shipping Act 1854, attested by one witness, accompanied by a declaration that the transferee is entitled to own a British ship, and registered at the port of registry. A mortgage is made in the same way; the mortgagee does not thereby become the owner, except so far as may be necessary to enforce his security; the mortgagee has a power to sell and to give receipts; the mortgagee is not affected by bankruptcy of the mortgagor; the mortgage ranks as from registration; and is discharged by the mortgage deed with a receipt indorsed being produced to the registrar who enters up satisfaction of it in the registry.

Q. A testator bequeathed a leasehold house to A, and appointed B his executor. A has agreed to sell the house to C, and B has agreed to sell it to D. Which contract can be enforced, and what compensation, if any, can the disappointed purchaser obtain?

A. The fact of B having contracted to sell the house shows he had not assented to the legacy; A's title is, therefore incomplete, and without that assent his contract to sell to C is valueless. As the house vests in the executor with all the other personalty for payment of debts, B's contract is a valid one, and D can enforce specific performance and have it enforced against him. If the executor had assented to the legacy, A would have had an absolute title, and his contract would have prevailed. The only remedy of the disappointed purchaser is by an action for damages, and the return of his deposit (if any).

Q. Freehold land was devised to A for life, remainder to

his son B in tail, remainder to the right heirs of A. A has died intestate, leaving B his heir. C has bought the land from B. How should he take the conveyance, and to whose acts should the covenants for title extend?

A. B possesses an estate tail in possession with a fee simple in remainder by descent, there being no merger of an estate tail. B must execute and enrol a disentailing deed, and then convey the absolute fee simple so acquired by ordinary deed of grant; or, as B has all the powers of a tenant for life under the Settled Land Act 1882, he may sell and convey the fee simple under that Act, but then the trusts of the settlement will attach to the purchase-money. In the former case, B will covenant for the acts of himself, of those claiming under him, and of those through whom he claims since the last conveyance for value, not being a marriage settlement; in the latter case, as the tenant for life is a trustee as regards the exercise of his powers under the Settled Land Acts, he will only covenant for his own acts.

Q. What are the essential attributes of mortis causa donations?

A. The donation must be made under the impression of impending death; to take effect if the donor does not recover from his present sickness, and does not revoke the gift before his death; must be of personal property; evidenced by delivery of the thing given, or the means of obtaining possession of it, or the title to it, to the donee, or some one for him, by the donor, or some one for him, in his presence and by his direction. It is liable to the donor's debts, to probate duty, and to legacy duty. It may be of a bond, of bills or notes, or cheques payable to the order of the donor, though not indorsed, or of a policy of life assurance, etc.; but not of the donor's own cheque, unless cashed in his lifetime.

Q. What is necessary to enable the assignee of a policy of life assurance to sue on the policy in his own name?

A. The assignment must be duly stamped, and the

assignee must have given notice to the assurance company. (30 & 31 Vict., c. 144; 51 & 52 Vict., c. 8, sec. 19.)

Q. How far is a voluntary settlement of (a) real estate, (b) chattels real, (c) pure personalty, void or voidable as against a subsequent purchaser for value?

A. (a) Under 27 Eliz., c. 4, the settlement would be void against the subsequent purchaser, even though he has notice of it, except in the one case of a charity. (b) When there is a substantial rent payable or any onerous covenant to perform, the voluntary assignee—by reason of the liability he incurs for the same—cannot be considered a volunteer, and the settlement would be good against the subsequent purchaser. (Price v. Jenkins. 4 Ch. Div., 483; *Ex parte* Hillman, 10 Ch. Div., 622.) (c) The settlement would be good, as 27 Eliz., c. 4, does not apply to pure personalty.

Q. Under what circumstances can a voluntary settlement be set aside by (a) the creditor, (b) the trustee in bankruptcy of the settlor?

A. (a) Under 13 Eliz., c. 5, where it can be deemed a fraud upon the creditors. (b) Under the Bankruptcy Act 1883—if the settlor becomes bankrupt within two years, or if he becomes bankrupt after two, but within ten, years unless it can be proved that he was solvent at the time of making the settlement, without the aid of the settled property, and that the settlor's interest in the property passed to the trustees on execution of the settlement.

Q. Under a grant to A B, and under a devise to A B, what estate would A B take under the present law?

A. Under the grant A B will take a life estate in the property granted. Under the devise A B now takes a fee simple or other the testator's whole interest, unless a contrary intention is expressed (1 Vict., c. 26, sec. 28); before this Act A B would have taken a life estate only, unless words were used showing that testator intended to give a larger estate.

Q. Under a limitation in a deed to A B and his heirs male; and under a devise to A B and his heirs male; what estate does A B take in each case, and why?

A. Under the deed, although the grantor clearly intended to give A B an estate in tail male, yet, as he failed to make use of the essential technical words "heirs male of his body," or "in fee tail," the word male is rejected as repugnant, and A B takes a fee simple. Under the will, A B takes an estate in tail male, because the cardinal rule for construction of wills is that the testator's intention must be observed.

Q. State the law relating to the ownership of title-deeds where the lands are the subject of settlements and other conveyances.

A. The title deeds of land so far partake of the nature of realty that they pass with the land itself on its devolution. The owner of the legal estate is the person entitled to them, and this rule is equally applicable to real and to personal estate. If, therefore, the legal interest in the settled lands is vested in trustees in trust to pay the rents and profits to a tenant for life, and after his death in trust for other persons, the trustees are, as a general rule, entitled to the custody of the title deeds (Garner v. Hannyngton, 22 Beav., 630); but the *cestui que trust* has a right to inspect and take copies at any time. If the tenant for life has both the legal and equitable estates, he is entitled to the custody, unless he has been guilty of misconduct endangering the safety of the deeds, or unless there is a suit pending as to the property, and it is more convenient for the purposes of the suit that they should be in Court. The trustee of a bare legal estate will be compelled to deliver the deeds to his *cestui que trust*. (2 Prideaux, 15th edition, 212, 213.) A purchaser is ordinarily entitled to such title deeds as his vendor possesses, unless they relate also to property retained by the vendor. On a sale in lots, the purchaser of the largest lot is entitled to deeds relating to all. A first mortgagee, legal or equitable, is entitled to the deeds. A lessee is entitled to possession of his lease.

10.—WILLS.

Q. Explain the difference of the mode of operation of a will of a real and a will of personal estate.

A. A will of real estate operates as a conveyance to the devisee, taking effect upon the death of the testator, so that the devisee's title accrues immediately upon the death of the testator and by force of the will alone. But a will of personal estate simply operates in the first instance to pass deceased's personalty as from the moment of the death to his legal personal representative to be applied by him in discharge of the debts of the deceased, and subject thereto in accordance with the directions of the will; and the will must be proved in common form or solemn form, and a legatee will only obtain his legacy with the executor's assent. (Edwards, 390, 391.)

Q. Give a short account of the measures by which the right of testamentary alienation of real estate has been secured.

A. The feudal system did not permit real estate to be disposed of by will. When uses were introduced, a conveyance was made to the uses to be declared by a will, and a devise then made of the use, which devise the Court of Equity enforced. 27 Hen. 8, c. 10, by turning the use into the legal estate, for a time put an end to devises. By 32 Hen. 8, c. 1, a will might be made of two-thirds of land in chivalry tenure and all lands in socage tenure. 12 Chas. 2, c. 24, turned the first-named tenure into socage tenure. The Statute of Frauds prescribed signature and attestation. The Wills Act, 1 Vict., c. 26, governs all wills made since 1837.

Q. How must a will be executed and attested? What would be the result if (1) an executor or (2) a legatee under the will were one of three attesting witnesses?

A. It must be signed, at the foot or end thereof, by the testator or by some one for him in his presence and by his direction; the signature must be made or acknowledged by the testator in the presence of two (or more) witnesses present at the same time; and the witnesses must attest and subscribe the will in the presence of the testator, but not necessarily in the presence of each other. (1 Vict., c. 26, sec. 9.) (1) The will and the appointment of the executor would both be valid (sec. 17). (2) The will would be good with the exception of the gift to the attesting legatee, which fails unless the legatee can satisfy the Probate Court he did not sign as a witness (*Re* Sharman, 1 P. & D. 661).

Q. Mention the changes introduced by the Wills Act 1837 as regards the execution, attestation, and revocation of wills of real and personal estate.

A. Before the Act, wills of realty had to be in writing, signed by the testator in the presence of three credible witnesses, but for wills of copyholds, chattels real and personalty, no formalities were prescribed by law; now, all wills must be signed at the foot or end thereof by the testator (or by some one for him in his presence and by his direction), and the signature must be made (or acknowledged) by the testator in the presence of two witnesses both present together, and each witness must sign in the testator's presence. Formerly, a gift to an attesting witness or the wife or husband of such witness made the whole will void; now, the witness simply loses that benefit. Now, cancellation does not revoke a will, but marriage does with one exception (see *post*, p. 136).

Q. What changes were made by the Wills Act of 1837 with regard to the exercise of testamentary powers of appointment, and the property passing by a will?

A. Formerly, in exercising a power of appointment by will all the formalities as to execution and attestation prescribed by the instrument creating the power had to be strictly observed or the exercise was bad; but now, as regards execution and attestation, the power is deemed to be complied with, provided the will is executed like any other will under 1 Vict., c. 26. As regards the property, formerly a will of real estate spoke from its date, and only passed the specific property of which the testator was then possessed; but now, a will speaks from the testator's death, and passes all his property at the time of death, except (1) where a contrary intention appears, or (2) the will is made by a married woman during coverture under the Married Woman's Property Act 1882, in which case it is specific and only passes property of which she actually becomes possessed during the coverture. (*In re* Price, Stafford v. Stafford, 28 Ch. D., 709; 54 L. J., Ch., 509.)

Q. State the several ways in which a will may be revoked, and how any obliteration, interlineation, or other alteration in a will after its execution must be made in order to be effectual.

A. A will is revoked—(1.) By marriage; except a will made in exercise of a power of appointment when the property appointed, would not, in default of appointment, go to the heir, customary heir, or next-of-kin of the appointor. (2.) By burning, tearing, or otherwise destroying it, with the intention of revoking it. (3.) By any writing executed as a will, and declaring an intention to revoke it. (4.) By a subsequent will or codicil, so far as inconsistent. No obliteration, interlineation, or other alteration in a will made after its execution is valid unless such alteration, &c., is executed as a will. (1 Vict., c. 26, secs. 18, 20.)

Q. Distinguish "specific," "general," and "demonstrative" legacies. How is the doctrine of ademption affected by the distinction? If a testator makes a will, leaving to A a sum described as now "owing to me on mortgage from B," and afterwards the mortgage is paid off, and the money received by the testator and invested on another mortgage, is A's legacy gone?

A. *A specific legacy* is a bequest of a particular thing, or sum of money, or debt, belonging to the testator, as distinguished from all others of the same kind, *e.g.*, my diamond ring, or the thousand pounds owing to me by C. *A general legacy* is a bequest to be satisfied out of the general personal estate, *e.g.*, a diamond ring, or a thousand pounds. *A demonstrative legacy* is a bequest, which in its nature is a general legacy, but there is a particular fund pointed out to satisfy it, *e.g.*, a thousand pounds out of my consols. A specific legacy alone is liable to ademption, *i.e.*, the legatee loses the particular thing if testator does not own it at his death; but general legacies and demonstrative legacies are not liable to ademption—except when given to a child and a subsequent portion is given by the parent during his life, which will be a satisfaction or ademption *pro tanto*. The legacy to A is specific and adeemed, for there exists nothing at the death on which the will can operate. (2 White & Tudor, 236, 282.)

Q. What is meant by "*ademption*"? In what different ways can it take place, and what alteration in the application of the doctrine resulted from the passing of the Wills Act (1 Vict., c. 26)?

A. Ademption usually means the failure of a specific devise or legacy because the testator does not own the particular thing given at the time of his death; but, by analogy to the ademption of a specific legacy, the equitable doctrine of satisfaction of portions is termed ademption when the parent makes a provision for a child by will, and subsequently during his lifetime makes a settlement upon that child, the idea being that money which would have passed under the will has been taken out of the will by reason of the subsequent settlement. The alteration made by the Wills Act was to annul the old rule that ademption took place if testator acquired an interest different from the one he possessed at the date of making his will in the subject of the devise or bequest. (Edwards, 407.)

Q. *Give an instance of a general, a specific, and a demonstrative legacy. And state out of what funds, or property, each kind of legacy is payable.*

A. A general legacy is one to be satisfied out of the general personal estate, *e.g.*, a horse, £100, a suit of mourning. A specific legacy is a gift of an ear-marked part of testator's personalty, *e.g.*, my brown horse, my railway stock, the plate presented to me by X; and is lost if the testator is not possessed of the thing given at his death. A demonstrative legacy is a gift of a certain sum directed to be satisfied out of a particular fund, *e.g.*, £100 out of my consols; and if the fund is non-existent, or so far as it is insufficient, at testator's death, the legacy is treated as a general legacy.

Q. What are the provisions of the Wills Act (1 Vict., c. 26) with regard to lapses of devises and bequests? A, in 1830, made a will, and thereby (inter alia) left certain land to a charity, and the residue of his real estate to B. He died in 1845. Who became entitled to the land? What would be the effect if the will had been made in 1840, and the death occurred in 1850? and what if the will had been made and death had occurred in 1892?

A. (1) That a devise of an estate tail shall not lapse if the devisee has heritable issue alive at testator's death; (2) that a devise or bequest to a child (or other lineal descendant) of testator shall not lapse if he leaves issue alive at testator's death, but shall take effect as if he had died immediately after testator; (3) that lapsed or void devises and bequests go to the residuary devisee or legatee. In the first case, the devise to the charity was void by the Mortmain Act then in force, and that land went to the heir as under an intestacy, for in wills prior to 1 Vict., c. 26, lapsed or void devises did not fall into the residue (see sec. 34); in the second case, the charitable devise was void, but under the Wills Act B takes the land; in the third case, the Mortmain Act 1891 says the charity shall take the land but must sell it within twelve months.

Q. A testator seised in fee simple of land, by his will, dated after 1837, devises it to his son X, who dies in his father's lifetime, leaving a son, Y, living at the testator's death. How will the land devolve on the testator's death?

A. This being a devise to a child of testator, who leaves issue alive at testator's death, the Wills Act prevents a lapse and says the devise shall take effect as if X had died immediately after the testator. Therefore, if X left a will, the land will pass under such will; but if X died intestate the land will go to his heir-at-law, *i.e.*, the son Y.

Q. Testator devises one freehold farm to each of his nephews, A, B, and C, in tail, and the residue of his real estates to the three nephews as tenants in common in fee. A died in testator's lifetime, leaving sons and daughters living at testator's death. To whom, and in what shares, do the farms and residuary real estate pass at testator's death?

A. A's farm goes to his eldest son as tenant in tail by descent, because of 1 Vict., c. 26, sec. 32; B is tenant in tail of his farm by purchase; so is C. B and C take two undivided third parts of the residue as tenants in common in fee; but A's undivided third part lapses, he not being a child or other issue of the testator. And as A's third is part of the residue, there is an intestacy as to it, and it goes to the testator's heir-at-law.

Q. What change did the Wills Act make in the ordinary interpretation of the words " died without issue " when occurring in a will?

A. Prior to the Act, the words were construed to mean an indefinite failure of issue and so gave an estate tail; but since the Act, they mean a want or failure of issue at the death of the person on whose death without issue the property is to go over, unless a contrary intention appears in the will by reason of such person having a prior estate tail, or of a preceding gift being, without implication by such words, a gift of an estate tail to such person or issue, or otherwise. (1 Vict., c. 26, sec. 29; see also Conveyancing Act 1882, sec. 10, *ante*, page 108.)

Q. Explain the difference between an executor and an

administrator. Under what circumstances are the following forms of letters of administration respectively granted, viz., (a) *during minority;* (b) *during absence;* (c) *with a will annexed;* (d) *of unadministered goods; and* (e) *when, in the first two cases, does the administrator's office cease?*

A. An executor is the person named by the testator in his will to carry out his wishes; all the personalty vests in him immediately the testator dies; and he may do any acts of administration short of going into Court before he takes probate, which is a mere authentication of his title. An administrator is an official appointed by the Court of Probate to wind up the deceased's affairs, where there is no executor, or the executor declines to act, or dies intestate without completely winding up the estate; he has no authority but the letters of administration, and cannot act without them. (*a*) Where a sole executor or the next-of-kin is a minor; (*b*) Where the sole executor is out of the kingdom at the death, or goes to reside abroad after taking a grant and remains there for a year; (*c*) where an executor dies before the testator, or renounces, or there is a will which does not appoint an executor; (*d*) where an executor dies intestate, or an administrator dies, without having fully administered the estate; (*e*) when the minor attains his majority and the absent one returns respectively.

Q. If a creditor appoints his debtor his executor, what is the effect at law, and in equity, respectively?

A. At law, this operated as an extinguishment of the debt, because the executor could not sue himself; but in equity, the executor is bound to account for the debt to the testator's estate.

Q. (a) *A bequeathed his watch to X, and appointed Y his executor. At the death of A the watch was in the hands of a watchmaker, who wrongfully refused to deliver it up. Who is the proper person to take proceedings for its recovery, and why?* (b) *A owed B £500 and C £200. The former debt was payable immediately, but the latter was payable three years hence. A by his will bequeathed £300 to B, and the same sum to C.*

Would either and which of the debts be satisfied by the legacy left to the creditor?

A. (*a*) The executor, for all the personalty vests in him the moment testator dies, and the legatee's title is incomplete until the executor has assented to the legacy. (*b*) The legacy to B will not satisfy his debt even *pro tanto*, but the legacy to C will satisfy his debt. The leaning of the Court is against satisfaction of debts by legacies; consequently there is only a satisfaction where the legacy is equal to or greater than the debt, and in all other respects equally beneficial, and the debt is owing when the will is made, and the will does not direct both debts and legacies to be paid.

Q. State briefly the duties of an executor with respect to the administration of the testator's estate.

A. He must bury the deceased in a manner suitable to his estate; make an inventory of the personal property; prove the will; collect and realize the personalty, bringing actions where necessary for that purpose; pay the debts in proper order; pay the legacies, pass the residuary account, and pay the duty; and pay the residue to the residuary legatee, or if none, to the next-of-kin. If there are no next-of-kin, he is personally entitled to the residue, unless the will evinces a contrary intention.

Q. What acts of administration can an executor do before probate?

A. He may do all ordinary acts of administration short of going into Court—*e.g.*, make inventories, sell and assign personalty, collect debts, pay debts and legacies, commence an action; but if he has occasion to go into Court in the action, he must produce the probate, as that is his only evidence of his title to sue.

Q. In what cases can executors and testamentary trustees respectively sell or mortgage their testator's real estate for payment of his debts or legacies?.

A. By 22 & 23 Vict., c. 35, secs. 14-17, if the testator has charged his real estate with payment of debts or legacies; then (1) if he has devised the same to trustees for his whole interest therein and has not made any express provision for raising such debts or legacies, the trustees may raise the same by sale or mortgage, notwithstanding the trusts actually declared; but (2) if testator has not devised his real estate to trustees for all his interest therein, the executors for the time being may so sell or mortgage. But the Act does not extend to a devise to any one in fee or in tail or for testator's entire interest, charged with debts or legacies, nor does it affect the power of such devisee to sell or mortgage.

Q. Is an executor bound to plead the Statute of Limitations to a demand for the payment of a debt which is statute-barred, or may he pay it if he thinks fit? If the estate is being administered in the Chancery Division, is any and what other person competent to take the objection although the executor may not have insisted upon it?

A. An executor may pay a debt proved to be justly due from his testator, although barred by the Statute of Limitations; but not where it is barred by any other statute (*In re* Rownson, Field v. White, 29 Ch. D., 358). If the estate is being administered in the Chancery Division, the plaintiff, or any person interested in the fund, may plead the Statute of Limitations against a claim set up by a creditor, although the executor refuse to take advantage of such plea. (Shewen v. Vanderhorst, 1 Russ & M., 347; 2 Russ & M., 75; Williams on Executors, 1810, 1811.)

Q. An owner in fee of land died in February, 1879, having devised the land to his son absolutely, and bequeathed his personal estate to his widow, whom he appointed executrix. Who can recover from the tenant the Lady-day rent, and who is entitled to it when recovered?

A. The rent accrues due after the testator's death, viz., on 25th March; consequently under the Apportionment Act 1870, the rent is only recoverable from the tenant by the son as devisee, who may distrain or sue ; and the son is personally liable to the executrix in an action for the apportioned part up to the death of the testator.

Q. Testator appointed A and B his executors. In administering his estate it becomes necessary to (a) sue a tenant of a freehold house for rent in arrear at testator's death; (b) sell and convey a leasehold house; (c) receive a debt due to testator; (d) assent to a legacy to A. State which of these acts can be done either by A or B solely, and which must be done by them jointly.

A. Both A and B must join in the action ; but as any one executor alone can perform all other ordinary acts of administration, either A or B solely, or the two jointly can do any of the other acts specified.

Q. (a) In the absence of any express direction upon the subject, from what period, and at what rate, do legacies carry interest? (b) If a legacy is left by a parent, or person in loco parentis, to an infant, from what period would the legatee be entitled to interest, and why? (c) If a legacy is given to an infant, or to a person beyond the seas, in what way can the executor obtain a proper discharge for it?

A. (a) From a year after the death of the testator, at 4 per cent. ; but interest runs from the death, if the legacy is to a child, or is charged on land, or is in satisfaction of an interest bearing debt, or is specific. (b) From the death unless some other fund is given for maintenance, because the legacy is presumed to be given for maintenance. (c) By paying it into Court under the Legacy Duty Act. (36 Geo. 3, c. 52.)

Q. A widower bequeathed his residuary personal estate equally amongst his six named children, of whom A and B subsequently died in his lifetime. A died a widower, and intestate, leaving two children, who survived testator. B died a bachelor, and testate. To whom, and in what shares, does the residuary personal estate belong?

A. The residuary bequest creates a tenancy in common ; the four surviving children, therefore, each take one-sixth of the residue; A's share does not lapse (1 Vict., c. 26, sec. 33), but passes to his two children in equal shares; but B's share does lapse, and is divided amongst testator's next-of-kin—viz., into five parts, one to each of the four surviving children, and the other to the two children of A *per stirpes*.

Q. If freehold land be limited to John and his heirs by Mary his wife, what estate has he (a) during her life (b) after her death without issue; and what power of disposition has he over the land during each of those periods?

A. If the limitations are by deed, John takes a fee simple estate in possession with absolute powers of disposition; the use of the words "heirs of the body" or "in fee tail" being necessary to create an estate tail. But if the limitation is by a will, then—as any words of procreation in a will are held to indicate an intention to create an estate tail in the absence of avowed intention to the contrary, and the cardinal maxim is that the intention of the testator shall be given effect to as nearly as may be—John takes an estate in special tail, which he can convert into a fee simple absolute at any time during the life of his wife Mary by disentailing deed under 3 & 4 Wm. 4, c. 74, but if he omits to do this before Mary's death without issue, he becomes tenant in tail after possibility of issue extinct, when he cannot bar the entail, and generally has the powers of a tenant for life.

Q. What points require attention in the preparation of a will giving legacies to (a) a creditor, (b) a debtor, (c) a child, for whom the testator has covenanted to make provision, (d) a charity?

A. (*a*) To consider whether the creditor is meant to have the legacy in addition to the debt owing to him by the testator (Talbot v. Duke of Shrewsbury, Indermaur's Conveyancing and Equity Cases, 124). (*b*) To consider whether the testator means the debt to be discharged, and the legacy to be in addition to this. (*c*) To consider whether the testator means the legacy to be something beyond the provision, or in satisfaction thereof (*Ex parte* Pye, *Ib*). (*d*) Formerly it was necessary to take care and make the legacy payable out of pure personalty only, so as not to be rendered bad either wholly or in part, by reason of the provisions of the Mortmain Act 1888; but if the testator dies since the Mortmain Act 1891, this precaution is unnecessary, as by that Act a charity can take land under a will, but must sell it within 12 months.

Q. A testator who died in 1835, devised Blackacre to A and his heirs, and the residue of his real estate to B and his heirs. A died intestate in the testator's lifetime. At the testator's death Blackacre was claimed by B, by A's heir, and by the testator's heir. Who was entitled to it? Would it have been different if the will had been made in 1840?

A. Where the testator died in 1835, his heir-at-law was entitled; because the devise to A lapsed, and a residuary devise did not then pass lapsed and void devises as it does now by 1 Vict., c. 26. But if the testator died in 1840, the devise to A lapsed, and under 1 Vict., c. 26 (sec. 24) the residuary devisee B would take, unless A were a child or other issue of testator and left issue living at testator's death, when A's residuary devisee, or heir, would take by sec. 32 of the same Act.

Q. What are the provisions of the Wills Act, 1 Vict., c. 26, with respect to the extent and duration of estates devised to trustees?

A. Where it is not specified what estate trustees are to take, they do not now as formerly, merely take such an estate as is necessary for the purposes of their trust, but under the 30th and 31st secs. of the Act, they in all cases take either an estate determinable on the life of a person taking a beneficial life interest in the property, or if the trust may endure beyond such life then they take the fee simple. (Goodeve's Realty, 398, 399.)

Q. A testator gave all his property to trustees upon trust for his daughter, subject to a condition that she would forfeit it

L

in case she married without their consent. This property consisted of real and personal estates, and money charged on land. The daughter married without the consent of the trustees. What was the effect of the marriage upon the property given by the will, and why?

A. As regards the real estate and the money charged on land, the daughter forfeits all her interest; but as regards the personal estate, the condition is regarded as merely *in terrorem* and void unless there is a gift over, and as there is here no gift over, the daughter does not lose the personal estate.

Q. State the steps by which the real property of deceased persons has become liable for payment of their debts. State how creditors can enforce their rights against real estate.

A. In the time of Edward 1, the real estate was liable in the hands of the heir for specialty debts, in which the heir was bound. If deceased devised his lands to trustees to pay debts, equity allowed specialty and simple contract debts to rank equally. 3 Wm. & Mary, c. 14, enabled specialty debts, in which the heir was bound, to be enforced against devisees. In 1807, the lands of dead traders were made liable for simple contract debts. In 1833, by 3 & 4 Wm. 4, c. 104, lands were made liable for simple contract debts, after payment of specialty debts. In 1869, by 32 and 33 Vict., c. 46, simple contract creditors were allowed to rank *pari passu* with specialty creditors. If judgment has been obtained in the debtor's lifetime, by writ of *elegit*: otherwise by administration proceedings in the Chancery Division, or, if the estate is insolvent, in the Bankruptcy Court under sec. 125 of the Bankruptcy Act 1883. (Williams' Real Property, 255-259.)

Q. X, by his will, gave an annuity of £100 to Y, and, after directing his executors to purchase same, went on to declare that Y should not be allowed to have the value of the said annuity in lieu thereof. Y nevertheless claims to be paid such value. Advise the executors as to the validity of the claim.

A. Y's claim is perfectly valid, for it is a perpetual annuity and he is entitled to the *corpus*. This right of Y might have been prevented by the testator having given the annuity over to some one else, or directing that it should fall into residue on any alienation or attempt to anticipate. (Hayes & Jarman, 10th ed., 142.)

11.—HUSBAND AND WIFE.—SETTLEMENTS.

Q. Give an outline of a marriage settlement of real property?

A. Date; Parties—(1) intended husband, (2) intended wife, (3) trustees; Testatum; in consideration of intended marriage the settlor conveys the real property to the trustees in fee simple—To use of settlor and his heirs until marriage, and afterwards—To use that the intended wife shall, during the joint lives of herself and her husband, receive a yearly rent charge (payable half yearly, the first payment to be made six calendar months after the marriage) as pin money for her separate use without power to anticipate; and subject thereto—To use of husband for life *sans* waste; with remainder—To use that the wife surviving her husband shall receive a jointure rent charge for life, commencing from the death, and payable half-yearly; and subject thereto—To use of trustees for 1000 years to raise portions for younger children: and subject thereto—To use of first and other sons of the marriage in tail male in succession, according to seniority; with remainder—To use of the daughters as tenants in common in tail, with cross-remainders amongst them; with remainder —To use of settlor in fee simple. There should be clauses (1) fixing amount of portions and giving husband power of appointment with a hotchpot clause; (2) declaring trusts of portion term; (3) advancement clause; (4) power for husband to jointure a future wife, and charge portions for children of future marriage; (5) naming trustees for Settled Land Acts and Conveyancing Act; (6) power for husband (and after his death for trustees) to mortgage for improvements; (7) husband to be the person to appoint new trustees; (8) any special clauses desired; (9) settlement to be void unless marriage takes place within 12 months. (Prideaux, Vol. II.)

Q. Sketch in outline a marriage settlement of £5,000 consols belonging to the wife, upon usual trusts, omitting all clauses and powers sufficiently provided for by statute.

A. Date; Parties—(1) intended husband, (2) intended wife, (3) trustees; Recitals—(1) of intended marriage, (2) of agreement for settlement, (3) of transfer of consols to trustees; Testatum—Declaration that trustees should hold consols (*a*) until marriage, in trust for wife, and (*b*) after marriage, upon the following trusts, *i.e.*, (1) Trusts to retain, or sell and invest, with power to vary investments; (2) Trust to pay income to wife for life, for her separate use without power of anticipation, with remainder to husband for life; (3) Trust in remainder as to *corpus* and income for children as husband and wife, or survivor, appoint, and, in default of appointment, equally—sons at 21, and daughters at 21 or marriage, with a hotchpot clause; (4) Trusts (on default of issue) for wife surviving coverture absolutely, but otherwise as wife by will appoints, and in default of appointment to her next-of-kin under the statutes excluding husband. Then come—Agreement to settle future acquired property on like trusts, if so intended; Investment Clause; Power to appoint new trustees to be vested in husband and wife and survivor; Solicitor trustee to charge costs; Settlement to be void unless marriage within 12 months; Testimonium (Prideaux, Vol. II.) If the settlement were of the husband's property, he would have the first life interest, and the trust (4) on default of issue would simply be for him absolutely.

Q. What is the object of adding a hotchpot clause to powers of appointment among children? Show how such a clause may operate favourably towards the representatives of a child dying before appointment.

A. To prevent a child to whom an appointment has been

made taking any share in the unappointed funds without bringing the appointed share into account. Under such a clause, the representative of such child will share the unappointed fund with the children to whom no appointments have been made; whereas in the absence of the clause, the children to whom appointments have been made will also be entitled to share in the unappointed funds.

Q. How can copyholds, leaseholds, and personal chattels be settled to accompany freeholds in strict settlement?

A. Copyholds should be surrendered to the use of trustees as joint tenants of a customary estate in fee simple upon trusts; and leaseholds and personal chattels should be assigned to the trustees absolutely to be held upon trusts and subject to powers and provisions—corresponding as nearly as law and circumstances permit with those relating to the freeholds. But as regards leaseholds and chattels, there must be a provision that they shall not vest absolutely in a tenant in tail by purchase unless he or she attains 21.

Q. (a) Can an infant, and if so, at what age, make a valid and binding settlement on marriage, and if so, how? (b) A married man conveyed an estate to trustees upon trust for his wife and children, and afterwards agreed to sell the same estate for value to a purchaser with notice of the settlement. Can the purchaser insist upon having the estate, or is the settlement valid as against him? (c) A, upon his marriage, settled a part of his own property upon trust for himself until he should dispose of the same, or become bankrupt. He afterwards became bankrupt. Would such a settlement be binding upon his trustee in bankruptcy?

A. (a) An infant not under 20, if a male, or 17, if a female, can make a binding settlement on his or her marriage, with the sanction of the Court of Chancery under 18 & 19 Vict., c. 43; but if such infant is a tenant in tail, and either bars the entail or exercises a power of appointment, he must attain 21 for the settlement to be good. If an infant makes a settlement without the sanction of the Court he may avoid it on coming of age, but if the infant does not avoid it within a reasonable time after coming of age then he or she will be bound by it (Carter v. Silber, 61 L. J., Ch., 401). (*b*) If the settlement is really a voluntary one, the settlement will be void as against the purchaser under 27 Eliz., c. 4. (*c*) No; such a settlement will not be binding on the trustee. If however, A acquired any property with his wife on the marriage, the settlement will be considered to be made with her property, and be valid up to the value of the property so received. (Prideaux, Vol. II.)

Q. Note the effect of marriage upon the wife's freeholds, leaseholds, choses in action, and choses in possession respectively.

A. *By the common law*—the husband became entitled to receive the rents and profits of the freeholds during the coverture, and, if he survived her, might have an estate by curtesy for his own life ; he could deal with the leaseholds in any way except dispose of them by will, and, so far as he did not dispose of them *inter vivos*, they passed to the survivor ; the choses in possession vested absolutely in him ; and the choses in action vested absolutely in him, provided he reduced them into possession during the coverture, otherwise they passed to the survivor, but, if he survived, he took as administrator. *Equity* permitted property to be given to the separate use of a woman, in which event the husband could only take (1) what the wife chose to give him, and (2) curtesy out of undisposed of freeholds of inheritance, and (3) undisposed of chattels real as her administrator; it also permitted the restraint on anticipation, which prevented her giving him anything beyond the income as it fell due ; it also gave the wife her equity (or right) to a settlement out of her choses in action, which the husband could only reduce into possession by the aid of a court of equity ; and it set aside a secret conveyance or settlement by a woman pending her marriage as a fraud on marital rights, except in a few rare instances. *The Legislature*, by 33 and 34 Vict., c. 93, enacted that (1) the wages, earnings, and savings of every married woman should be her separate property; and (2) that all personalty acquired as next-of-kin, and money not exceeding £200 under a deed or will, and the rents and profits of freeholds and copyholds acquired by descent, should be separate property where the marriage was after the 9th August, 1870, and the property was acquired during coverture. Lastly, by 45 & 46 Vict., c. 75, it is enacted (1) that all real and personal property belonging to a woman married after 1882, or coming to her during the marriage, shall be her separate property; and (2) that where a woman was married before 1883, all property, "her title to which, whether vested or contingent, and whether in possession, reversion, or remainder shall accrue" after 1882, shall be separate property. In construing the words in inverted commas, the Court of Appeal held, in Reid v. Reid, 55 L. J., Ch., 294, that where a reversionary interest was acquired before 1883 by a married woman, but it fell into possession after 1882, the Act does not make this separate property, as there can only be one accrual of title.

Q. What power of testamentary disposition of real and personal property respectively had a married woman before 1st January, 1883, and what additional power of testamentary disposition does she possess since that date?

A. Before that date—a married woman could only make a will of real or personal estate settled to her separate use as of right; and a will of personalty, which was not separate property, with her husband's consent, which he might revoke at any time before probate. Since that date, she has also the added powers (1) if married before 1883, of making a will of all property coming to her during the coverture after 1882, and (2) if married after 1882, of willing all her property at the date of, and also acquired during, the coverture. (*In re* Price, Stafford v. Stafford, 28 Ch. D., 709; 54 L. J., Ch., 509.)

Q. How far is a provision that a life interest given to any person under a settlement shall cease on bankruptcy or alienation valid?

A. Unless there is a gift over, it is simply void. But assuming there is a gift over, then (1) if the property settled comes from the life tenant, the gift over is good against his alienees, but void against the trustee under his bankruptcy; but (2) as regards property coming from any other person (*e.g.*, where such an interest is given to the husband in a settlement of the intended wife's fortune) the provision is altogether good; and (3) if a husband has received part of his wife's fortune on the marriage, and settled his own property with such a life interest for himself, the provision is good to the extent of the wife's fortune which he so received. (Prideaux, Vol. II., 250, 251.)

Q. What are the requisites and incidents of dower and freebench?

A. *Dower* is a life estate which a widow takes in a portion (usually a third) of her husband's lands of inheritance. At Common Law, it attached the instant the husband became solely seised in possession, unless barred by a conveyance to user to bar dower or jointure or a fine. As regards marriages since 1834, its requisites under 3 & 4 Wm. 4, c. 105, are (1) marriage, (2) death of the husband, leaving some estate of inheritance (either legal or equitable) not disposed of by him, and without his having barred the dower, which he may do by a simple declaration in any deed or his will. *Freebench* is dower out of copyholds. Its requisites are (1) a custom in the particular manor allowing it, (2) death of the husband leaving some estate undisposed of by him out of which, according to the custom, she may claim it. 3 & 4 Wm. 4, c 105, does not apply to freebench.

Q. Describe the nature and incidents of a tenancy by the curtesy.

A. It is a life estate which the husband takes in all his

wife's lands of inheritance in possession, of which she was the legal or equitable owner in severalty or in common, provided (1) he survives her, (2) there was a legal marriage subsisting at her death, and (3) issue born alive capable of inheriting. It attaches to separate use property, unless the wife has disposed of it by deed or will. (Hope v. Hope, 61 L. J., Ch., 441.) As to gavelkind lands, it is independent of the birth of issue, but only extends to a moiety, and ceases on re-marriage. A tenant by curtesy (but not a tenant in dower) has all the powers of a tenant for life under the Settled Land Acts.

Q. By what methods can dower be barred? State the rule as to legacies in satisfaction of dower.

A. If the parties were married since 1st January, 1834, the dower may be barred by a simple declaration under 3 & 4 Wm. 4, c. 105, contained in any deed or will, or by any disposition of the lands. If prior to that date, it can be barred by legal jointure, a fine, or uses to bar dower. The point as to a legacy in satisfaction of dower would practically only apply to persons married on or before 1st January, 1834. Where the will contains provisions inconsistent with the right to dower, the legacy will satisfy it in the sense that she will be put to her election and not allowed to claim the dower and the legacy. Even at the present day if a husband, married since 1833, dies intestate as to land, out of which his widow would be dowable, but makes a will of personalty giving her a legacy in lieu of dower, such a legacy is entitled to priority over other legacies. (Greenwood v. Greenwood, 61 L. J., Ch., 558.)

Q. What was the modern form of a limitation to uses to bar dower, and in what does its efficacy exist?

A. A general power of appointment was given to the purchaser by limiting the land to such uses as he should appoint—this enabled him to dispose of the fee without his wife's concurrence; in default of an appointment, the land was limited to the use of the purchaser for life; and on determination of that estate, by any means, in the purchaser's life, a vested remainder was given to a trustee and his heirs during the purchaser's natural life in trust for him; with an ultimate remainder to the use of the purchaser and his heirs. The efficacy was that it prevented dower attaching, for during the life of the purchaser he had no estate of inheritance in possession because the vested estate given to the trustee prevented the legal life estate of the purchaser merging in the legal fee simple remainder.

Q. What are a wife's pin-money, jointure, and paraphernalia; and what arrears of pin-money are recoverable by her and her legal personal representative respectively?

A. Pin-money is a yearly allowance secured to the wife by ante-nuptial settlement for dress and personal expenses suitable to the position of the husband. The wife can recover one year's arrears, unless the husband has paid all her personal expenses, in which case she can recover nothing; unless she has complained and been assured by her husband that she will have it ultimately, in which case she can recover all the arrears. The wife's representatives cannot (from the very nature of the property) recover any arrears. *Legal jointure* is a competent livelihood of freehold for the life of the wife at least, to take effect presently in possession or profit after the death of the husband; it was an effectual bar of dower; it had to be made to the wife directly and not to any one in trust for her, and in lieu of her whole dower, and before marriage. *Equitable jointure* is a provision out of freeholds lacking any of the above-mentioned particulars, or a provision out of personalty; and only put the wife to her election between it and her dower. *Paraphernalia* comprise the wife's wearing apparel and ornaments and gifts of jewels, &c., from her husband, to which she is entitled, beyond her dower, provided the husband predeceases her without having disposed of them in his life. They are liable to the husband's debts, and must carefully be distinguished from separate estate.

12.—INCORPOREAL HEREDITAMENTS.

Q. Enumerate and classify the principal kinds of incorporeal hereditaments.

A. According to Blackstone, incorporeal hereditaments are chiefly of 10 sorts. 1. Advowsons. 2. Tithes. 3. Commons. 4. Ways. 5. Offices. 6. Dignities. 7. Franchises. 8. Corrodies or pensions. 9. Annuities. 10. Rents. They have been classified as 1. Appendant. 2. Appurtenant. 3. In gross.

Q. Mention the characteristics of commons, (a) appendant; (b) appurtenant; (c) in gross.

A. *Common appendant* arose from necessity, and was the Common Law right of every free tenant of *arable* land to depasture on the lord's wastes all cattle needed for tillage and manurance of the land (*i.e.*, horses, cattle, and sheep, which are thence called commonable beasts); the number of beasts put on was not to exceed as many as the common would feed during the winter; as it is of common right it need not be prescribed for, and on a sale of part of the lands in respect of which it arises, it can be apportioned; and it passes along with the lands in respect of which it arises. *Common appurtenant* is annexed to some corporeal hereditament, but is against common right because it depends on a special grant (either express or implied from long usage); it cannot be apportioned, and fails altogether when it cannot be exercised in its integrity; it may be created at the present day; and it also passes along with the property in respect of which it is claimed. *Common in gross* is the right of the owner to a *profit à prendre* out of the lands of another, arising by express grant to the commoner, and not as appendant or appurtenant to any corporeal hereditament; it requires a deed for its transfer. (See Tyrringham's Case.)

Q. Explain the rule that rent-charges and rights of common appurtenant should be regarded as being "against common right." What consequences have been deduced from the rule with respect to hereditaments of these kinds?

A. They are not of common right, for they do not arise by implication of law only as did common appendant, but by express grant, or (as to common appurtenant) by prescription or custom; and, unlike common appendant, they may be created at the present day. Common appendant was extinguished by purchase of all the lands over which the right existed; but rent-charges and commons appurtenant were regarded as entire and issuing out of every part of the land charged. Consequently, the purchase or release of any part of the lands subject to a rent-charge, or common appurtenant, destroyed the charge or common. By 17 & 18 Vict., c. 97, the rent-charge was made apportionable, and by 22 & 23 Vict., c. 35, the release of a portion of the lands from the rent-charge no longer destroys the whole rent-charge.

Q. What are the principal methods by which rights of common may be extinguished?

A. By express release; unity of seisin; or abandonment.

Q. What is an easement? State what is meant by an affirmative easement, and what is meant by a negative easement. Give an instance of each.

A. An easement is a privilege without profit which the owner of one tenement, which is called the dominant tenement, has over another, which is called the servient tenement, to compel the owner thereof—(1) to permit to be done, or (2) to refrain from doing, something on the servient tenement for the advantage of the dominant tenement. The former is called an affirmative easement, and the second a negative easement. An instance of the former would be where the owner of Whiteacre has a right-of-way over Blackacre, he can compel the owner of Blackacre to permit him to go along the way. An instance of the second would be where the owner of Whiteacre has ancient lights in a house on his estate, he can restrain the owner of Blackacre from doing any act on Blackacre which will deprive him of his accustomed light and air.

Q. Explain prescription and custom; continuous and discontinuous easements.

A. Prescription, which is personal, is for the most part applied to persons being made in the name of a certain person and his ancestors, or of those whose estate he held, or in bodies politic or corporate and their predecessors; but a custom, which is local, is alleged in no person, but laid within some manor or other place. Continuous easements are those of which the enjoyment is, or may be, continual without the necessity of any actual interference by man, as a waterspout, or right to light and air, or drains; discontinuous easements are those the enjoyment of which can only be had by the interference of man, as rights-of-way or a right to draw water.

Q. Under what circumstances does there arise a way of necessity? How is it limited, and by whom is it to be selected, where more than one way is available?

A. A way of necessity arises either where a man grants a piece of land in the middle of his field, or where the grantor conveys all the lands surrounding his field and retains the field, provided in neither case an express right-of-way is granted or reserved. It is limited to such a right-of-way as will enable the owner of the close to enjoy it in the same condition as at the time of the grant, *e.g.*, if the close is arable or meadow, the owner may not put up houses and claim a right-of-way to them for his tenants. (Corporation of London v. Riggs, 13 Ch. Div., 798.) The grantee is restricted to such one way as will be convenient for the reasonable enjoyment of the premises; but, subject to this rule, the grantor is probably justified in assigning such a way as he can best spare. (Woolrych on Ways, 34.)

Q. Distinguish easements from those rights which, though similar to them in other respects, are not annexed to the ownership of land.

A. The distinction is that easements are rights of property enjoyed by a person *as accessory to his* ownership of land, and for its convenience over the land of another, by reason whereof the latter is bound to permit some definite use (not involving participation in the soil or its produce) of his land, or to refrain from some particular use of it; whilst an easement in gross is a right similar in extent but not annexed to the ownership of land, and exists because of a licence to do on another person's land that which, without such licence, would be a trespass, and is not alienable, and may be determined at any time by the withdrawal of the licence. (Edwards, 297, 298.)

Q. Define the easement of watercourse, and explain the various methods by which it may be acquired.

A. The right which a man has to the benefit of the flow of water in a defined channel. It may be acquired by express grant, or implied grant, or prescription under 2 & 3 Wm. 4, c. 71, or statute. (Sury v. Pigot, Indermaur's Conveyancing and Equity Cases, 11.)

Q. By what means may easements be extinguished?

A. They may be extinguished by express release, by Act of Parliament, by unity of seisin, or by abandonment. As to abandonment, it is not necessary to show any definite period of non-user; it is not so much the duration of the cesser as the nature of the act done by the grantee of the easement, or of the adverse act acquiesced in by him and the intention in him which either the one or the other indicates, which are material. As to extinguishment by unity of seisin, this will not occur where the easement is one of necessity, or is some right arising *ex jure naturæ*. (Sury v. Pigot, and Notes, Indermaur's Conveyancing and Equity Cases, 11.)

Q. Explain what is meant by prescription. What change was made by the Prescription Act?

A. *Prescription* means the acquisition of a title to an incorporeal right by means of immemorial user, which implies a grant. The right can be claimed either as being exercised in gross by the claimant and his ancestors; or, as being exercised as appendant or appurtenant to lands held by the claimant and his ancestors. Formerly a title by prescription could only be acquired by enjoyment time out of mind, *i.e.*, since the first day of the reign of Richard 1; then the judges established an artificial rule by which 20 years adverse and uninterrupted enjoyment of an incorporeal hereditament uncontradicted and unexplained, was cogent evidence from which the jury should be conclusively directed to presume a grant or other lawful origin of the possession. The Prescription Act, 2 & 3 Wm. 4, c. 71, enacted that if the right is claimed as appendant or appurtenant and not in gross—rights to light are to be indefeasible after enjoyment without interruption for 20 years, unless enjoyed by consent in writing; and that rights-of-way and other easements (except light) are not to be defeated, after 20 years of such enjoyment by merely showing the precise time when they began to be enjoyed, and after 40 years are to be indefeasible; and as to rights of common and other *profits à prendre* (except tithes, rent, and services) fixed the periods of thirty and sixty years. The time must be reckoned back from the date of action brought; and interruption must be acquiesced in for a year after notice, or it is of no avail.

Q. What interest has the owner of an advowson in the parsonage house and glebe lands? If he sells the advowson during a vacancy of the living, what result ensues?

A. As patron, he enjoys the perpetual right of presentation to the benefice; but he has no property or interest as such in the parsonage house and glebe lands. The advowson passes with the exception of the right to present on that particular vacancy, which is considered too sacred a thing to be bought and sold, the sale of such a right being simony; the vendor accordingly presents whom he will, and, if he does not present within six months, the right lapses to the bishop, and in turn to the archbishop and, finally the Crown.

Q. Define a rent-charge. How can it be created, and in what different ways can it be determined?

A. A rent-charge is a rent payable by the owner of land, otherwise than as a tenant, and expressly charged upon the land. It may be created by grant *inter vivos* or by will. It may be determined (1) by effluxion of time where granted for a limited period; (2) by determination of the estate on which it is charged; (3) by merger; (4) by release; (5) by redemption under the provision in the Conveyancing Act 1881; and (6) by the Statute of Limitations. (Edwards, 276, 280, 281, 451.)

Q. Mention any peculiarities of the law relating to tithes and tithe rent-charge.

A. Tithes constituted the provision for the ministers of the Church, consisting of a tenth part of the yearly increase of the soil, and under various Acts of Parliament of the present reign, a rent charge varying with the price of corn has now been substituted for tithes in kind. On the sale of land, tithe is a burden, the existence of which is presumed in the absence of agreement, but from the dissolution of the monasteries it has arisen that not only the lands of many laymen (being derived from the Crown) are discharged from tithes, but that an existing right of tithe is vested in lay hands. Under the Tithe Commutation Acts, the person entitled to tithes is enabled by deed, to be approved by the Commissioners and confirmed under their seal, to merge the tithes or tithe rent-charge in the land out of or in respect of which they issue. Tithes in lay hands are capable of sale as a distinct incorporeal hereditament, and on an open contract for the sale of tithes a purchaser is entitled to call for the production of the original grant, and then to have the title deduced for a period of 40 years preceding the sale. They always descend by Common Law rules, and are not subject to any particular customs, *e.g.*, gavelkind. (Goodeve's Realty, 357-360.)

Q. In what cases, and subject to what restrictions, can quit-rents and other perpetual charges be compulsorily redeemed?

A. Where there was, at the end of 1881, a quit rent, chief rent, rent-charge, or other annual sum issuing out of land—which is perpetual and is *not* tithe rent-charge, or a rent reserved on a sale or lease, or a rent payable under a building grant—any person interested in the land may, by signed writing, require the Land Department of the Board of Agriculture to assess under seal the sum for which the rent can be redeemed; and may then give one month's notice in writing to the person who is absolute owner of the rent, or can absolutely dispose thereof, or can give an absolute discharge for its capital value; and may then pay or tender the certified value to such person, and on proof thereof get a certificate from the Department that the land is freed. (Conveyancing Act 1881, sec. 45.)

Q. State the meaning of franchise, lay-impropriator.

A. A *franchise* is a royal privilege subsisting in the hands of a subject, *e.g.*, to have a market, forest, fishery. *Lay-impropriator* denotes the owner of an advowson who has obtained it because it was vested in Henry 8 by statute and was afterwards granted by the Crown to a layman as a lay interest. (Edwards, 15, 283.)

Q. Explain the meaning of the term "free-fishery."

A. A *free-fishery* is the exclusive right of fishing in a public river, and is a franchise granted by the Crown to, or vested by prescription in, a private person and his heirs; the owner has a qualified property in the fish before they are caught; grants of this description can no longer be made by the Crown, being prohibited by Magna Charta. (Stephen's Commentaries, 11th edition, Vol. I., 642, 643.)

Q. Describe the legal nature and incidents of personal annuities.

A. A personal annuity is an incorporeal chattel and personal property; it consists of an annual payment not charged on real estate; it may be limited to the grantee, or to him and his heirs, or the heirs of his body; if given to the grantee and his heirs, it will descend to the heir on an intestacy, but will pass under a bequest of all the grantee's personalty; if given to the grantee and the heirs of his body, the grantee takes a fee-simple conditional on his having issue and not an estate tail, but on his death without having had issue the annuity ceases; if given to the grantee *for ever*, it will devolve on the grantee's legal personal representative and not on his heir.

13.—COPYHOLDS.

Q. What is a manor? Who has seisin of the copyholds? To whom do the minerals under the copyholds belong? What services are always due from the copyholders? How are copyholds conveyed?

A. A manor is an aggregate of rights vested in the lord; it comprises demesne lands (occupied by the lord and his lessees and his customary tenants, and the wastes) and tenemental lands (occupied by at least two freehold tenants in fee simple) as regards which the lord has a seignory and is entitled to services; and the right to hold a court baron and a court leet, with incidental rights of escheat, fines, reliefs, heriots, &c. The seisin of the copyholds is in the lord, and he is entitled to the minerals under them, but he may not enter to work them without the consent of the tenant. The services due include fealty and suit of court, escheat, rent, reliefs, fines, heriots, &c. Copyholds are conveyed by surrender and admittance on payment of the proper fine. (Goodeve's Realty, 310, 311.)

Q. What was the origin of manors? Can they now be created? Mention the legal incidents of a manor.

A. They originated in the large tracts of land granted by the Conqueror to his followers; which, being much larger than the *tenant in capite* could make use of in person, were subinfeudated or granted out by him to be held of him under certain services. They were all created prior to the statute of Quia Emptores, 18 Edw. 1, c. 1, which put an end to subinfeudation. The grant of "a manor" will pass the demesne lands, the freehold of lands held by copyhold or customary tenants, the pastures, wastes, commons, mines, minerals, quarries, woods, and the ground and soil thereof, fisheries, fealty, suit of court, rents, and generally all the services, Courts Baron with the fines and perquisites annexed thereto, Courts Leet with the like fines and perquisites, franchises and advowsons appendant.

Q. What are the necessary parts of a "manor"? What is a "reputed manor"? What is the meaning and user of "seizure quousque" by the lord of a manor?

A. These must be demesne lands which include those occupied by the lord and by his lessees and by his customary tenants, and the waste; and tenemental lands, which are held of the lord by freehold tenants, and in regard to which the lord has a seignory and is entitled to services; there must be at least two tenants in fee simple who hold of the lord and constitute the court baron; the manor must date back prior to 18 Edw. 1, c. 1. A reputed manor is where there cease to be two freehold tenants. If a copyhold tenant dies and no person comes forward to be admitted after proclamation at three successive courts, the lord seizes the copyholds until the tenant comes forward to claim them. (Edwards' Compendium, 26, 27, 28, 33.)

Q. Explain the nature of the lord's right to a fine on the alienation of copyholds.

A. It is a right founded on the custom of manors. In

some manors the fine was always fixed; in others it was anciently arbitrary. An arbitrary fine is limited now to two years improved value of the land after deducting quit rents.

Q. Describe the different kinds of fines payable by custom in respect of copyhold estates.

A. Fines have been classified as payable (1) on the death of the lord, (2) on change of the tenant, and (3) for licences to empower the tenant to alienate, to demise for more than one year, and the like. Admittance-fines are either certain or arbitrary, but the arbitrary fine must be reasonable and must not exceed two years' clear intrinsic value (except in the case of joint tenants and of remainder-men for lives) where the copyholder has a right to demand admission. (Elton on Copyholds, 128.)

Q. What difference is there between copyholds and customary freeholds? To whom, in each case, do the minerals belong, and what rights has the owner of getting them?

A. The former are always expressed to be held " at the will of the lord," whilst the latter were never expressed to be so held. In both cases the freehold, and consequently the minerals, belong to the lord; but he may not enter on the surface of the lands to work them without the tenant's consent, although he may work them from a shaft sunk on adjoining land, taking care he does not injure the surface.

Q. How far can estates tail be created in copyhold, and how, when created, can they be barred? Explain the origin of the differences between freeholds and copyholds with regard to estates tail.

A. Only where there is a custom of the particular manor allowing estates tail; if there is no such custom, a surrender of copyholds to A and the heirs of his body gives him an estate analogous to the fee simple conditional created by a like grant of freeholds prior to 13 Edw. 1, c. 1. Estates tail in copyholds are barred—(1) if legal, by surrender; (2) if equitable, by surrender or deed. The consent of the protector (if any) is necessary ; and the transaction is enrolled, not in Chancery, but in the court rolls of the manor within six months (3 & 4 Wm. 4, c. 74). The distinction between copyholds and freeholds arises from the fact that the former are regulated by custom, which is their very life, and are not included in the statute *De Donis*, which relates only to freeholds.

Q. In what manner are copyholds conveyed ? How is a mortgage of copyholds usually effected ?

A. By surrender and admission, duly enrolled on the court rolls of the manor. They are mortgaged by conditional surrender. The mortgagee, to avoid payment of the fine, does not usually take admission unless he wishes to sell under his power of sale. When the mortgage is paid off, no re-surrender is necessary, unless the mortgagee has been admitted; but a memorandum signed by the mortgagee acknowledging satisfaction of the mortgage is entered on the court rolls, and this vacates the conditional surrender.

Q. State shortly the history of the law as to devising copyholds.

A. Copyholds were not devisable at common law except under a special custom. The Statute of Wills of Henry 8 did not affect them. Under the custom the copyholder surrendered to the uses of his will. The copyhold passed by the surrender and not by the will which merely declared the uses of the surrender. By 55 Geo. 3, c. 192, a will of copyholds is good without any such surrender; and this continues to be the law under the Wills Act 1837, which now regulates the power of devising copyholds and the form of all wills. (Goodeve's Realty, 378.)

Q. In what different ways may the enfranchisement of copyhold lands be effected ? Show the difference of their operation as regards the rights of the lord of the manor.

A. *At Common Law* voluntarily by the fee simple owner of the manor conveying a fee simple estate in the land or releasing his seignorial rights to the copyholder—and this absolutely extinguishes all the rights and incidents of copyhold tenure. *Under the Copyhold Acts* 1841 to 1887, either voluntarily or compulsorily through the award of the Board of Agriculture—but this does not affect any rights of common possessed by the copyholder or (unless expressly so agreed) the lord's right to minerals or any right of fair or market or in respect of game or fish or the lord's right of escheat. (Edwards, 34-37.)

Q. What is the best mode of devising copyholds in trust for sale?

A. They should not be actually devised to the trustees; but a simple direction should be given to the trustees to sell, by which means the necessity of the trustees' admittance will be avoided.

14.—LEASEHOLDS, &c.

Q. Describe and distinguish the chief varieties of chattel interests in land.

A. They are those estates in land which are less than freehold, viz., (1) estates for years, (2) at will, and (3) at sufferance. The first is an estate for a fixed period of time, having a certain ending; the second is an estate determinable at the will of either party; and the third is the estate held by a person who has lawfully come into possession, and is now holding over after the termination of that tenancy. A mortgage and a tenancy by elegit are also chattel interests in land.

Q. How could a term of years be created at common law? What alterations were made in the law in this respect by the Statute of Frauds, and the Act to amend the law of Real Property respectively?

A. A term of years could have been created by word of mouth at Common Law. The Statute of Frauds enacted that if the term exceeded three years from the making thereof, or the rent was less than two-thirds of the full improved value of the land, the lease should have the effect of an estate at will only unless made by signed writing; and the Real Property Amendment Act 1845 provided that all leases required by law to be in writing should be void at law, unless made by deed. (Goodeve's Realty, 142, 143.)

Q. Can a lease for years be created or assigned by parol? Give an analysis of an assignment of a lease for years on sale. Set out the habendum at length.

A. It may be created by parol, provided the term does not exceed three years and the rent is not less than two-thirds of the improved value (29 Chas. 2, c. 3, sec. 2); but it can only be assigned by deed (*Ibid.*, sec. 3; 8 & 9 Vict., c. 106, sec. 3.) Date; Parties (1) assignor, (2) assignee; Recitals (1) of lease, (2) agreement for sale; Testatum, consideration, receipt; A, as beneficial owner, assigns to B the parcels (as described in lease) To hold to B for all the residue now unexpired of the term created by the lease subject to the rent reserved by the lease and to the covenants and conditions therein contained and which henceforth ought on the part of the lessee to be observed and performed; Covenant by purchaser to pay rent and observe the covenants and conditions and indemnify A therefrom; Testimonium. (1 Prideaux, 235.)

Q. What covenants in a lease run with the land demised and bind the assigns (whether named in the covenants or not) of the lessee and lessor respectively?

A. A covenant is said to run with the land or with the reversion respectively when either the liability to perform it, or the right to take advantage of it, passes to the assignee of the land or reversion respectively. At Common Law covenants ran with the land, but not with the reversion, so that the assignee of the lessee could sue, whilst the assignee of the lessor could not sue except under a power of attorney in the lessor's name. By 32 Hen. 8, c. 34, it was provided that the assignee of the reversion should have the like remedies against the lessee and his assigns as the lessor had, and *vice versa*, that the lessee and his assigns should have the like remedies against the lessor's assignee as he had against the lessor. This statute was, however, held only to extend to covenants which touch and concern the thing demised, and not to collateral covenants. Thus, (1) all implied covenants run with the land; also (2) covenants touching a thing in *esse*, parcel of the demise, although assignees are not mentioned; and (3) covenants to do some act upon the thing demised, if the assignee is mentioned. Now, by 44 & 45 Vict., c. 41, it is provided—as to leases made after 31st December, 1881—that (sec. 10) the rent reserved by, and the benefit of every covenant or provision contained in, the lease having reference to the subject matter thereof, and on the lessee's part to be observed, and every condition of re-entry and other condition, shall go with the reversion expectant on the lease, even if severed, and shall be recovered, enforced, and taken advantage of by the person entitled to the income of the land leased; and that (sec. 11) the obligation of the lessor's covenants is to run with the reversion, so far as the lessor had power to bind the reversioners, and may be taken advantage of and enforced against the owner for the time being of the reversion.*

Q. *Distinguish between a tenancy at will and a tenancy at sufferance. To what notice to quit is a tenant from year to year entitled by common law and by statute?*

A. A tenancy at will arises where premises are let for so long as both parties like, and reserving a compensation accruing *de die in diem*. This is the original nature of the

---

* As regards covenants relating to the fee simple—the burden of such a covenant never runs with the land at law (Austerberry v. Corporation of Oldham, 29 Ch. D., 750) but in equity restrictive or negative covenants will be enforced against a purchaser with notice by an injunction (Tulk v. Moxhay, L. R., 2 Ch., 774); and the benefit will only run with the land if it is really connected with the enjoyment thereof (Austerberry v. Corporation of Oldham). (1 Smith's Leading Cases, 9th edition, 103, 104.)

tenancy. A tenancy at sufferance is where a tenant has had a fixed tenancy, and is holding over after the expiration of that tenancy. Such tenancies are both capable of being converted into yearly tenancies by the payment of rent referable to any aliquot part of a year. A yearly tenant is at common law entitled to half a year's notice to quit expiring at the end of the current year of the tenancy; but as regards agricultural property and market gardens, a year's notice so expiring is now required under the provisions of the Agricultural Holdings Act 1883. (See Richardson v. Langridge and Notes in Indermaur's Conveyancing and Equity Cases, 7th edition, 1-3.)

Q. A lease for 99 years at £60 a year rent having expired, it is found that the tenant has not paid rent, or otherwise acknowledged the lessor's title, for the last 15 years. What are the reversioner's rights with respect to (a) the rent; (b) the land?

A. (a) If the lessee is still in possession, he can distrain for the rent accrued due within the six years immediately preceding the distress (3 & 4 Wm. 4, c. 27, sec. 42); and, the demise being by deed, he may sue the lessee for the rent which accrued due within twenty years preceding the issue of the writ (3 & 4 Wm. 4, c. 42, sec. 3; Lewis v. Graham, 80 *Law Times* Newspaper, 66.) (b) The reversioner may bring an action for recovery of the land at any time within twelve years after the lease expires, as the possession of the lessee does not become adverse until then (37 & 38 Vict., c. 57.)

Q. State the provisions of the Conveyancing Act 1881, sec. 14, respecting restrictions on, and relief against, forfeiture of leases.

A. A lessor cannot take advantage of a right of forfeiture reserved on breach of conditions of a lease, until he has first served on the lessee notice (1) specifying the breach complained of, (2) requiring the lessee to remedy the breach, if

possible, and (3) requiring money compensation for the
breach; and the lessee has failed to comply with such notice
for a reasonable time. Even then the lessee may apply to
the Court for relief from forfeiture, and the Court may exercise its discretion, and impose terms. The section applies to
leases, underleases, and grants at fee farm-rent, or at a rent
upon condition; although the right of re-entry is reserved
pursuant to the directions of a statute; and affects all
leases notwithstanding stipulation otherwise. A lease *until*
breach of condition takes effect for as long a term as it can
legally exist, subject to the proviso for re-entry on such
breach. The section does *not* extend to covenants or conditions against assigning or underletting; nor to a condition
for forfeiture on bankruptcy of lessee, or on execution against
lessee's interest*; nor (in a mining lease) to a covenant or
condition for lessor to have access to, or inspect accounts, or
machinery, or the mine or workings—and against forfeiture
for these no relief can be had. Nor does the section affect
the law of forfeiture or relief for non-payment of rent.

*Q. What is the effect of the assignment of a lease upon the
rights and liabilities of the lessor, the lessee, and the assignee?*

A. The lessor still keeps all his rights against the lessee,
who cannot get rid of his liability without the lessor's consent; and also acquires rights of action against the assignee
in respect of the rent and covenants which relate to the
demised property during the period for which he remains
assignee. The lessee, to protect himself, should take a
covenant from the assignee to pay the rent and perform the
covenants after assignment. The assignee acquires the right
to sue the lessor upon the lessor's covenants in the lease.

*Q. The purchaser of an underlease requires the seller to
prove that all the covenants and provisions in both the underlease and the superior lease have been performed and observed*

---

* As to bankruptcy and execution, see now Conveyancing Act 1892, *ante*, page 27.

down to the time of actual completion of the purchase. How shall the seller comply with the requisition?

A. By production of the receipt for the last payment for rent due under the underlease before the date of actual completion of the purchase. (Conveyancing Act 1881, sec. 2.)

Q. (a) *What are the relative advantages and disadvantages of mortgaging leaseholds by demise and by assignment, respectively?* (b) *How can a trustee in bankruptcy get rid of the liabilities attaching to the bankrupt's leaseholds?*

A. (a) A mortgage of leaseholds should always be by underlease, as thereby the mortgagee incurs no liability on the rents and covenants contained in the original lease. (b) By disclaiming, but the leave of the Bankruptcy Court must usually be obtained.

Q. *What effect has the disclaimer of a lease by the trustee in bankruptcy of the lessee upon the lessor, the lessee, and persons claiming under the lessee respectively?*

A. It determines the rights, interests, and liabilities of the bankrupt and his property in respect of the lease as from the date of the disclaimer; but does not, except so far as is necessary for the release of the bankrupt and his property, and the lessee from liability, affect the rights or interests of others. Any person claiming under the lessee (*e.g.*, a mortgagee or underlessee) may apply to the Bankruptcy Court for an order vesting the disclaimed lease in him, subject, however, to the same liabilities and obligations as the bankrupt was subject to under the lease in respect of the property at the date when the bankruptcy petition was filed. Under the Bankruptcy Act 1890 (sec. 13), the Court may, however, make the person in whose favour the vesting order is made, subject only to the same liabilities as if the lease had been assigned to him at the date when the bankruptcy petition was filed.

Q. *If a term of years be bequeathed to A for his life, and after his death to B, in whom does the whole term vest, and what interest has B therein, during A's lifetime?*

A. The whole term of years is considered as vesting in the legatee for life, A, but on his decease the term is held to shift away from him, and to vest, by way of executory bequest, in the person next entitled, B. During A's life, B has technically no vested estate, but a mere possibility.

Q. How may a lease for years be surrendered? What difference does it make to an underlessee whether the lessee surrenders the lease, or the lessor re-enters on a forfeiture?

A. By a surrender in law, *i.e.*, the grant of a new lease either to the tenant or to a third person, with the tenant's consent, which operates in law as the surrender of the existing one; or by a surrender in fact, where the lessee assigns his interest in the lease to the remainderman or reversioner, which must be by deed (8 & 9 Vict., c. 106), unless the lease is one which by law could have been created without writing, and is called a surrender, or bequeaths his interest to the remainderman or reversioner in his own right. If the lessee surrenders a lease, his underlessee is not prejudiced, but by 4 Geo. 2, c. 28, and 8 & 9 Vict., c. 106, the reversioner next after the lessee becomes his landlord; but if the lessee's term is put an end to by re-entry under the forfeiture clause, the underlessee's term (which is carved out of the lessee's interest) is gone also, unless the underlessee gets a vesting order under sec. 4 of the Conveyancing Act 1892, *ante*, page 28.

Q. In what ways may a term of years, created by lease, be determined?

A. By effluxion of time. By an express surrender of the term. By a surrender in law, *e.g.*, where the tenant accepts a new lease from the landlord to take effect *in praesenti*. By merger, if the tenant acquires in his own right an ulterior estate immediately subsequent to the term. By re-entry for condition broken, subject to sec. 14 of 44 & 45 Vict., c. 41.

Q. Explain the doctrine of estoppel with reference to leases for years.

A. If a lease is made by deed, the lessor is estopped from disputing the grant, and the lessee is estopped from denying the lessor's right to make it; and this although the lessor had not, at the time of making the lease, either the lands or the title. But, if the lessor during the lease becomes entitled to the lands, the lease at once takes effect for all purposes. If the lessor had, at the time of making the lease, any interest in the lands, that interest only will pass, and the lease will have no further effect by estoppel, although the lessor had professed to grant more than he really had.

Q. By what methods can long terms of years be enlarged into fee simple, and what is the effect of such enlargement?

A. By a mere declaration to that effect in a deed executed by the beneficial or legal owner of the term, which vests in him, a fee simple estate—subject to all the trusts, powers, executory limitations over, rights, equities, and covenants, and provisions as to use and enjoyment, and all obligations to which the unconverted term was subject; and if the term had been settled along with freeholds in strict settlement, the fee simple shall devolve exactly like those freeholds, unless some person had previously to the enlargement become absolute owner of the term; and the fee simple shall include minerals which have not previously been severed in right or in fact, or reserved by an Inclosure Act or award. (Conveyancing Act 1881, sec. 65.)

15.—Mortgages, &c.

Q. Distinguish the different kinds of security created by mortgages, liens, charges and pledges respectively.

A. *A mortgage* is a transfer of ownership from the mortgagor to the mortgagee, subject to a proviso for redemption and reconveyance on payment of the mortgage money with interest and costs; the legal ownership is in the mortgagee, and the beneficial ownership is in the mortgagor; if the money is not paid on the covenanted day, the mortgagee can enforce his security in a variety of active ways; the mortgagor usually retains possession until the mortgagee seeks to enforce his security. *A lien* (*a*) at common law is a mere passive right to keep certain goods until claims against the owner are paid; it is general or special; it gives active rights to an innkeeper under the Innkeepers Act 1878, and a solicitor under the Solicitors Act 1860; it is neither a right of property in the thing nor of action to the thing; it is not barred by statutes of limitation, but is lost by parting with possession; (*b*) an equitable lien (*e.g.*, vendor of land for unpaid purchase-money) exists apart from possession, and can be enforced by action. *A charge* is an obligation imposed on property, and creates a trust which equity will enforce, *e.g.*, portions or legacies charged on land. *A pledge* gives possession of the article to the pledgee, together with qualified rights of property therein.

Q. Describe the methods of creating legal and equitable mortgages of leaseholds and copyholds respectively.

A. A legal mortgage of leaseholds may be by assignment or underlease: of copyholds, by conditional surrender. An equitable mortgage is always by deposit of the muniments of title, with or without a memorandum, or by a mere memorandum of a charge. The distinction is that a legal mortgage transfers legal ownership to the mortgagee, with legal rights against the property; while an equitable mortgage transfers no legal ownership, but simply gives the mortgagee rights enforceable in equity.

Q. Give an analysis of a mortgage in fee simple, and state at length the provisions of the power of sale formerly inserted in such a mortgage.

A. Date; parties, (1) mortgagor, (2) mortgagee; recitals (if any); first testatum, consideration, receipt; covenant to pay principal on day named with agreed interest, and to pay interest half-yearly; second testatum, mortgagor as beneficial owner conveys, parcels, habendum to use of mortgagee in fee simple; proviso for redemption; testimonium. (1 Prideaux, 531.) The provisions were, (1) permission to sell, (2) owner of legal estate to convey, (3) when power of sale could be exercised, (4) purchaser protected if power exercised improperly by mortgagee, (5) power to give receipts, (6) application of purchase-money, and (7) any one entitled to give receipt may exercise power of sale. (Elphinstone, 150-153.)

Q. Describe succinctly the powers conferred on mortgagors and mortgagees respectively, by the Conveyancing and Law of Property Act 1881.

A. The mortgagor can—(1) compel the mortgagee to transfer the mortgage debt, if the mortgagee is not in possession and the right to redeem still exists, (2) inspect and copy the title deeds in mortgagee's hands, if mortgage made since 1881, (3) redeem without fear of consolidation any mortgage made since 1881 unless otherwise agreed, (4) grant leases when in possession unless otherwise agreed, and (5) compel a sale if he sues for redemption or sale. (Secs. 15-18, 25.) The mortgagee can—(1) grant leases when in possession, (2) sell and convey and give valid receipts for sale monies, (3) insure, (4) appoint a receiver, and (5) cut ripe timber when in possession. (Secs. 18-24.)

Q. Discuss the nature, properties, and liabilities of an equity of redemption in real estate subject to a mortgage.

A. It is an equitable estate in the land; it means that the mortgagor retains the right to redeem his property on payment of principal, interest and costs *after* the day named for redemption in the deed has gone by; it cannot be restricted by any condition in the mortgage deed, *e.g.*, a clause, that if the property is not redeemed within five years it cannot be redeemed, is void; it can be lost (1) by sale under mortgagee's powers, (2) by foreclosure, (3) by making a second mortgage without disclosing the first; or (4) by mortgagee being in possession for 12 years without any signed acknowledgment of the right to redeem ; it is alienable ; and devolves on intestacy like the land itself, but subject under Locke King's Acts to the mortgage debt. (Edwards, 223-226.)

Q. After sale of the equity of redemption by the mortgagor, can the mortgagee sue the purchaser or the mortgagor for the principal and interest due on the mortgage? Give reasons.

A. The mortgagee can still sue the mortgagor on his covenant. He cannot sue the purchaser of the equity of redemption, for there is no privity between him and such person. But the mortgagor is, in the absence of any contrary intention, entitled to be indemnified by the purchaser of the equity (Waring v. Ward, 7 Ves., 337), the principle being that there is an implied covenant on the part of the purchaser to this effect. (Goodeve's Realty, 207.)

Q. What are the general powers and liabilities of a mortgagee in possession of land?

A. He can make building leases for 99 years and occupation leases for 21 years ; he can cut and sell ripe timber ; he must account for what he has received, or but for his wilful default might have received ; he is chargeable with an occupation rent in respect of property in hand, and is liable for voluntary waste ; he is allowed the cost of necessary repairs ; he may charge actual expenses. (See Goodeve's Realty, 197, 198.)

Q. (a) What provisions are implied in a statutory mortgage of land under the Conveyancing Act 1881, sec. 26 : and (b) what remedies, under the Act generally, has a statutory mortgagee for enforcing his security?

A. (a) In a statutory mortgage there are implied by sec. 26 of the Conveyancing Act 1881 : (1) a covenant with the mortgagee by the mortgagor to pay the stated mortgage money on the stated day with interest at the stated rate, and thereafter, so long as any of the mortgage money remains unpaid, to pay interest on the unpaid portion at the stated rate by equal half yearly payments commencing at the end of six calendar months from the day stated for payment of the mortgage money; and (2) a proviso for redemption and reconveyance on payment of the mortgage money and interest on the stated day. (*b*) The remedies of a statutory mortgagee—and of every mortgagee, if the mortgage deed was made since 1881—are: (1) Sale when the mortgage money is due, secs. 19 (1) 20, and 21. (2) Insurance, secs. 19 (2) and 23. (3) Appointment and removal of a receiver, secs. 19 (3), 24. (4) Power to give receipts for purchase and other moneys and securities, sec. 22. (5) Recovery of the title-deeds after his power of sale becomes exerciseable, except against persons having prior claims, sec 21 (7). (6) Obtain an order for sale in an action for foreclosure and redemption, sec. 25 (2). (7) When in possession make or agree to make agricultural or occupation leases not exceeding 21 years, and building leases not exceeding 99 years, by sec. 18, unless excluded. (8) When in possession cut and sell timber, sec. 19.

Q. Against what persons respectively is an unregistered bill of sale valid or invalid?

A. The subject of bills of sale is governed by two Acts passed respectively in 1878 and 1882 (41 and 42 Vict., c. 31; and 45 & 46 Vict., c. 43). The 1882 Act applies to all bills of sale given by way of security for money, and the 1878 Act to instruments given other than as security for money, *i.e.*, absolute bills of sale. The effect of non-registration of a bill of sale under the 1878 Act is to render the instrument void (if the chattels are allowed to remain in the apparent possession of the grantor) as against execution creditors and trustees in bankruptcy, but not as between the parties; but under the 1882 Act, a bill of sale is absolutely void if not duly registered.

Q. A proposes to borrow from B £1000 on the security of A's possessory life interest in Consols in Court in an admin-

istration action, and his absolute reversion under a settlement, and (subject to his mother's life interest therein) in railway stocks standing in the names of trustees. What precautions before, and after, the loan should B take, and what risks would he run by neglecting them?

A. Prior to the loan, B must satisfy himself as to the sufficiency of the proposed security, by ascertaining the nature and extent of A's life's interest in the property proposed to be mortgaged; that such interest is in possession; that there are no charging orders and stop orders on the funds in Court; that the reversion under the settlement is unincumbered; that the railway stock is intact, and there is no distringas upon it, and that the trustees have no notice of any charges. Otherwise B would run the risk of obtaining a fraudulent or insufficient security. After the advance, B should at once obtain a stop order on A's life interest in the fund in Court; give notice to the settlement trustees (if any); register his security, if the settled lands are in a register county; put a distringas on the stock to prevent its being dealt with except on notice to him; and serve the trustees of the stock with notice of his security. Otherwise he might be postponed to a *bonâ fide* purchaser without notice, or a mortgagee who had perfected his security, or to successful fraudulent dealings with the property.

Q. Explain how the title of a mortgagor may become barred by the Statutes of Limitation.

A. It will become so barred, if the mortgagee enters into possession and holds for 12 years without giving any acknowledgment in writing of the mortgagor's right to redeem. (37 & 38 Vict., c. 57, sec. 7.) It has been decided that in this case there is no further period allowed for disabilities. (Forster v. Paterson, 17 Ch. Div., 132.)

Q. (a) On the death of a sole mortgagee of freeholds to whom should the mortgage debt be paid, and by whom may the mortgaged estate be conveyed to the mortgagor? State what

the law formerly was upon this point, and how it was altered.
(b) *On the death of a mortgagor, out of what property is the mortgage debt primarily payable? What was the old law upon this point, and how was it altered?*

A. (a) Under sec. 30 of the Conveyancing Act 1881, the mortgage money will be paid to the personal representatives of the mortgagee, who are also the proper persons to reconvey. Formerly, the money would have been paid to the personal representatives, and the heir or devisee, as the case may be, would have been the person to reconvey. (b) Formerly, out of the general personal estate, but now, under 17 & 18 Vict., c. 113, out of the mortgaged estate itself, unless there is a contrary intention expressed in the mortgagor's will, and a mere general direction for payment of debts is not a sufficient contrary intention. (30 & 31 Vict., c. 69.) The 17 & 18 Vict., c. 113, did not formerly apply to leaseholds (Solomon v. Solomon, 33 L. J., Ch., 473); but it does now (40 & 41 Vict., c. 34).

Q. *Define the equitable doctrine of tacking, and show how it has been affected by recent legislation.*

A. It is the uniting of two incumbrances with the view of squeezing out an intervening one, prior in point of time to the security tacked, and it depends on the maxim, "Where the equities are equal, the law shall prevail." The third advance must have been made without notice of the second. Tacking was abolished by the Vendor and Purchaser Act 1874, which came into operation on 7th August, 1874; but this provision was repealed by the Land Transfer Act 1875, except as to anything done before 1st January, 1876. (Marsh v. Lee, and Notes, Indermaur's Conveyancing and Equity Cases.)

Q. *A mortgaged Blackacre to B for one sum: he afterwards mortgaged Whiteacre to B for another sum. Blackacre is an insufficient security for the money lent upon it, and A, therefore, does not wish to redeem it; but he wishes to redeem White-*

acre, which is an ample security for the money lent upon it. State what, under the aforesaid circumstances, were the rights of the mortgagee, before the Conveyancing Act 1881 came into operation, and what change in the law upon the subject was made by that Act?

A. Before the Conveyancing Act 1881, the mortgagee might have consolidated his mortgages, and refused to allow the mortgagor to redeem one without redeeming all. By sec. 17 of that Act, a mortgagor may redeem the property comprised in one mortgage, without paying any money due under a separate mortgage, provided one, at least, of the mortgages is made after 1881, unless the contrary is expressed in one of the mortgages. (See Vint v. Padgett, and Notes in Indermaur's Conveyancing and Equity Cases.)

Q. When, and to whom, is a mortgagee bound to transfer the mortgage, and to assign the mortgage debt?

A. He has always been bound, on payment off by any person entitled to redeem, to reconvey or transfer the estate. He was not, however, formerly bound to assign the mortgage debt itself, but he is now, under sec. 15 of the Conveyancing Act 1881. The Conveyancing Act 1882 provides that a requisition for conveyance and assignment made by an incumbrancer shall prevail over a like requisition by the mortgagor; and as between incumbrancers, a requisition of a prior incumbrancer shall prevail over that of a subsequent incumbrancer.

Q. What statutory powers does the owner of a legal rent charge possess where the rent charge was created by deed since 1881?

A. (*a*) If the rent charge is in arrear for 21 days a power of distress; (*b*) if in arrear for 40 days, power to enter into possession and take the income till satisfaction; or instead, or in addition, (*c*) power to demise the land to a trustee for a term of years on trust (by way of mortgage, or sale, or demise, of the whole, or any part, of the term) to raise the money to satisfy arrears. These powers are subject to any contrary provisions in the instrument creating the rent charge.

Q. What are the provisions of Locke King's Acts, otherwise known as the Real Estates Charges Acts?

A. The general effect of these Acts is that—when real estate (17 & 18 Vict., c. 113) or chattels real (40 & 41 Vict., c. 34) are devised to a devisee, or descend on intestacy (17 & 18 Vict., c. 113, and 40 & 41 Vict., c. 34) charged with any mortgage debt (17 & 18 Vict., c. 113) or lien for unpaid purchase-money (30 & 31 Vict., c. 69, and 40 & 41 Vict., c. 34)—in all cases the devisee or heir-at-law takes the property, subject to the charge, unless a contrary intention appears by the will. A charge or direction for the payment of debts is not a contrary intention (30 & 31 Vict., c. 69).

Q. Explain the nature of an equitable mortgage, and describe the various remedies to which the mortgagee is entitled.

A. It is created by a deposit of title deeds with or without a memorandum in writing, or by a memorandum without deposit; and is permitted from necessity, notwithstanding sec. 4 of the Statute of Frauds (Russell v. Russell). The remedies are (1) action of debt; (2) action of foreclosure, in which the Court has a discretion to order a sale under sec. 25 (2) of the Conveyancing Act 1881; and (3) if there is a memorandum agreeing to give a legal mortgage, the mortgagee has a right to a sale, enforceable by action.

Q. Describe the different forms of debenture, and show in what cases such securities are assignable free from equities affecting the assignor.

A. (1) Mortgage debentures, *i.e.*, secured by a mortgage on property; bonds, *i.e.*, deeds; and instruments not under seal containing a promise to pay. (2.) Terminable, *i.e.*, payable after a certain time, or notice, or being drawn for redemption; and Perpetual, *i.e.*, payable on default in paying interest. They are usually issued by joint stock companies to secure repayment of money borrowed or to pay for property bought or services rendered. The *prima facie* rule is that debentures can only be assigned, subject to the equities existing between the original parties to the contract; but this rule will yield to a contrary intention appearing from the nature or terms of the contract, *e.g.*, where payable to bearer or holder.

16.—TITLE AND MISCELLANEOUS POINTS.

Q. What are the enactments of the Vendor and Purchaser Act 1874, and the Conveyancing Acts 1881 and 1882, with respect to the title to be shown by a vendor of freehold and leasehold land respectively?

A. As to freeholds, 40 years' title must be shown; but if a deed 20 years old at the date of sale contains a recital that the then owner was seised in fee simple free from incumbrances, the purchaser cannot call for any prior title unless he can prove that statement to be false. As to leaseholds, the title always begins with the lease itself, and the purchaser cannot call for the title to the freehold or leasehold reversion. See fully as to details, secs. 1 and 2 of the 1874 Act; secs. 3 and 13 of the 1881 Act; and sec. 4 of the 1882 Act.

Q. What title to land is a purchaser, in the absence of special stipulation entitled to require in the following cases:—(a) freeholds, (b) leaseholds, (c) enfranchised copyholds, (d) an advowson, (e) tithes?

A. (*a*) Forty years. (*b*) The lease itself and the subsequent title thereto not exceeding forty years. (*c*) Forty years; but if the enfranchisement took place within that period, the Conveyancing Act 1881 forbids him calling for the title of the lord to make the enfranchisement. (*d*) 100 years. (*e*) The original grant from the Crown must be produced, and forty years' tite prior to the contract shown.

Q. State shortly the provisions of the statutes now governing the right to bring an action for the recovery of land. What are the special provisions with respect to actions by a tenant in tail?

A. The Act really governing this subject is the Real Property Limitation Act 1874 (37 & 38 Vict., c. 57), though to a certain extent the prior statutes of 3 & 4 Wm. 4, c. 27, and 7 Wm. 4 and 1 Vict., c. 28, remain in force. The law may be shortly summarised as being that an action to recover land, rent, mortgages, legacies, &c., must be brought within 12 years, with a further period of six years in the case of disabilities, but no action to be brought after 30 years. In the case of concealed fraud, however, time does not begin to run until the fraud has, or with reasonable diligence might have, been discovered. Special provisions are made with regard to estates in remainder, and with regard to tenants in tail it is provided (sec. 6) that in case of possession under an assurance by a tenant in tail which shall not bar the remainders, they shall nevertheless be barred at the end of 12 years after that period at which the assurance, if then executed, would have barred them.

Q. Explain the difference in form between a deed of covenant and a bond for securing payment of money. What advantage has the covenantee or obligee over a simple contract creditor of the covenantor or obligor?

A. The difference is that, in the deed of covenant, the covenantor covenants to pay the sum of money which he is meant to, and is actually liable to, pay; whilst in a bond, the person giving it is bound in a certain penal sum, and then follows a condition or provision stating that if a certain smaller sum, being the actual debt, is paid on a certain day, then the bond is to be void. In either case, now, only the actual amount due can be recovered. The only advantage that the covenantee or obligee would have over a simple contract creditor would be that he would have twenty years within which to sue instead of six. Formerly, he had a priority in payment on the death of the covenantor or obligor, but this is no longer so by 32 & 33 Vict., c. 46.

Q. State the law relating to insurable interests as affecting policies of life insurance.

A. By 14 Geo. 3, c. 48, contracts of life insurance are void, unless the person for whose benefit the assurance is effected has an insurable interest in the life insured at the time when the insurance is effected; the name of the person in whose favour the policy is taken out must be stated in it; and only the amount of the insurable interest can be recovered. A man may insure his own life; husband and wife may insure in each other's favour; a creditor may insure his debtor's life to the amount of his debt.

Q. Describe the nature of the contract of life assurance, and state the effect of the Married Women's Property Act 1882, on contracts of this kind.

A. It is not a mere contract of indemnity, but is a contract to pay a certain sum of money on the death of a person in consideration of due payment of an annuity for his life, Dalby v. India and London Life Assurance Company (Indermaur's Common Law Cases). By sec. 11, the wife may effect an insurance on her own life, or her husband's, for her separate use; and either may effect an insurance on his or her life, expressed to be for the benefit of the other, or the children or both, which will create a trust for the declared objects, and prevent the policy moneys (so long as any object of the trust remains unperformed) forming part of the estate or being responsible for the debts of the insured; but on proof that the policy was effected and premiums were paid to defraud the insured's creditors, the creditors are entitled to receive such premiums out of the policy moneys. The insured may, by the policy or a signed memorandum, appoint trustees of the policy moneys, and appoint new trustees, and provide for so doing and for investment of the moneys. If no other trustee is appointed, the insured is trustee. The Court can appoint new trustees under the Trustee Act 1850. The receipt of the trustee, or (if none, or if he gives no notice to the insurance office) of the insured's personal representative, is to be a good discharge for the policy monies.

Q. What is a satisfied term, and what protection can it afford to the inheritance? Refer to the Satisfied Terms Act.

A. A satisfied term is a term, the object for the creation of which has been accomplished; the term still exists, unless there was a proviso for its cessor in the instrument creating it. It was generally a long term of years vested in the trustees of a settlement for raising portions for younger children. It can now afford no protection to the inheritance because of the Act. But formerly where the owner in possession was liable to be evicted by some one claiming under a title, prior to his own but subsequent to the creation of the term, the owner used to take an assignment from the trustees in trust for himself to attend upon and protect his inheritance. And if, afterwards, the owner's title were assailed, he could set up the term and hold under it till it expired. But by 8 & 9 Vict., c. 112, all terms satisfied and attendant on 31st December, 1845, were to cease, but afford the same protection as if they still existed; and all satisfied terms becoming attendant after that date were to cease without affording any protection.

Q. Describe the incidents of a corporation, and state the principal classes into which corporations may for legal purposes be divided.

A. A corporation is an artificial personage created by law and endowed by it with the quality of a perpetual existence and a corporate seal. It may be either *ecclesiastical, e.g.*, a bishop, or a dean and chapter, in which case it is formed solely of spiritual persons and for the furtherance of religion and perpetuation of the rights of the Church, or *lay*. Lay corporations are either *civil* or *eleemosynary*. Any corporation may be either *aggregate*, composed of more persons than one, or *sole*. It may arise by special Act of Parliament or Royal Charter, or under the Companies Act 1862, or may exist as a corporation at common law or by prescription.

Q. In what different ways may a corporation be dissolved?

A. (1) By Act of Parliament; (2) by the natural death of all its members in the case of a corporation aggregate; (3) by surrender of its franchises; (4) by forfeiture of its charter. As regards a company registered under the Companies Act 1862, that is liable to be wound up either voluntarily, or under the supervision of the Court, or compulsorily by the order of the Court.

Q. State the rules under which protection is attainable for paintings, drawings, and photographs.

A. By 25 & 26 Vict., c. 68, the author (being a British subject or resident within the Dominions of the Crown) of any painting or drawing, or the negative of any photograph, shall have the copyright therein for his life and seven years; but if the same shall, for the first time after 29th July, 1862, be sold or disposed of, or made or executed for a good or valuable consideration, the vendor or author shall not have the copyright therein unless expressly reserved to him at the time by signed agreement, but it shall belong to the purchaser or person for whom executed, nor shall the vendee or assignee be entitled to the copyright unless expressly so agreed in signed writing. Such copyright is personal estate; must be registered at Stationers' Hall to give a right enforceable by action; and assigned by writing. Penalties are imposed by infringement.

Q. Define a "patent." State shortly the provisions of the present law regulating the grant and protection of patents, as regards the mode of application for, extent and duration, and revocation and assignment, of patents.

A. The privilege granted by the Crown to the first

inventor of any new contrivance in the manufactures that he alone, for a limited time, shall make a profit out of his invention. The grant and protection of a patent is now regulated by the Patents Designs and Tradenarks Acts 1883-1888. Anyone may apply for a patent, the application is sent to the Patent Office with a declaration that the applicant (or one of them) is the true and first inventor in this realm, and a specification (provisional or complete) giving the details of the invention; the comptroller refers the application to the examiner; if the latter reports favorably, the application is accepted and advertised; and if no successful opposition is made, the patent is sealed. The patent extends through the United Kingdom and the Isle of Man, and endures for 14 years, but may then be renewed for 7 (or 14) years if the patentee has not gained adequate remuneration. Revocation is by a petition to the High Court by the Attorney General, or his nominee, or any one who alleges the patent was obtained by fraud, or that he is the true inventor, or that the invention is not new. The assignment must be by deed, and may be partial. (Goodeve's Personalty, c. 9; Indermaur's Common Law, 6th edition, 199.)

INDEX.

Accumulation of income, 107.
Accumulations Act, 107.
Ademption, 137.
Administrators and executors, 140.
Advowsons, 63, 159, 160.
Alienation *inter vivos*, 122.
Alienation of personal chattels, 123.
Allodial land, 65.
Ancestor can inherit, 86.
Annuities, 146, 147, 162.
Appointment of trustees under Settled Land Act, 73, 74.
Apportionment of rent, 70, 71.
Assignment of leaseholds, 167.
——— life policy, 131.
Assurance, 131, 132, 184.
Attorney, power of, 114.

Bargain and sale, 118, 120.
Barring dower, 153.
Base fee, 67, 81-85.
" Beneficial owner," covenants implied by these words, 126.
Bills of sale, 177.
Bonds, 183, 184.
Borough English, 87.
Business, sale of, 129.

Capital money under Settled Land Acts, 80.
Capite, tenants *in*, 65.
Charge, definition of, 174.
Charity, gift to, 145.
Chattel interests in land, 166-173.
Chief rent, 63.
Choses in action, 129, 130, 150, 151.
——— in possession, wife's, 150, 151.
Collateral powers, 111, 112.
Commons—
    Appendant, 155, 156.
    Appurtenant, 155, 156.
    How extinguished, 156.
    In gross, 155.
Conditional estates, 66, 67.
Conduit pipe, 120.
Consolidation of mortgages, 180.
Constructive notice, 128, 129.
Contingency with double aspect, 103.
Contingent remainders, 99-103.

Contract for sale, effect of, 123, 130.
Conveying to one's self, 123.
Conveyance, outline of a, 127.
Conveyancing Acts, Epitome of, 6-28.
Coparcenary, 94.
Copyholds—
    Conveyance of, 162.
    Covenants on sale of, 125.
    Devising, 165, 166.
    Enfranchisement of, 165, 166.
    Estates tail in, 164, 165.
    Fines in, 164.
    Generally as to, 162-166.
    Minerals, 162.
    Mortgage of, 165.
Corporations, 185, 186.
——— how dissolved, 186.
Course of reading, 1-5.
Covenants—
    Deed of, 183, 184.
    Implied by use of certain words, 126.
    On sales and mortgages, 125.
    Running with land, 126, 127, 167, 168.
Curtesy, 153.
Custom, 157.
Customary freeholds, 164.
——— heir, 64.
Cy-près, doctrine of, 114, 115.

Death without issue, 108, 139.
Debentures, 181, 182.
Debts, how realty became liable for, 146.
Decline of feudal system, 65.
Deed of covenant, 183, 184.
Delivery of a deed, 123.
Demesne lands, 162.
Demonstrative legacy, 137.
Descent, 85-89.
Devises, 134-147.
Devise to trustees, 145.
Devolution on death, 86-93.
Disclaimer, 171.
Distribution of personal estate, 89-93.
Donatio mortis causâ, 131.
Dower—
    Definition of, 152.
    How barred, 153.
    Uses to bar, 153.

Dying without issue, 139.

Easements, 62, 156, 157, 158.
——— affirmative and negative, 156, 157.
——— continuous and discontinuous, 157.
——— extinguishment of, 158.
Enfranchisement, 63.
Enlargement of leasehold into fee simple, 173.
Entails, 81-85.
Entireties, tenancy by, 94.
Epitome of Conveyancing Acts, 6-28.
——— Settled Land Acts, 29-44.
Equitable mortgage, 174.
Equity of redemption, 175, 176.
Escheat, 62.
Escrow, 123.
Estates on condition, 66.
Estates—
   Definitions of various, 67.
   For life, varieties of, 67.
   In severalty, 93.
   Quantity and quality of, 69.
   Tail, 81-85.
   Vesting under a statute, 68.
   Words necessary to create different, 68.
Estate in land, 67.
——— in personalty, 60.
——— pur autre vie, 62.
Estoppel, 173.
Excessive execution of powers, 112.
Executors, 140, 141, 142, 143.
Executory interests, 99.
——— limitations, 108.
Exclusive appointments, 112.

Feoffment, 63, 122.
Feudal lands, 65.
——— system, decline of, 65.
Fines, 163, 164.
Fines and Recoveries Act, 82.
Fixtures, 60, 61.
Forfeiture on marriage, 145, 146.
Franchise, 161.
Frauds, Statute of, 64, 65.
Freebench, 152, 153.
Free fishery, 161.
Future estates and interests, 98-116.

Gavelkind land, 87.
General legacy, 136, 137.
General occupant, 62.
General power, 110.
Goodwill, 129.
Grant, 118.

Habendum, 125.

Half-blood, 86.
Heir—
   Apparent, 64.
   At law, 64.
   Presumptive, 64.
Heirs male, 83.
Heirlooms, 76.
Hotchpot, 93, 148.
Husband and wife, 147-155.

Illusory appointments, 112.
Impropriator, 161.
Income, accumulation of, 107, 108.
Incorporeal hereditaments, 155-162.
Infants' settlements, 149.
Inheritance, 85-89.
Innkeepers Act 1878, 174.
Insurable interests, 184.
Insurance, 184, 185.
Intestacy, 89-93.
Investments for capital money, 80.

Joint tenancy, 93-98.
Jointure, 154.
Jus accrescendi, 96, 97.

Land, recovery of by action, 183.
Lapse 92, 93, 138, 139.
Lay-impropriator, 161.
Leaseholds—
   Assignment of, 167, 170, 171.
   Covenants running with land, 167, 168.
   Demise of, 171.
   Determination of, 172.
   Disclaimer of, 171.
   Enlargement into fee simple, 173.
   Estoppel, 173.
   Forfeiture of, 169, 170.
   Generally as to, 166-173.
   Mortgage of, 171.
   Notice to quit, 168, 169.
   Of wife, 150, 151.
   Parol, 167.
   Rent in respect of, 169.
   Severance of reversion, 172.
   Surrender of, 172.
   Title to, 172.
Leases—
   By tenant for life under Settled Land Acts, 71, 72.
   By tenant in tail, 85.
Lease, 118.
Lease and release, 120.
Legacy—
   Ademption, 137.
   Demonstrative, 136, 137.
   Executor's assent, 150.
   General, 136, 137.

Legacy—*continued.*
    Interest on, 143.
    Lapse, 138, 139.
    Specific, 136, 137.
    Vested and contingent, 104.
Lien of vendor, 128.
Liens, 174.
Life estates, generally as to, 69-81.
———, proviso for cesser of, 152.
Limitation, Statutes of, 183.
Locke King's Acts, 181.
Lord paramount, 65.

Manors—
    Incidents of, 162.
    Origin of, 163.
Marriage—
    Condition of forfeiture, 145, 146.
    Effect of on property, 150, 151.
    Settlement on, 147, 148.
Married women, testamentary powers of, 151.
Maxims—
    Mobilia sequuntur personam. 60, 61, 62.
    Nemo est hæres viventis, 64.
    Quicquid plantatur solo, solo cedit, 61.
    Seisina facit stipitem, 86.
    Solus deus hæredem facere potest, non homo, 64.
    The father to the bough, the son to the plough, 61, 62.
Merger, 115, 116.
Mesne lord, 65.
Minerals, right to in copyholds, 162.
Mortgages—
    Analysis of mortgage in fee simple, 174, 175.
    Consolidation of, 180.
    Equitable, 181.
    Generally as to, 173-182.
    Locke King's Acts, 181.
    Of chattels, 181.
    Of copyholds, 174.
    Of leaseholds, 174.
    Payment of mortgage money after death of mortgagee, 179.
    Powers of mortgagor and mortgagee, 175, 176.
    Remedies of mortgagee, 177.
    Statute of Limitations as to, 178.
    Statutory, 176, 177.
    Tacking, 179.
    Transfers of, 180.
Mortmain, 145.

Necessity, way of. 157.
Next-of-kin, 89-91.
Notice, constructive, 128, 129.

Ownership of real and personal property, 59, 60.

Paintings, &c., protection of, 186.
Paraphernalia, 154.
Partition, 97.
Pasture, common of, 155.
Patents, 186, 187.
Perpetuities, rule against, 106, 107.
Personal annuities, 162.
Personal property, estate in, 60.
Per stirpes, 88.
Pin money, 154.
Pledge, 174.
Policy of insurance, 131, 132.
Possibility of issue extinct, 83.
Possibility of reverter, 103.
Powers, 109-114.
Powers of attorney, 114.
Prescription, 157, 159.
Property, meanings of, 59.
Protector of settlement, 84.
Proviso for cesser of life interest, 152.
Purchase deed, analysis of, 127.
Purchaser, 86.

Quantity and quality of estates, 69.
Questions and answers, digest of, 59-187.
Quit rents, 63.
——— redemption of, 161.

Reading, course of, 1-5.
Real and personal property, 59, 60.
Recitals, 124.
Redemption of quit rents, 161.
Release, 118.
Remainders, 98, 99.
Rent-charge, 156, 160, 180.
——— powers of owner of, 180, 181.
Rent on leases, 169.
Reputed manor, 163.
Restraint of trade, 129.
Resulting use, 119.
Reversions, 98.
Rights of common, 155, 156.
Rule in Shelley's case, 105.
——— of perpetuities, 106.

Sales under Settled Land Acts, 71, 78.
Satisfied terms, 185.
Scintilla juris, 121, 122.
Scutage, 66.
Seizure quousque, 163.
Settled Land Acts—
    Epitome of, 29-44.
    Questions and answers on, 71-81.
Settled Land Act 1887, 32.
——————— 1889, 29.

Settlement by infant, 149.
———— by way of trusts for sale, 79.
———— of realty on marriage, 147.
———— personalty, 148.
———— of chattels to accompany freeholds, 149.
Severalty, 93.
Severance of reversion, 172.
Shelley's case, rule in, 105.
Shifting use, 63.
Ships, 130.
Solicitors Act 1860, 174.
Special occupant, 62.
Special power, 110.
Specific legacy, 136, 137.
Springing use, 62.
Statute of Frauds, Epitome of, 64.
Statutes, list of important, 45-47.
Statutes—
    De Donis, 81.
    Frauds, 64.
    Prescription Act, 159.
    Quia Emptores, 66.
    Real Estate Charges Acts, 181.
    Tenures, 66.
    Uses, 116.
Statutory mortgage, 176, 177.
Strict settlement, 147, 148.
Subinfeudation, 66.
Surrender, 115, 118.
Survivorship of covenants, 97, 98.
———— estates, 97, 98.
———— powers, 97, 98.

Tacking, 179.
Tenancy at sufferance, 168, 169.
———— at will, 168, 169.
———— by entireties, 94.
———— in common, 93-98.
Tenant for life, regulations on exercise of powers, 71.
Tenant for life, assignment of powers, 73.
———— cutting timber, 74.
———— effect of conveyance, 74.
———— infant, 72.
———— lunatic, 72.
———— married woman, 72.
———— who has powers of, 70.

Test Questions, 48-58.
Thellusson Act, 107.
Tithes, 160, 161.
Tithe rent-charge, 160, 161.
Title, generally as to, 182.
Title to advowson, 182.
———— enfranchised copyholds, 182.
———— freeholds, 182.
———— leaseholds, 182.
———— tithes, 182.
Title deeds, who entitled to possession of, 133.
Transmutation of possession, 117.
Trust distinguished from use, 117.
Trusts, generally as to, 117.
Trustees under Conveyancing Act, 73.
Trustees under Settled Land Acts, 73, 74, 80, 81.
Trusts to preserve contingent remainders, 102.

Uses and trusts, 116, 122.
Use distinguished from trust, 117.
Uses, Statute of, 116, 117.
Uses to bar dower, 153.

Vendor's lien, 128.
Vested estate subject to being divested, 103.
Vested remainders, 99.
Vesting of estates by statute, 68.
Voluntary settlements, 132.

Waste, 69, 70.
Watercourse, 158.
Way of necessity, 157.
Wills—
    By married women, 151, 152.
    Devise to trustees, 145.
    Execution of, 134.
    Execution of power of appointment by, 135.
    Generally as to, 134-147.
    History of power of devise, 134.
    How executed, 134, 135.
    Operation of, 134.
    Property passing by, 135.
    Revocation of, 135, 136.

A CATALOGUE

OF

LAW WORKS

PUBLISHED AND SOLD BY

STEVENS & HAYNES,

𝔏𝔞𝔴 𝔓𝔲𝔟𝔩𝔦𝔰𝔥𝔢𝔯𝔰, 𝔅𝔬𝔬𝔨𝔰𝔢𝔩𝔩𝔢𝔯𝔰 & 𝔈𝔵𝔭𝔬𝔯𝔱𝔢𝔯𝔰,

13, BELL YARD, TEMPLE BAR,

LONDON.

BOOKS BOUND IN THE BEST BINDINGS.

Works in all Classes of Literature supplied to Order.

FOREIGN BOOKS IMPORTED.

LIBRARIES VALUED FOR PROBATE, PARTNERSHIP, AND OTHER PURPOSES.

LIBRARIES OR **SMALL COLLECTIONS** OF **BOOKS PURCHASED.**

A large Stock of Reports of the various Courts of England, Ireland, and Scotland, always on hand.

Catalogues and Estimates Furnished, and Orders Promptly Executed.

NOTE.—*To avoid confusing our firm with any of a similar name, we beg to notify that we have no connexion whatever with any other house of business, and we respectfully request that Correspondents will take special care to direct all communications to the above names and address.*

INDEX OF SUBJECTS.

ABSTRACT DRAWING—
  Scott 32
ADMINISTRATION ACTIONS—
  Walker and Elgood 18
ADMINISTRATORS—
  Walker 6
ADMIRALTY LAW—
  Kay 17
  Smith 23
ARBITRATION—
  Slater 7
ARTIZANS AND LABOURERS'
  DWELLINGS—Lloyd 13
BANKRUPTCY—
  Baldwin 15
  Hazlitt 29
  Indermaur (Question & Answer) 28
  Ringwood 15, 29
BAR EXAMINATION JOURNAL 39
BIBLIOGRAPHY 40
BILLS OF LADING—
  Campbell 9
  Kay 17
BILLS OF SALE—
  Baldwin 15
  Indermaur 28
  Ringwood 15
BUILDING LEASES AND CON-
  TRACTS—
  Emden 8
  Hudson 12
CAPITAL PUNISHMENT—
  Copinger 42
CARRIERS—
  See RAILWAY LAW.
  ,, SHIPMASTERS.
CHANCERY DIVISION, Practice of—
  Brown's Edition of Snell . . . 22
  Indermaur 25
  Williams 7
  And see EQUITY.
CHARITABLE TRUSTS—
  Cooke 10
  Whiteford 20
CHURCH AND CLERGY—
  Brice 9
CIVIL LAW—See ROMAN LAW.
CLUB LAW—
  Wertheimer 32
CODES—Argles 32
COLLISIONS AT SEA—Kay . . 17
COLONIAL LAW—
  Cape Colony 38
  Forsyth 14
  Tarring 41
COMMERCIAL AGENCY—
  Campbell 9

COMMERCIAL LAW—
  Hurst and Cecil 11
COMMON LAW—
  Indermaur 24
COMPANIES LAW—
  Brice 16
  Buckley 17
  Reilly's Reports 29
  Smith 39
  Watts 47
COMPENSATION—
  Browne 19
  Lloyd 13
COMPULSORY PURCHASE—
  Browne 19
CONSTABLES—
  See POLICE GUIDE.
CONSTITUTIONAL LAW AND
  HISTORY—
  Forsyth 14
  Taswell-Langmead 21
  Thomas 28
CONSULAR JURISDICTION—
  Tarring 42
CONVEYANCING—
  Copinger, Title Deeds 45
  Copinger, Precedents in . . . 40
  Deane, Principles of 23
COPYRIGHT—
  Copinger 45
CORPORATIONS—
  Brice 16
  Browne 19
COSTS, Crown Office—
  Short 41
COVENANTS FOR TITLE—
  Copinger 45
CREW OF A SHIP—
  Kay 17
CRIMINAL LAW—
  Copinger 42
  Harris 27
CROWN LAW—
  Forsyth 14
  Hall 30
  Kelyng 35
  Taswell-Langmead 21
  Thomas 28
CROWN OFFICE RULES—
  Short 10
CROWN PRACTICE—
  Corner 10
  Short and Mellor 10
CUSTOM AND USAGE—
  Browne 19
  Mayne 38
DAMAGES—
  Mayne 31
DICTIONARIES—
  Brown 26

INDEX OF SUBJECTS—*continued.*

DIGESTS—
   Law Magazine Quarterly Digest . 37
   Menzies' Digest of Cape Reports . 38
DISCOVERY—Peile 7
DIVORCE—Harrison 23
DOMESTIC RELATIONS—
   Eversley 9
DOMICIL—*See* PRIVATE INTERNATIONAL LAW.
DUTCH LAW 38
ECCLESIASTICAL LAW—
   Brice 9
   Smith 23
EDUCATION ACTS—
   See MAGISTERIAL LAW.
ELECTION LAW and PETITIONS—
   Hardcastle 33
   O'Malley and Hardcastle . . 33
   Seager 47
EQUITY—
   Blyth 22
   Choyce Cases 35
   Pemberton 32
   Snell 22
   Story 43
   Williams 7
EVIDENCE—
   Phipson 20
EXAMINATION OF STUDENTS—
   Bar Examination Journal . . . 39
   Indermaur . . . . . 24 and 25
   Intermediate LL.B. 21
EXECUTORS—
   Walker and Elgood 6
EXTRADITION—
   Clarke 45
   See MAGISTERIAL LAW.
FACTORIES—
   See MAGISTERIAL LAW.
FISHERIES—
   See MAGISTERIAL LAW.
FIXTURES—Brown 33
FOREIGN LAW—
   Argles 32
   Dutch Law 38
   Foote 36
   Pavitt 32
FORESHORE—
   Moore 30
FORGERY—*See* MAGISTERIAL LAW
FRAUDULENT CONVEYANCES—
   May 29
GAIUS INSTITUTES—
   Harris 20
GAME LAWS—
   See MAGISTERIAL LAW.
GUARDIAN AND WARD—
   Eversley 9
HACKNEY CARRIAGES—
   See MAGISTERIAL LAW.

HINDU LAW—
   Coghlan 28
   Cunningham . . . . 38 and 42
   Mayne 38
HISTORY—
   Taswell-Langmead 21
HUSBAND AND WIFE—
   Eversley 9
INDEX TO PRECEDENTS—
   Copinger 40
INFANTS—
   Eversley 9
   Simpson 43
INJUNCTIONS—
   Joyce 44
INSTITUTE OF THE LAW—
   Brown's Law Dictionary . . . 26
INSURANCE—
   Porter 6
INTERNATIONAL LAW—
   Clarke 45
   Cobbett 43
   Foote 36
   Law Magazine 37
INTERROGATORIES—
   Peile 7
INTOXICATING LIQUORS—
   See MAGISTERIAL LAW.
JOINT STOCK COMPANIES—
   See COMPANIES.
JUDGMENTS AND ORDERS—
   Pemberton 18
JUDICATURE ACTS—
   Cunningham and Mattinson . . 7
   Indermaur 25
   Kelke 6
JURISPRUDENCE—
   Forsyth 14
   Salmond 13
JUSTINIAN'S INSTITUTES—
   Campbell 47
   Harris 20
LANDLORD AND TENANT—
   Foa 11
LANDS CLAUSES CONSOLIDATION ACT—
   Lloyd 13
LAND, IMPROVEMENT OF, by Buildings—
   Emden 8
LATIN MAXIMS 28
LAW DICTIONARY—
   Brown 26
LAW MAGAZINE and REVIEW . 37
LEADING CASES—
   Common Law 25
   Constitutional Law 28
   Equity and Conveyancing . . 25
   Hindu Law 28
   International Law 43

INDEX OF SUBJECTS—*continued.*

	PAGE
LEADING STATUTES—	
Thomas	28
LEASES—	
Emden	8
Copinger	45
LEGACY AND SUCCESSION—	
Hanson	10
LEGITIMACY AND MARRIAGE—	
See PRIVATE INTERNATIONAL LAW.	
LICENSES— *See* MAGISTERIAL LAW.	
LIFE ASSURANCE—	
Buckley	17
Reilly	29
LIMITATION OF ACTIONS—	
Banning	42
LUNACY—	
Williams	7
MAGISTERIAL LAW—	
Greenwood and Martin	46
MAINTENANCE AND DESERTION.	
Martin	7
MARRIAGE and LEGITIMACY—	
Foote	36
MARRIED WOMEN'S PROPERTY ACTS—	
Brown's Edition of Griffith	40
MASTER AND SERVANT—	
Eversley	9
See MAGISTERIAL LAW.	
,, SHIPMASTERS & SEAMEN.	
MERCANTILE LAW	32
Campbell	9
Duncan	33
Hurst and Cecil	11
Slater	7
See SHIPMASTERS.	
,, STOPPAGE IN TRANSITU.	
MERCHANDISE MARKS—	
Daniel	42
MINES—	
Harris	47
See MAGISTERIAL LAW.	
MORTMAIN—	
See CHARITABLE TRUSTS.	
NATIONALITY— *See* PRIVATE INTERNATIONAL LAW.	
NEGLIGENCE—	
Deven	14
Campbell	40
NEWSPAPER LIBEL—	
Elliott	14
OBLIGATIONS—	
Brown's Savigny	20
PARENT AND CHILD—	
Eversley	9
PARLIAMENT—	
Taswell-Langmead	21
Thomas	28

	PAGE
PARTITION—	
Walker	43
PASSENGERS—	
See MAGISTERIAL LAW.	
,, RAILWAY LAW.	
PASSENGERS AT SEA—	
Kay	17
PATENTS—	
Daniel	42
Frost	12
PAWNBROKERS—	
See MAGISTERIAL LAW.	
PETITIONS IN CHANCERY AND LUNACY—	
Williams	7
PILOTS—	
Kay	17
POLICE GUIDE—	
Greenwood and Martin	46
POLLUTION OF RIVERS—	
Higgins	30
PRACTICE BOOKS—	
Bankruptcy	15
Companies Law	29 and 39
Compensation	13
Compulsory Purchase	19
Conveyancing	45
Damages	31
Ecclesiastical Law	9
Election Petitions	33
Equity	7, 22 and 32
Injunctions	44
Magisterial	46
Pleading, Precedents of	7
Railways	14
Railway Commission	19
Rating	19
Supreme Court of Judicature	25
PRACTICE STATUTES, ORDERS AND RULES—	
Emden	11
PRECEDENTS OF PLEADING—	
Cunningham and Mattinson	7
Mattinson and Macaskie	7
PRIMOGENITURE—	
Lloyd	1
PRINCIPLES—	
Brice (Corporations)	16
Browne (Rating)	19
Deane (Conveyancing)	23
Harris (Criminal Law)	27
Houston (Mercantile)	32
Indermaur (Common Law)	24
Joyce (Injunctions)	44
Ringwood (Bankruptcy)	15
Snell (Equity)	22
PRIVATE INTERNATIONAL LAW—	
Foote	36

INDEX OF SUBJECTS—*continued*.

	PAGE
PROBATE—	
Hanson	10
Harrison	23
PROMOTERS—	
Watts	47
PUBLIC WORSHIP—	
Brice	9
QUARTER SESSIONS—	
Smith (F. J.)	6
QUEEN'S BENCH DIVISION, Practice of—	
Indermaur	25
QUESTIONS FOR STUDENTS—	
Aldred	21
Bar Examination Journal	39
Indermaur	25
Waite	22
RAILWAYS—	
Browne	19
Godefroi and Shortt	47
See MAGISTERIAL LAW.	
RATING—	
Browne	19
REAL PROPERTY—	
Deane	23
Edwards	16
Tarring	26
REGISTRATION—	
Elliott (Newspaper)	14
Seager (Parliamentary)	47
REPORTS—	
Bellewe	34
Brooke	35
Choyce Cases	35
Cooke	35
Cunningham	34
Election Petitions	33
Finlason	32
Gibbs, Seymour Will Case	10
Kelyng, John	35
Kelynge, William	35
Reilly	29
Shower (Cases in Parliament)	34
ROMAN DUTCH LAW—	
Van Leeuwen	38
ROMAN LAW—	
Brown's Analysis of Savigny	20
Campbell	47
Harris	20
Salkowski	14
Whitfield	14
SALVAGE—	
Jones	47
Kay	17
SANITARY ACTS—	
See MAGISTERIAL LAW.	
SAVINGS BANKS—	
Forbes	18
SCINTILLAE JURIS—	
Darling (C. J.)	18

	PAGE
SEA SHORE—	
Hall	30
Moore	30
SHIPMASTERS AND SEAMEN—	
Kay	17
SOCIETIES—	
See CORPORATIONS.	
STAGE CARRIAGES—	
See MAGISTERIAL LAW.	
STAMP DUTIES—	
Copinger	40 and 45
STATUTE OF LIMITATIONS—	
Banning	42
STATUTES—	
Craies	6
Hardcastle	9
Marcy	26
Thomas	28
STOPPAGE IN TRANSITU—	
Campbell	9
Houston	32
Kay	17
STUDENTS' BOOKS	20—28, 39, 47
SUCCESSION DUTIES—	
Hanson	10
SUCCESSION LAWS—	
Lloyd	13
SUPREME COURT OF JUDICATURE, Practice of—	
Cunningham and Mattinson	7
Indermaur	25
TELEGRAPHS—	
See MAGISTERIAL LAW.	
TITLE DEEDS—	
Copinger	45
TORTS—	
Ringwood	13
TOWNS IMPROVEMENTS—	
See MAGISTERIAL LAW.	
TRADE MARKS—	
Daniel	42
TREASON—	
Kelyng	35
Taswell-Langmead	21
TRIALS—Bartlett, A. (Murder)	32
Queen *v.* Gurney	32
ULTRA VIRES—	
Brice	16
USAGES AND CUSTOMS—	
Browne	19
Mayne	38
VOLUNTARY CONVEYANCES—	
May	29
WATER COURSES—	
Higgins	30
WILLS, CONSTRUCTION OF—	
Gibbs, Report of Wallace *v.* Attorney-General	10

Second Edition, in 8vo. Price 21s., cloth,

THE LAWS OF INSURANCE:
Fire, Life, Accident, and Guarantee.
EMBODYING
CASES IN THE ENGLISH, SCOTCH, IRISH, AMERICAN, AND CANADIAN COURTS.

By JAMES BIGGS PORTER,
OF THE INNER TEMPLE AND SOUTH EASTERN CIRCUIT, BARRISTER-AT-LAW.

ASSISTED BY

W. FEILDEN CRAIES, M.A.,
OF THE INNER TEMPLE AND WESTERN CIRCUIT, BARRISTER-AT-LAW.

"In reviewing the first edition of this book we expressed an opinion that it was a painstaking and useful work. Its utility has been shown by the speedy appearance of the present edition, and the labour of its authors is still apparent to anyone who will glance through its pages."—*Solicitors' Journal.*

"The success of the first edition proves its value. It is clearly and concisely compiled, and upwards of 1,500 cases are quoted."—*Law Times.*

"Mr. Porter's useful book on insurance law has reached a second edition in less than three years, which is not common in a book of this class. The fact is, that in taking up insurance law in all its branches, except marine insurance, he hits upon a popular subject. . . . . Mr. Porter well fills the gap thus made for him, and he has called to his aid a useful coadjutor in the person of Mr. Craies."—*Law Journal.*

"When writing on the first edition in 1884, we ventured to predict for Mr. Porter's work a great success. We spoke in terms of unqualified commendation concerning the lucidity of the author's style, the thoroughness of his work and his happy gift of narrowing down broad and diffusive subjects into a small space. Practical experience of the contents of the volume during the past three years has, we may say, fully confirmed our favourable views."—*Insurance Record.*

In Royal 12mo, price 20s., cloth,

QUARTER SESSIONS PRACTICE,
A VADE MECUM OF GENERAL PRACTICE IN APPELLATE AND CIVIL CASES AT QUARTER SESSIONS.

By FREDERICK JAMES SMITH,
OF THE MIDDLE TEMPLE, BARRISTER-AT-LAW, AND RECORDER OF MARGATE.

Second Edition. In one volume, 8vo, price 21s., cloth,

A COMPENDIUM OF THE LAW RELATING TO
EXECUTORS AND ADMINISTRATORS,
With an Appendix of Statutes, Annotated by means of References to the Text. Second Edition. By W. GREGORY WALKER, B.A., of Lincoln's Inn, Barrister-at-Law, and EDGAR J. ELGOOD, B.C.L., M.A., of Lincoln's Inn, Barrister-at-Law.

"We highly approve of Mr. Walker's arrangement. . . . . The Notes are full, and as far as we have been able to ascertain, carefully and accurately compiled. . . . . We can commend it as bearing on its face evidence of skilful and careful labour, and we anticipate that it will be found a very acceptable substitute for the ponderous tomes of the much esteemed and valued Williams."—*Law Times.*

"Mr. Walker is fortunate in his choice of a subject, and the power of treating it succinctly for the ponderous tomes of Williams, however satisfactory as an authority, are necessarily inconvenient for reference as well as expensive. . . . . On the whole we are inclined to think the book a good and useful one."—*Law Journal.*

In royal 12mo, price 4s., cloth,

A DIGEST OF THE LAW OF
PRACTICE UNDER THE JUDICATURE ACTS AND RULES,
AND THE CASES DECIDED IN THE CHANCERY AND COMMON LAW DIVISIONS FROM NOVEMBER 1875 TO AUGUST 1880.

By W. H. HASTINGS KELKE, M.A., Barrister-at-Law.

In 8vo, price 5s., cloth,

THE LAW OF MAINTENANCE AND DESERTION,
AND THE ORDERS OF THE JUSTICES THEREON. By TEMPLE CHEVALLIER MARTIN, Chief Clerk of the Lambeth Police Court, and Joint Author of the "Magisterial and Police Guide," &c.

Second Edition. Crown 8vo, price 8s. 6d., cloth,

THE LAW OF ARBITRATION AND AWARDS;
With Appendix containing Lord Denman's ARBITRATION BILL, AND STATUTES RELATING TO ARBITRATION, and a collection of Forms and Index. Second Edition. With a Supplement containing an Abstract of the Arbitration Act, 1889. By JOSHUA SLATER, of Gray's Inn, Barrister-at-Law.

*** *The Supplement can be had separately, price 6d.*

In crown 8vo, price 6s., cloth,

THE PRINCIPLES OF MERCANTILE LAW. By
JOSHUA SLATER, of Gray's Inn, Barrister-at-Law, Author of "The Law of Arbitration and Awards."

In 8vo, price 12s., cloth,

THE LAW AND PRACTICE OF DISCOVERY in
the SUPREME COURT of JUSTICE. WITH AN APPENDIX OF FORMS, ORDERS, &c., AND AN ADDENDA GIVING THE ALTERATIONS UNDER THE NEW RULES OF PRACTICE. By CLARENCE J. PEILE, of the Inner Temple, Barrister-at-Law.

"Mr. Peile has done well in writing this book. The subject is carefully yet tersely treated."—*Law Times.*

In one volume, 8vo, price 18s., cloth,

THE LAW AND PRACTICE RELATING TO

PETITIONS IN CHANCERY AND LUNACY,
INCLUDING THE SETTLED ESTATES ACT, LANDS CLAUSES ACT, TRUSTEE ACT, WINDING-UP PETITIONS, PETITIONS RELATING TO SOLICITORS, INFANTS, ETC., ETC. WITH AN APPENDIX OF FORMS AND PRECEDENTS. By SYDNEY E. WILLIAMS, of Lincoln's Inn, Barrister-at-Law.

Second Edition, in 8vo, price 28s., cloth,

A SELECTION OF PRECEDENTS OF PLEADING
UNDER THE JUDICATURE ACTS IN THE COMMON LAW DIVISIONS. With Notes explanatory of the different Causes of Action and Grounds of Defence; and an Introductory Treatise on the Present Rules and Principles of Pleading as illustrated by the various Decisions down to the Present Time.

By J. CUNNINGHAM and M. W. MATTINSON.

SECOND EDITION.

By MILES WALKER MATTINSON, of Gray's Inn, Barrister-at-Law, and STUART CUNNINGHAM MACASKIE, of Gray's Inn, Barrister-at-Law.

REVIEWS.
"The notes are very pertinent and satisfactory: the introductory chapters on the present system of pleading are excellent, and the precedents will be found very useful."—*Irish Law Times.*

"A work which, in the compass of a single portable volume, contains a brief Treatise on the Principles and Rules of Pleading, and a carefully annotated body of Forms which have to a great extent gone through the entirely separate sifting processes of Chambers, Court, and Judges' Chambers, cannot fail to be a most useful companion in the Practitioner's daily routine."—*Law Magazine and Review.*

Second Edition, in 8vo, price 25s., cloth,

REMODELLED, MUCH ENLARGED, WITH SEVERAL NEW CHAPTERS ON "LIGHT," "SUPPORT," ETC.

EMDEN'S LAW RELATING TO

BUILDING, BUILDING LEASES, AND BUILDING CONTRACTS.

WITH A FULL COLLECTION OF PRECEDENTS,

TOGETHER WITH THE

STATUTE LAW RELATING TO BUILDING,

WITH NOTES AND THE LATEST CASES UNDER THE VARIOUS SECTIONS.

By ALFRED EMDEN,

OF THE INNER TEMPLE, ESQ., BARRISTER-AT-LAW; AUTHOR OF THE "PRACTICE IN WINDING-UP COMPANIES," "A COMPLETE COLLECTION OF PRACTICE STATUTES, ORDERS, AND RULES, FROM 1275 TO 1885," "THE SHAREHOLDER'S LEGAL GUIDE," ETC., ETC.

"We were able to speak in terms of commendation of the First Edition of this book, but we can say much more for the present edition. Mr. Emden has re-written and enlarged his work, and in its present form it constitutes a complete, and so far as our examination has gone, an accurate treatise on the branch of the law to which it relates."—*Solicitors' Journal.*

"We had occasion to speak favourably of the First Edition of Mr. Emden's work, and we have nothing but commendation to award to the Second Edition, which has practically been re-written and very much enlarged."—*The Field.*

"With the revisions and additions, Mr. Emden's treatise claims in a higher degree to be considered the most comprehensive text-book of the law relating to building, that has been published in a single volume." —*The Building News.*

"This work viewed as a whole, is in all ways a standard authority on all the subjects treated, and it is in reality a small Law Library on building subjects, ingeniously and most lucidly compressed in a single volume."—*The Building World.*

"No more useful book for architect, contractor, or building owner, has been published than 'Emden's Law of Building, Building Leases, and Building Contracts,' and its re-issue as a revised and extended work will be generally appreciated."—*The Architect.*

"A second edition of Mr. Alfred Emden's useful work on *The Law relating to Building Leases, and Building Contracts*, has just been issued by Messrs. Stevens & Haynes, Bell Yard, Temple Bar. The first edition soon became exhausted, and the learned author has entirely rewritten, remodelled, and considerably enlarged the previous edition. There is a good collection of precedents with respect to matters connected with building, together with the Statute Law relating to building, with notes, and the latest cases under the various sections. A new and comprehensive index has been compiled, and last, but not least, is an excellent glossary of architectural and building terms used in the Building Act, building leases and contracts, &c."—*Law Times.*

"We have been asked from time to time which is the text-book of the *Law relating to Building, Building Leases, and Building Contracts*, and we have had to reply that, so far as we know, the comprehensive work published by Messrs. Stevens & Haynes, of Bell Yard, Temple Bar, by Mr. Alfred Emden, is the best and most generally useful we know. We mention this fact because a second edition has just been published, 'rewritten, remodelled, and enlarged,' on the law relating to buildings, with new chapters on damage to property or person caused by building, gas and water, support, party walls, and light. Voluminous precedents are also given, with a comprehensive view of the Statute Law, which has materially changed since the first edition was published in 1882. It is well that those engaged in the building trade should bear this in mind, as much litigation would therefore be avoided, with its consequent expense and annoyance. The book is rendered more valuable from its glossary and well-arranged index." —*Building Times.*

"The present treatise of Mr. Emden deals with the subject in an exhaustive manner, which leaves nothing to be desired. . . . The book contains a number of forms and precedents for building leases and agreements which are not to be found in the ordinary collection of precedents."—*The Times.*

"Mr. Emden has obviously given time and labour to his task, and therefore will save time and labour to those who happen to be occupied in the same field of enquiry."—*Law Journal.*

"It may safely be recommended as a practical text-book and guide to all people whose fortune or misfortune it is to be interested in the construction of buildings and other works."—*Saturday Review.*

"To supply this want is the writer's object in publishing this work, and we have no hesitation in expressing our opinion that it will be found valuable by several distinct classes of persons . . . . it seems to us a good and useful book, and we recommend the purchase of it without hesitation."—*The Builder.*

"From the point of view of practical utility the work cannot fail to be of the greatest use to all who require a little law in the course of their building operations. They will find both a sound arrangement and a clear sensible style, and by perusing it with ordinary attention many matters of which they were before doubtful will become quite comprehensible."—*City Press.*

In royal 8vo, 1100 pages, price 52s. 6d., cloth,

THE LAW OF THE DOMESTIC RELATIONS,
INCLUDING

HUSBAND AND WIFE: PARENT AND CHILD: GUARDIAN AND WARD: INFANTS: AND MASTER AND SERVANT.

By WILLIAM PINDER EVERSLEY, B.C.L., M.A.,
OF THE INNER TEMPLE, BARRISTER-AT-LAW.

"It is essentially readable and interesting, and ought to take a high place among text books. . . . We say, without hesitation, that this is a learned book, written in a peculiarly fascinating style, having regard to the nature of the subject. . . . It can only be said, therefore, that the book is deserving of success upon the merits; and that the attempt to combine the treatment of three branches of the law which have hitherto been unnaturally divided shows, in itself, a comprehensive grasp of principle."—*Law Times*.

"The author may be congratulated upon having produced an excellent treatise on this branch of the law, well arranged, clearly written, and complete. A word of praise, too, must be accorded to the laborious care with which he has accumulated references to the various Reports, and constructed his very full index."—*Solicitors' Journal*.

Second Edition, in one volume, royal 8vo, price 32s., cloth,

THE LAW RELATING TO THE
SALE OF GOODS AND COMMERCIAL AGENCY.
SECOND EDITION.

By ROBERT CAMPBELL, M.A.,
OF LINCOLN'S INN, BARRISTER-AT-LAW; ADVOCATE OF THE SCOTCH BAR;
AUTHOR OF THE "LAW OF NEGLIGENCE, ETC."

"An accurate, careful, and exhaustive handbook on the subject with which it deals. The excellent index deserves a special word of commendation."—*Law Quarterly Review*.

"We can, therefore, repeat what we said when reviewing the first edition—that the book is a contribution of value to the subject treated of, and that the writer deals with his subject carefully and fully."—*Law Journal*.

Second Edition, in one volume, 8vo, price 28s., cloth,

A TREATISE ON
THE CONSTRUCTION AND EFFECT OF STATUTE LAW.

WITH APPENDICES CONTAINING WORDS AND EXPRESSIONS USED IN STATUTES WHICH HAVE BEEN JUDICIALLY OR STATUTABLY CONSTRUED, AND THE POPULAR AND SHORT TITLES OF CERTAIN STATUTES.

By HENRY HARDCASTLE, BARRISTER-AT-LAW.

SECOND EDITION, REVISED AND ENLARGED, BY W. F. CRAIES,
BARRISTER-AT-LAW.

"The result of Mr. Craies' industry is a sound and good piece of work, the new light thrown on the subject since 1879 having been blended with the old in a thoroughly workmanlike manner. Though less a student's manual than a practitioner's text book, it is the sort of volume an intelligent perusal of which would educate a student better than the reading of much substantial law."—*Saturday Review*.

In one volume, 8vo, price 28s., cloth,

THE LAW RELATING TO PUBLIC WORSHIP;

With special reference to Matters of Ritual and Ornamentation, and the Means of Securing the Due Observance thereof, and containing in extenso, with Notes and References, The Public Worship Regulation Act, 1874; The Church Discipline Act; the various Acts of Uniformity; the Liturgies of 1549, 1552, and 1559, compared with the Present Rubric; the Canons; the Articles; and the Injunctions, Advertisements, and other Original Documents of Legal Authority. By SEWARD BRICE, LL.D., of the Inner Temple, Barrister-at-Law.

STEVENS & HAYNES, BELL YARD, TEMPLE BAR.

In 8vo, price 30s., cloth,

THE PRACTICE ON THE CROWN SIDE

Of the Queen's Bench Division of Her Majesty's High Court of Justice

(Founded on CORNER'S CROWN OFFICE PRACTICE), including
APPEALS FROM INFERIOR COURTS; WITH APPENDICES OF RULES AND FORMS.

By FREDERICK HUGH SHORT,

Chief Clerk of the Crown Office, Author of "Taxation of Costs in the Crown Office," and Editor of "Crown Office Rules and Forms, 1886;" and

FRANCIS HAMILTON MELLOR, M.A.,

Trin. Coll. Camb., Northern Circuit, Inner Temple, Barrister-at-Law.

In 8vo, price 12s., cloth,

THE CROWN OFFICE RULES AND FORMS, 1886.

The Supreme Court of Judicature Acts and Rules of the Supreme Court 1883, relating to the Practice on the Crown side of the Queen's Bench Division; including Appeals from Inferior Courts, Tables of Court Fees, Scales of Costs; together with Notes, Cases, and a Full Index. By F. H. SHORT, Chief Clerk of the Crown Office.

In 8vo, price 6s. 6d., cloth,

THE CUSTOMS AND INLAND REVENUE ACTS,

1880 and 1881 (43 VICT. CAP. 14, and 44 VICT. CAP. 12),

So far as they Relate to the Probate, Legacy, and Succession Duties, and the Duties on Accounts. With an Introduction and Notes. By ALFRED HANSON, Esq., Comptroller of Legacy and Succession Duties.

*** This forms a Supplement to the Third Edition of the Probate, Legacy, and Succession Duty Acts by the same Author.

Third Edition, in 8vo, 1876, price 25s., cloth,

THE ACTS RELATING TO PROBATE, LEGACY, AND SUCCESSION DUTIES.

Comprising the 36 Geo. III. c. 52; 45 Geo. III. c. 28; 55 Geo. III. c. 184; and 16 & 17 Vict. c. 51; with an Introduction, Copious Notes, and References to all the Decided Cases in England, Scotland, and Ireland. An Appendix of Statutes, Tables, and a full Index. By ALFRED HANSON, of the Middle Temple, Esq., Barrister-at-Law, Comptroller of Legacy and Succession Duties. Incorporating the Cases to Michaelmas Sittings, 1876.

"It is the only complete book upon a subject of great importance.
"Mr. Hanson is peculiarly qualified to be the adviser at such a time. Hence a volume without a rival."—*Law Times.*

"His book is in itself a most useful one; its author knows every in and out of the subject, and has presented the whole in a form easily and readily handled, and with good arrangement and clear exposition."—*Solicitors' Journal.*

In royal 8vo, 1877, price 10s., cloth,

LES HOSPICES DE PARIS ET DE LONDRES.

THE CASE OF LORD HENRY SEYMOUR'S WILL

(WALLACE v. THE ATTORNEY-GENERAL).

Reported by FREDERICK WAYMOUTH GIBBS, C.B., Barrister at-Law,
LATE FELLOW OF TRINITY COLLEGE, CAMBRIDGE.

In 8vo, 1867, price 16s., cloth,

CHARITABLE TRUSTS ACTS, 1853, 1855, 1860;

THE CHARITY COMMISSIONERS' JURISDICTION ACT, 1862;
THE ROMAN CATHOLIC CHARITIES ACTS:

Together with a Collection of Statutes relating to or affecting Charities, including the Mortmain Acts, Notes of Cases from 1853 to the present time, Forms of Declarations of Trust, Conditions of Sale, and Conveyance of Charity Land, and a very copious Index. Second Edition.

By HUGH COOKE and R. G. HARWOOD, of the Charity Commission.

In one Volume, 8vo, price 20s., cloth,

THE
PRINCIPLES OF COMMERCIAL LAW;
WITH AN APPENDIX OF STATUTES, ANNOTATED BY MEANS OF REFERENCES TO THE TEXT.

By JOSEPH HURST AND LORD ROBERT CECIL,
OF THE INNER TEMPLE, BARRISTERS-AT-LAW.

"Their compendium, we believe, will be found a really useful volume, one for the lawyer and the business man to keep at his elbow, and which, if not giving them all that they require, will place in their hands the key to the richer and more elaborate treasures of the Law which lie in larger and more exhaustive works."—*Law Times.*

"The object of the authors of this work, they tell us in their preface, is to state, within a moderate compass, the principles of commercial law. Very considerable pains have obviously been expended on the task, and the book is in many respects a very serviceable one."—*Law Journal.*

In one Volume, 8vo, price 20s. cloth,

THE
RELATIONSHIP OF LANDLORD AND TENANT.
By EDGAR FOA,
OF THE INNER TEMPLE, BARRISTER-AT-LAW.

"Will be found of much value to practitioners, and when a second edition has given the author the opportunity of reconsidering and carefully revising his statements in detail, we think it will take its place as a very good treatise on the modern law of landlord and tenant."—*Solicitors' Journal.*

"Mr. Foa is a bold man to undertake the exposition of a branch of law so full of difficulties and encumbered by so many decisions as the Law of Landlord and Tenant. But his boldness is justified by the excellent arrangement and by the lucid statements which characterise his book."—*Law Quarterly Review.*

"Mr. Foa's is a compact work, treating (1) of the creation of the relationship; (2) the incidents of creation (distress) and determination of the relationship; (3) modes and incidents of determination. We commend it to the attention of the Profession, and predict for Foa on Landlord and Tenant a very useful and very permanent future."—*Law Times.*

"We have nothing but praise for the work, and we shall be astonished if it does not take rank in course of time as one of the best—if not the best—work for every-day practice on the subject of Landlord and Tenant."—*Law Notes.*

"Without making any invidious comparison with existing works on the subject, we may frankly say that Mr. Foa's work indisputably possesses merit. . . . Our verdict on the book must be a decidedly favourable one."—*Law Students' Journal.*

"'The Relationship of Landlord and Tenant,' written by Mr. Edgar Foa, Barrister-at-Law, affords a striking instance of accuracy and lucidity of statement. The volume should be found useful not only by lawyers but by landlords and tenants themselves, the law in each particular being stated with a simplicity and clearness which bring it within the grasp of the lay mind."—*Law Gazette.*

Second Edition, in one Volume, medium 8vo, price 35s., cloth,

EMDEN'S COMPLETE COLLECTION
OF
PRACTICE STATUTES,
ORDERS AND RULES.

Being a Selection of such Practical Parts of all Statutes, Orders and Rules, as are now in force, and relate to the Practice and Procedure of the Supreme Court. From **1275 to 1886**. With Tabulated Summaries of the Leading Cases and Analytical Cross-references.

By ALFRED EMDEN,
OF THE INNER TEMPLE, ESQ., BARRISTER-AT-LAW; AUTHOR OF "THE PRACTICE IN WINDING-UP COMPANIES;" "THE LAW RELATING TO BUILDING, BUILDING LEASES, AND CONTRACTS;" "THE SHAREHOLDER'S LEGAL GUIDE," ETC.

ASSISTED BY
HERBERT THOMPSON, M.A.,
OF THE INNER TEMPLE, BARRISTER-AT-LAW.

Just published, in royal 8vo, cloth, 28s.,

A TREATISE ON THE
LAW AND PRACTICE
RELATING TO
LETTERS PATENT FOR INVENTIONS.
WITH AN
APPENDIX OF STATUTES, INTERNATIONAL CONVENTION, RULES, FORMS AND PRECEDENTS, ORDERS, &c.

By ROBERT FROST, B.Sc. (LOND.),
FELLOW OF THE CHEMICAL SOCIETY; OF LINCOLN'S INN, ESQUIRE, BARRISTER-AT-LAW.

"In our view a good piece of work may create a demand, and without disparaging existing literature upon the subject of patents, we think the care and skill with which the volume by Mr. Frost has been compiled, entitles it to recognition at the hands of the profession. . . . Judging Mr. Frost on this ground, we find him completely satisfactory. A careful examination of the entire volume satisfies us that great care and much labour have been devoted to the production of this treatise, and we think that patent agents, solicitors, the bar and the bench, may confidently turn for guidance and instruction to the pages of Mr. Frost."—*Law Times*.

"Few practice books contain so much in so reasonable a space, and we repeat that it will be found generally useful by practitioners in this important branch of the law. . . . A capital index concludes the book."—*Law Journal*.

"The book is, as it professes to be, a treatise on patent law and practice, the several topics being conveniently arranged and discussed in the thirteen chapters which form the body of the work, to which are appended statutes, rules, and forms. The statements of the law, so far as we have been able to test them, appear to be clear and accurate, and the author's style is pleasant and good. . . . The book is a good one, and will make its way. The index is better than usual. Both paper and type are also excellent."—*Solicitors' Journal*.

In royal 8vo, price 36s., in cloth,

A PRACTICAL TREATISE ON THE
LAW OF BUILDING AND ENGINEERING CONTRACTS,
AND OF THE DUTIES AND LIABILITIES OF ENGINEERS, ARCHITECTS, SURVEYORS AND VALUERS,
WITH AN APPENDIX OF PRECEDENTS,
ANNOTATED BY MEANS OF REFERENCE TO THE TEXT AND TO CONTRACTS IN USE.

AND AN APPENDIX OF UNREPORTED CASES
ON BUILDING AND ENGINEERING CONTRACTS.

By ALFRED A. HUDSON,
OF THE INNER TEMPLE, BARRISTER-AT-LAW.

"A very full index completes the book. Mr. Hudson has struck out a new line for himself, and produced a work of considerable merit, and one which will probably be found indispensable by practitioners, inasmuch as it contains a great deal that is not to be found elsewhere. The Table of Cases refers to all the reports."—*Law Journal*.

"Mr. Hudson, having abandoned his profession of an architect to become a barrister, hit upon the idea of writing this work, and he has done it with a thoroughness which every houseowner would like to see bestowed upon modern houses. . . . The Index and Table of Cases reveal a vast amount of industry expended upon detail, and we shall be much surprised if Mr. Hudson does not reap the reward of his labours by obtaining a large and appreciative public."—*Law Times*.

"The author of this somewhat bulky volume has, within the compass of some 900 pages, dealt in a practical and exhaustive manner with the Law of Building and Engineering Contracts. . . . An Index of Precedents and a good General Index will be found at the end of the work."—*Solicitors' Journal*.

". . . has enabled him to produce a work which, regarded both from the lawyer's and from the architect's and builder's point of view, must be pronounced excellent. It is good from the lawyer's standpoint as being logical in arrangement, clear in statement, and generally accurate in the law laid down. The architect or engineer will also give it praise for answering the questions precisely which arise in his dealings with his employers."—*Scotsman*.

OUTLINES OF THE LAW OF TORTS.

In 8vo, price 10s. 6d., cloth,

By RICHARD RINGWOOD, M.A.,

OF THE MIDDLE TEMPLE, BARRISTER-AT-LAW; AUTHOR OF "PRINCIPLES OF BANKRUPTCY," &c.,
AND LECTURER ON COMMON LAW TO THE INCORPORATED LAW SOCIETY.

"This is a work by the well-known author of a student's book on Bankruptcy. Its groundwork is a series of lectures delivered in 1887 by Mr. Ringwood, as lecturer appointed by the Incorporated Law Society. It is clear, concise, well and intelligently written and one rises from its perusal with feelings of pleasure. . . . After perusing the entire work, we can conscientiously recommend it to students."—*Law Students' Journal.*

"The work is one we well recommend to law students, and the able way in which it is written reflects much credit upon the author."—*Law Times.*

"Mr. Ringwood's book is a plain and straightforward introduction to this branch of the law."—*Law Journal.*

In 8vo, price 25s., cloth,

THE LAW OF COMPENSATION FOR LANDS, HOUSES, &c.

UNDER THE LANDS CLAUSES, RAILWAY CLAUSES CONSOLIDATION AND METROPOLITAN ACTS,

THE ARTIZANS AND LABOURERS' DWELLINGS IMPROVEMENT ACT, 1875,

WITH A FULL COLLECTION OF FORMS AND PRECEDENTS.

FIFTH EDITION, ENLARGED, WITH ADDITIONAL FORMS, INCLUDING PRECEDENTS OF BILLS OF COSTS.

By EYRE LLOYD,

OF THE INNER TEMPLE, BARRISTER-AT-LAW.

"The work is eminently a practical one, and is of great value to practitioners who have to deal with compensation cases."—*Solicitors' Journal.*

"It is with much gratification that we have to express our unhesitating opinion that Mr. Lloyd's treatise will prove thoroughly satisfactory to the profession, and to the public at large. Thoroughly satisfactory it appears to us in every point of view—comprehensive in its scope, exhaustive in its treatment, sound in its exposition."—*Irish Law Times.*

"In providing the legal profession with a book which contains the decisions of the Courts of Law and Equity upon the various statutes relating to the Law of Compensation, Mr. Eyre Lloyd has long since left all competitors in the distance, and his book may now be considered the standard work upon the subject. The plan of Mr. Lloyd's book is generally known, and its lucidity is appreciated; the present quite fulfils all the promises of the preceding editions, and contains in addition to other matter a complete set of forms under the Artizans and Labourers Act, 1875, and specimens of Bills of Costs, which will be found a novel feature, extremely useful to legal practitioners."—JUSTICE OF THE PEACE.

In 8vo, price 7s., cloth,

THE SUCCESSION LAWS OF CHRISTIAN COUNTRIES,

WITH SPECIAL REFERENCE TO

THE LAW OF PRIMOGENITURE AS IT EXISTS IN ENGLAND.

By EYRE LLOYD, B.A.,

OF THE INNER TEMPLE, BARRISTER-AT-LAW; AUTHOR OF "THE LAW OF COMPENSATION UNDER THE LANDS CLAUSES CONSOLIDATION ACTS," ETC.

In crown 8vo, price 6s., cloth,

ESSAYS IN JURISPRUDENCE AND LEGAL HISTORY.

By JOHN W. SALMOND, M.A., LL.B. (LOND.),

A BARRISTER OF THE SUPREME COURT OF NEW ZEALAND.

In one volume, royal 8vo, price 42s., cloth,

PRINCIPLES OF THE LAW OF NEGLIGENCE.

By THOMAS BEVEN,

OF THE INNER TEMPLE, BARRISTER-AT-LAW; AUTHOR OF "THE LAW OF EMPLOYER'S LIABILITY FOR THE NEGLIGENCE OF SERVANTS CAUSING INJURY TO FELLOW SERVANTS."

"He has treated the well-known subject of Negligence in a scientific way, and has not been content with merely collecting, in more or less relevant positions, a number of cases which anyone could find for himself in any Digest of Law Reports, but has endeavoured to reduce from the chaos of decided cases a systematic study of the subject, with clear enunciations of the principles he finds governing the various decisions. In the arrangement of the book the author has been very happy in his method, a by no means easy task in the treatment of a subject in which each branch of it in reality overlaps another. . . . A good index and clear type increase the value of a book which will without doubt receive the hearty commendation of the profession as a successful completion of the author's ambitious task."—*Law Times.*

"The reader who takes these as samples of the work, will find how careful and exhaustive Mr. Beven has been, and how valuable a contribution he has made to the important branch of the law with which he has undertaken to deal."—*Solicitor's Journal.*

"In respect of the style of treatment of the subject, the book must be highly commended. It will be of service to every lawyer who wishes rather to get an intelligent understanding of the Law of Negligence, than merely to find correct and reliable legal propositions for practical use and that whether he be a student or a practitioner. To the student the work is valuable for the searching and well-sustained discussion of the cases; and to the practitioner there are presented all the cases that bear on most points for which he may be in search of authority. One of the chief merits of the work is, that all the available authority on each point is collected and so arranged that it can be easily found."—*Juridical Review.*

"Contains evidence of much serious work, and ought to receive a fair trial at the hands of the profession."—*Law Quarterly Review.*

"This is the most elaborate work on the Law of Negligence which has yet appeared in England. . . . His treatment is original, and has evidently not been adopted without great research, care, and revision."—*Law Journal.*

In one large vol., 8vo, price 32s., cloth,

INSTITUTES AND HISTORY OF ROMAN PRIVATE LAW,

WITH CATENA OF TEXTS.

By Dr. CARL SALKOWSKI, Professor of Laws, Königsberg.

Translated and Edited by E. E. WHITFIELD, M.A. (Oxon.).

In 8vo, price 4s. 6d., cloth,

THE

NEWSPAPER LIBEL AND REGISTRATION ACT, 1881.

With a statement of the Law of Libel as affecting Proprietors, Publishers, and Editors of Newspapers. By G. ELLIOTT, Barrister-at-Law, of the Inner Temple.

In one volume, royal 8vo, price 30s., cloth,

CASES AND OPINIONS ON CONSTITUTIONAL LAW,

AND VARIOUS POINTS OF ENGLISH JURISPRUDENCE.

Collected and Digested from Official Documents and other Sources; with Notes. By WILLIAM FORSYTH, M.A., M.P., Q.C., Standing Counsel to the Secretary of State in Council of India, Author of "Hortensius," "History of Trial by Jury," "Life of Cicero," etc., late Fellow of Trinity College, Cambridge.

Fifth Edition, in 8vo, price 10s. 6d., cloth,

THE PRINCIPLES OF BANKRUPTCY.

WITH AN APPENDIX,

CONTAINING

THE CONSOLIDATED RULES OF 1886 & 1890, SCALE OF COSTS, 1886, AND THE BILLS OF SALE ACTS 1878, 1882 & 1890,

Etc., Etc.

By RICHARD RINGWOOD, M.A.,

OF THE MIDDLE TEMPLE, BARRISTER-AT-LAW; LATE SCHOLAR OF TRINITY COLLEGE, DUBLIN.

"This edition is a considerable improvement on the first, and although chiefly written for the use of Students, the work will be found useful to the practitioner."—*Law Times*.

"Those who have to deal with the subject in any of its practical legal aspects will do well to consult Mr. Ringwood's unpretending but useful volume."—*Law Magazine*.

"His book does not profess to be an exhaustive treatise on bankruptcy law, yet in a neat and compact volume we have a vast amount of well-digested matter. The reader is not distracted and puzzled by having a long list of cases flung at him at the end of each page, as the general effect of the law is stated in a few well-selected sentences, and a reference given to the leading decisions only on the subject. . . An excellent index, and a table of cases where references to four sets of contemporary reports may be seen at a glance, show the industry and care with which the work has been done."—*Daily Paper*.

Sixth Edition, 1890, in royal 12mo, price 20s., cloth,
With Supplement, 1891, containing the Act and Rules, 1890,

A TREATISE UPON

THE LAW OF BANKRUPTCY

AND

BILLS OF SALE.

WITH AN APPENDIX

CONTAINING

THE BANKRUPTCY ACT, 1883; GENERAL RULES AND FORMS OF 1886; SCALE OF COSTS AND FEES OF 1886; RULES UNDER S. 122 OF 1888; BANKRUPTCY (COUNTY COURT APPEALS) ACT, 1884; BANKRUPTCY DISCHARGE ACT, 1887; RULES AND FORMS; BANKRUPTCY (PREFERENTIAL PAYMENTS) ACT, 1888; DEEDS OF ARRANGEMENT ACT, 1887; RULES AND FORMS; BOARD OF TRADE AND COURT ORDERS; DEBTORS ACTS, 1869, 1878, AND RULES, 1889; BILLS OF SALE ACTS, 1878, 1882, AND RULES, 1883.

By EDWARD T. BALDWIN, M.A.,

OF THE INNER TEMPLE, BARRISTER-AT-LAW.

*** *The Supplement may be had separately, price 3s. cloth.*

"His new edition is in every respect satisfactory."—*Law Times*.

"It is a thoroughly good and reliable work. . . . We think—as practitioners—that we would rather have this book than any other on the same subject in our library."—*Law Students' Journal*.

"Mr. Baldwin's book has a well-earned reputation for conciseness, clearness, and accuracy. . . . As a terse and readable treatise on Bankruptcy law his work may be commended to our readers. . . . There is a good index."—*Solicitors' Journal*.

"The present edition appears to be quite equal in excellence to its predecessors, and for practitioner's purposes the book is all that can be desired."—*Law Notes*.

Second Edition, in one vol., price 20s., cloth,

A COMPENDIUM OF THE LAW OF PROPERTY IN LAND.

FOR THE USE OF STUDENTS AND THE PROFESSION.

SECOND EDITION.

By WILLIAM DOUGLAS EDWARDS, LL.B.,
OF LINCOLN'S INN, BARRISTER-AT-LAW.

"We consider it one of the best works published on Real Property Law."—*Law Students' Journal*.

"Another excellent compendium which has entered a second edition is Mr. Edwards' 'Compendium of the Law of Property in Land.' No work on English law is written more perspicuously. . . . Mr. Edwards has manifestly bestowed the utmost care in putting into the most modern dress a treatise which we think will continue to grow in the estimation of the profession."—*Law Times*.

"We formed a very favourable opinion of the first edition of this little book, and our opinion is confirmed by the perusal of the second edition. The author has the merit of being a sound lawyer, a merit perhaps not always possessed by the authors of legal text books for students. He writes in good English, and generally speaking states the law correctly. We are glad to hear of the rapid sale of the book, as we feel certain that no student will repent having studied it."—*Law Quarterly Review*.

"The book is certainly destined to take a high place as a standard work on the Law of Property in Land. The style is good, the conclusions of law are accurate, and the authorities are well selected. . . . The amount of detail is much greater than in Williams . . . . . As a companion volume to it, we can with great confidence recommend it to the student; and the practitioner will find it a very useful epitome of the modern law. Altogether it is a work for which we are indebted to the author, and is worthy of the improved notions of law which the study of jurisprudence is bringing to the front."—*Solicitors' Journal*.

"This book shows signs of thorough work throughout. . . . The book is a business-like and useful performance."—*Law Journal*.

"Mr. Edwards has produced a most comprehensive, and in many ways most valuable, piece of work . . . . We consider this book preferable in many respects to the standard works usually placed in the hands of students. . . . In arrangement, the book has more good method in it than any other book we know on the same subject."—*The Oxford Review*.

Third Edition, royal 8vo, in preparation,

A TREATISE ON THE DOCTRINE OF

ULTRA VIRES:

BEING

An Investigation of the Principles which Limit the Capacities, Powers, and Liabilities of

CORPORATIONS,

AND MORE ESPECIALLY OF

JOINT STOCK COMPANIES.

THIRD EDITION.

By SEWARD BRICE, LL.D.,
OF THE INNER TEMPLE, ONE OF HER MAJESTY'S COUNSEL.

REVIEWS.

". . . . On the whole, we consider Mr. Brice's exhaustive work a valuable addition to the literature of the profession."—SATURDAY REVIEW.

"It is the Law of Corporations that Mr. Brice treats of (and treats of more fully, and at the same time more scientifically, than any work with which we are acquainted), not the law of principal and agent; and Mr. Brice does not do his book justice by giving it so vague a title."—*Law Journal*.

"On this doctrine, first introduced in the Common Law Courts in *East Anglian Railway Co.* v. *Eastern Counties Railway Co.*, BRICE ON ULTRA VIRES may be read with advantage."—*Judgment of* LORD JUSTICE BRAMWELL, *in the Case of Evershed* v. *L. & N. W. Ry. Co.* (L. R., 3 Q. B. Div. 141.)

Sixth Edition, in royal 8vo, price 34s., cloth,

BUCKLEY ON THE COMPANIES ACTS.

SIXTH EDITION BY THE AUTHOR.

THE LAW AND PRACTICE UNDER THE COMPANIES ACTS, 1862 TO 1890,

AND

THE LIFE ASSURANCE COMPANIES ACTS, 1870 TO 1872,

INCLUDING THE COMPANIES (MEMORANDUM OF ASSOCIATION) ACT,

THE COMPANIES (WINDING-UP) ACT, AND THE DIRECTORS' LIABILITY ACT.

A Treatise on the Law of Joint Stock Companies.

CONTAINING THE STATUTES, WITH THE RULES, ORDERS, AND FORMS, TO REGULATE PROCEEDINGS.

By H. BURTON BUCKLEY, M.A.,

OF LINCOLN'S INN, ESQ., ONE OF HER MAJESTY'S COUNSEL.

Second Edition in preparation.

THE LAW RELATING TO

SHIPMASTERS AND SEAMEN.

THEIR APPOINTMENT, DUTIES, POWERS, RIGHTS, LIABILITIES, AND REMEDIES.

By JOSEPH KAY, Esq., M.A., Q.C.,

OF TRIN. COLL. CAMBRIDGE, AND OF THE NORTHERN CIRCUIT;
SOLICITOR-GENERAL OF THE COUNTY PALATINE OF DURHAM; ONE OF THE JUDGES OF THE COURT OF RECORD FOR THE HUNDRED OF SALFORD;
AND AUTHOR OF "THE SOCIAL CONDITION AND EDUCATION OF THE PEOPLE IN ENGLAND AND EUROPE."

REVIEWS OF THE WORK:

From the LIVERPOOL JOURNAL OF COMMERCE.

"'The law relating to Shipmasters and Seamen'—such is the title of a voluminous and important work which has just been issued by Messrs. Stevens and Haynes, the eminent law publishers, of London. The author is Mr. Joseph Kay, Q.C., and while treating generally of the law relating to shipmasters and seamen, he refers more particularly to their appointment, duties, rights, liabilities, and remedies. It consists of two large volumes, the text occupying nearly twelve hundred pages, and the value of the work being enhanced by copious appendices and index, and by the quotation of a mass of authorities. . . . *The work must be an invaluable one to the shipowner, shipmaster, or consul* at a foreign port. The language is clear and simple, while the legal standing of the author is a sufficient guarantee that he writes with the requisite authority, and that the cases quoted by him are decisive as regards the points on which he touches."

From the LAW JOURNAL.

"The author tells us that for ten years he has been engaged upon it. . . . Two large volumes containing 1181 pages of text, 81 pages of appendices, 98 pages of index, and upwards of 1800 cited cases, attest the magnitude of the work designed and accomplished by Mr. Kay.

"Mr. Kay says that he has 'endeavoured to compile a guide and reference book for masters, ship agents, and consuls.' He has been so modest as not to add lawyers to the list of his pupils; but *his work will, we think, be welcomed by lawyers who have to do with shipping transactions, almost as cordially as it undoubtedly will be by those who occupy their business in the great waters.*"

Fourth Edition, in Royal 8vo, price 40s., cloth,

THE JUDGMENTS, ORDERS, AND PRACTICE OF THE SUPREME COURT,

CHIEFLY in RESPECT to ACTIONS ASSIGNED to the CHANCERY DIVISION.

By LOFTUS LEIGH PEMBERTON,

One of the registrars of the Supreme Court of Judicature; and Author of "The Practice in Equity by way of Revivor and Supplement."

"The work under notice ought to be of considerable service to the profession. . . . . . The forms throughout the work—and they are the most important element in it—appear to us to be accurate, and of the most approved type. This fact alone will commend the new edition to practitioners in the Chancery Division. There is a useful table of the Lord Chancellors and Judges at the beginning of the book, and a very full index concludes it."—*Law Times.*

In demy 12mo, price 5s.,

THE STATUTORY LAW RELATING TO TRUSTEE

SAVINGS BANKS (1863—1891), together with the Treasury Regulations (1888—1889), and the Scheme for the Appointment of the Inspection Committee of Trustee Savings Banks. By URQUHART A. FORBES, of Lincoln's Inn, Esq., Barrister-at-Law, Author of "The Law Relating to Savings Banks;" the "Law of Savings Banks since 1878;" and joint Author of "The Law Relating to Water."

In demy 12mo, price 6s., cloth,

THE LAW OF SAVINGS BANKS SINCE 1878;

With a Digest of Decisions made by the Chief Registrar and Assistant Registrars of Friendly Societies from 1878 to 1882, being a Supplement to the Law relating to Trustee and Post Office Savings Banks.

By U. A. FORBES, of Lincoln's Inn, Barrister-at-Law.

⁎ *The complete work can be had, price 10s. 6d., cloth.*

In 8vo, price 15s., cloth,

THE LAW AND PRACTICE RELATING TO

THE ADMINISTRATION OF DECEASED PERSONS

BY THE CHANCERY DIVISION OF THE HIGH COURT OF JUSTICE;

WITH AN ADDENDA giving the alterations effected by the NEW RULES of 1883,

AND AN APPENDIX OF ORDERS AND FORMS, ANNOTATED BY REFERENCES TO THE TEXT.

By W. GREGORY WALKER and EDGAR J. ELGOOD,

OF LINCOLN'S INN, BARRISTERS-AT-LAW.

"In this volume the most important branch of the administrative business of the Chancery Division is treated with conciseness and care. Judging from the admirable clearness of expression which characterises the entire work, and the labour which has evidently been bestowed on every detail, we do not think that a literary executorship could have devolved upon a more able and conscientious representative . . . . Useful chapters are introduced in their appropriate places, dealing with the 'Parties to administration actions,' 'The proofs of claims in Chambers,' and 'The cost of administration actions.' To the last-mentioned chapter we gladly accord special praise, as a clear and succinct summary of the law, from which so far as we have tested it, no proposition of any importance has been omitted . . . . An elaborately constructed table of cases, with references in separate columns to all the reports, and a fairly good index, much increase the utility of the work."—*Solicitors' Journal.*

In Foolscap 8vo, superfine paper, bound in Vellum, price 3s. 6d. nett.

⁎ *A limited number of copies have been printed upon large paper, price 7s. 6d. nett.*

SCINTILLAE JURIS.

By CHARLES J. DARLING, Q.C., M.P. With a Frontispiece and Colophon by FRANK LOCKWOOD, Q.C., M.P. Fourth Edition (Enlarged).

"'Scintillae Juris' is that little bundle of humorous essays on law and cognate matters which, since the day of its first appearance, some years ago, has been the delight of legal circles. . . . It has a quality of style which suggests much study of Bacon in his lighter vein. Its best essays would not be unworthy of the Essays, and if read out, one by one, before a blindfolded *connoisseur*, might often be assigned to that wonderful book."—*Daily News.*

Second Edition, in 8vo, price 25s., cloth,
THE PRINCIPLES OF
THE LAW OF RATING OF HEREDITAMENTS
IN THE OCCUPATION OF COMPANIES.
By J. H. BALFOUR BROWNE,
OF THE MIDDLE TEMPLE, Q.C.,
And D. N. McNAUGHTON, of the Middle Temple, Barrister-at-Law.

"The tables and specimen valuations which are printed in an appendix to this volume will be of great service to the parish authorities, and to the legal practitioners who may have to deal with the rating of those properties which are in the occupation of Companies, and we congratulate Mr. Browne on the production of a clear and concise book of the system of Company Rating. There is no doubt that such a work is much needed, and we are sure that all those who are interested in, or have to do with, public rating, will find it of great service. Much credit is therefore due to Mr. Browne for his able treatise—a work which his experience as Registrar of the Railway Commission peculiarly qualified him to undertake."—*Law Magazine.*

In 8vo, 1875, price 7s. 6d., cloth,
THE LAW OF USAGES & CUSTOMS:
A Practical Law Tract.
By J. H. BALFOUR BROWNE,
OF THE MIDDLE TEMPLE, Q.C.

"We look upon this treatise as a valuable addition to works written on the Science of Law."—*Canada Law Journal.*

"As a tract upon a very troublesome department of Law it is admirable—the principles laid down are sound, the illustrations are well chosen, and the decisions and *dicta* are harmonised so far as possible and distinguished when necessary."—*Irish Law Times.*

"As a book of reference we know of none so comprehensive dealing with this particular branch of Common Law. . . . In this way the book is invaluable to the practitioner."—*Law Magazine.*

In one volume, 8vo, 1875, price 18s., cloth,
THE PRACTICE BEFORE THE RAILWAY COMMISSIONERS
UNDER THE REGULATION OF RAILWAY ACTS, 1873 & 1874;
With the Amended General Orders of the Commissioners, Schedule of Forms, and Table of Fees: together with the Law of Undue Preference, the Law of the Jurisdiction of the Railway Commissioners, Notes of their Decisions and Orders, Precedents of Forms of Applications, Answers and Replies, and Appendices of Statutes and Cases.
By J. H. BALFOUR BROWNE,
OF THE MIDDLE TEMPLE, Q.C.

"Mr. Browne's book is handy and convenient in form, and well arranged for the purpose of reference: its treatment of the subject is fully and carefully worked out: it is, so far as we have been able to test it, accurate and trustworthy. It is the work of a man of capable legal attainments, and by official position intimate with his subject; and we therefore think that it cannot fail to meet a real want and to prove of service to the legal profession and the public."—*Law Magazine.*

In 8vo, 1876, price 7s. 6d., cloth,
ON THE COMPULSORY PURCHASE OF THE UNDERTAKINGS OF COMPANIES BY CORPORATIONS,
And the Practice in Relation to the Passage of Bills for Compulsory Purchase through Parliament. By J. H. BALFOUR BROWNE, of the Middle Temple, Q.C.

"This is a work of considerable importance to all Municipal Corporations, and it is hardly too much to say that every member of these bodies should have a copy by him for constant reference. Probably at no very distant date the property of all the existing gas and water companies will pass under municipal control, and therefore it is exceedingly desirable that the principles and conditions under which such transfers ought to be made should be clearly understood. This task is made easy by the present volume. The stimulus for the publication of such a work was given by the action of the Parliamentary Committee which last session passed the preamble of the 'Stockton and Middlesborough Corporations Water Bill, 1876.' The volume accordingly contains a full report of the case as it was presented both by the promoters and opponents, and as this was the first time in which the principle of compulsory purchase was definitely recognised, there can be no doubt that it will long be regarded as a leading case. As a matter of course, many incidental points of interest arose during the progress of the case. Thus, besides the main question of compulsory purchase, and the question as to whether there was or was not any precedent for the Bill, the questions of water compensations, of appeals from one Committee to another, and other kindred subjects were discussed. These are all treated at length by the Author in the body of the work, which is thus a complete legal compendium on the large subject with which it so ably deals."

Now ready, in crown 8vo, price 10s., 6d. cloth,

THE LAW OF EVIDENCE,

By S. L. PHIPSON, M.A., of the Inner Temple, Barrister-at-Law.

"This book condenses a head of law into a comparatively small compass—a class of literary undertaking to which every encouragement should be given. . . . The volume is most portable, most compendious, and as far as we have been able to examine it, as accurate as any law book can be expected to be."—*Law Times*.

"We are of opinion that Mr. Phipson has produced a book which will be found very serviceable, not only for practitioners, but also for students. We have tried it in a good many places, and we find that it is well brought down to date."—*Law Journal*.

In 8vo, 1878, price 6s., cloth,

THE

LAW RELATING TO CHARITIES,

ESPECIALLY WITH REFERENCE TO THE VALIDITY AND CONSTRUCTION OF

CHARITABLE BEQUESTS AND CONVEYANCES.

By FERDINAND M. WHITEFORD, of Lincoln's Inn, Barrister-at-Law.

In 8vo, 1872, price 7s. 6d., cloth,

AN EPITOME AND ANALYSIS OF

SAVIGNY'S TREATISE ON OBLIGATIONS IN ROMAN LAW.

By ARCHIBALD BROWN, M.A.

EDIN. AND OXON., AND B.C.L. OXON., OF THE MIDDLE TEMPLE, BARRISTER-AT-LAW.

"Mr. Archibald Brown deserves the thanks of all interested in the science of Law, whether as a study or a practice, for his edition of Herr von Savigny's great work on 'Obligations.' Mr. Brown has undertaken a double task—the translation of his author, and the analysis of his author's matter. That he has succeeded in reducing the bulk of the original will be seen at a glance; the French translation consisting of two volumes, with some five hundred pages apiece, as compared with Mr. Brown's thin volume of a hundred and fifty pages. At the same time the pith of Von Savigny's matter seems to be very successfully preserved, nothing which might be useful to the English reader being apparently omitted."—*Law Journal*.

THE ELEMENTS OF ROMAN LAW.

Second Edition, in crown 8vo, price 6s., cloth,

A CONCISE DIGEST OF THE

INSTITUTES OF GAIUS AND JUSTINIAN.

With copious References arranged in Parallel Columns, also Chronological and Analytical Tables, Lists of Laws, &c. &c.

Primarily designed for the Use of Students preparing for Examination at Oxford, Cambridge, and the Inns of Court.

By SEYMOUR F. HARRIS, B.C.L., M.A.,

WORCESTER COLLEGE, OXFORD, AND THE INNER TEMPLE, BARRISTER-AT-LAW
AUTHOR OF "UNIVERSITIES AND LEGAL EDUCATION."

"*Mr. Harris's digest ought to have very great success among law students both in the Inns of Court and the Universities. His book gives evidence of praiseworthy accuracy and laborious condensation.*"—LAW JOURNAL.

"*This book contains a summary in English of the elements of Roman Law as contained in the works of Gaius and Justinian, and is so arranged that the reader can at once see what are the opinions of either of these two writers on each point. From the very exact and accurate references to titles and sections given he can at once refer to the original writers. The concise manner in which Mr. Harris has arranged his digest will render it most useful, not only to the students for whom it was originally written, but also to those persons who, though they have not the time to wade through the larger treatises of Poste, Sanders, Ortolan, and others, yet desire to obtain some knowledge of Roman Law.*"—OXFORD AND CAMBRIDGE UNDERGRADUATES' JOURNAL.

"*Mr. Harris deserves the credit of having produced an epitome which will be of service to those numerous students who have no time or sufficient ability to analyse the Institutes for themselves.*"—LAW TIMES.

Fourth Edition, in 8vo, price 21s., cloth,

ENGLISH CONSTITUTIONAL HISTORY:

FROM THE TEUTONIC INVASION TO THE PRESENT TIME.

Designed as a Text-book for Students and others,

By T. P. TASWELL-LANGMEAD, B.C.L.,

OF LINCOLN'S INN, BARRISTER-AT-LAW, FORMERLY VINERIAN SCHOLAR IN THE UNIVERSITY
AND LATE PROFESSOR OF CONSTITUTIONAL LAW AND HISTORY,
UNIVERSITY COLLEGE, LONDON.

Fourth Edition, Revised throughout, with Notes and Appendices.

By C. H. E. CARMICHAEL, M.A. OXON.

"Mr. Carmichael has performed his allotted task with credit to himself, and the high standard of excellence attained by Taswell-Langmead's treatise is worthily maintained. This, the third edition, will be found as useful as its predecessors to the large class of readers and students who seek in its pages accurate knowledge of the history of the constitution."—*Law Times.*

"To the student of constitutional law this work will be invaluable. . . . . The book is remarkable for the raciness and vigour of its style. The editorial contributions of Mr. Carmichael are judicious, and add much to the value of the work."—*Scottish Law Review.*

"The work will continue to hold the field as the best class-book on the subject."—*Contemporary Review.*

"The book is well known as an admirable introduction to the study of constitutional law for students at law. . . . . Mr. Carmichael appears to have done the work of editing, made necessary by the death of Mr. Taswell-Langmead, with care and judgment."—*Law Journal.*

"The work before us it would be hardly possible to praise too highly. In style, arrangement, clearness, and size, it would be difficult to find anything better on the real history of England, the history of its constitutional growth as a complete story, than this volume."—*Boston (U.S.) Literary World.*

"As it now stands, we should find it hard to name a better text-book on English Constitutional History."—*Solicitors' Journal.*

"Mr. Taswell-Langmead's compendium of the rise and development of the English Constitution has evidently supplied a want. . . . . The present Edition is greatly improved. . . . We have no hesitation in saying that it is a thoroughly good and useful work."—*Spectator.*

"It is a safe, careful, praiseworthy digest and manual of all constitutional history and law."—*Globe.*

"The volume on English Constitutional History, by Mr. Taswell-Langmead, is exactly what such a history should be."—*Standard.*

"Mr. Taswell-Langmead has thoroughly grasped the bearings of his subject. It is, however, in dealing with that chief subject of constitutional history—parliamentary government—that the work exhibits its great superiority over its rivals."—*Academy.*

Second Edition, in 8vo, price 6s., cloth,

HANDBOOK TO THE INTERMEDIATE AND FINAL LL.B. OF LONDON UNIVERSITY;

(PASS AND HONOURS).

INCLUDING A COMPLETE SUMMARY OF "AUSTIN'S JURISPRUDENCE," AND THE EXAMINATION PAPERS OF LATE YEARS IN ALL BRANCHES.

By A B.A., LL.B. (Lond.).

"Increased in size and usefulness. . . . The book will undoubtedly be of help to those students who prepare themselves for examination. . . . The Appendix contains a good selection of papers set at the different examinations."—*Law Times.*

"A very good handbook to the Intermediate and Final LL.B. by a B.A., LL.B."—*Law Notes.*

In Crown 8vo, price 3s.; or Interleaved for Notes, price 4s.,

CONTRACT LAW.

QUESTIONS ON THE LAW OF CONTRACTS. WITH NOTES TO THE ANSWERS. *Founded on "Anson," "Chitty," and "Pollock."*

By PHILIP FOSTER ALDRED, D.C.L., Hertford College and Gray's Inn; late Examiner for the University of Oxford.

"This appears to us a very admirable selection of questions, comparing favourably with the average run of those set in examinations, and useful for the purpose of testing progress."—*Law Journal.*

Tenth Edition, in 8vo, price 25s., cloth,

THE PRINCIPLES OF EQUITY.

INTENDED FOR THE USE OF STUDENTS AND THE PROFESSION.

By EDMUND H. T. SNELL,

OF THE MIDDLE TEMPLE, BARRISTER-AT-LAW.

TENTH EDITION.

By ARCHIBALD BROWN, M.A. EDIN. & OXON., & B.C.L. OXON.,

OF THE MIDDLE TEMPLE, BARRISTER-AT-LAW; AUTHOR OF "A NEW LAW DICTIONARY," "AN ANALYSIS OF SAVIGNY ON OBLIGATIONS," AND THE "LAW OF FIXTURES."

REVIEWS.

"Mr. Brown's long experience (he has edited seven editions of this book) has enabled him so to treat the subject as to be invaluable to students."—*Law Journal.*

"This work on the 'Principles of Equity' has, since the publication of the First Edition, been recognised as the best elementary treatise on the subject, and it would not be necessary to say more of this Edition, than to mention the fact of its publication, were it not for the fact that the author, Mr. Snell, is dead, and the late Editions have been brought out under the care of Mr. Brown. It seldom happens that a new editor is able to improve on the work of his predecessor in its plan or its details. But in the case of the present work we find that each edition is a manifest improvement on the former ones, and well as Mr Snell did his work we discover that Mr. Brown has done it better."—*Irish Law Times.*

"This is the Ninth Edition of certainly one of the best, and probably the most widely read, text-book which deals with any part of the English law."—*Oxford Magazine.*

"It is ample proof of the popularity of 'Snell's Principles of Equity,' that it has now reached its Ninth Edition in the hands of Mr. Archibald Brown."—*Law Times.*

"This is now unquestionably the standard book on Equity for students."—*Saturday Review.*

"On the whole we are convinced that the Sixth Edition of Snell's Equity is destined to be as highly thought of as its predecessors, as it is, in our opinion, out and out the best work on the subject with which it deals."—*Gibson's Law Notes.*

"*We know of no better introduction to the Principles of Equity.*"— CANADA LAW JOURNAL.

"Within the ten years which have elapsed since the appearance of the first edition of this work, its reputation has steadily increased, and it has long since been recognised by students, tutors, and practitioners, as the best elementary treatise on the important and difficult branch of the law which forms its subject." —*Law Magazine and Review.*

Fourth Edition, in 8vo, price 6s., cloth,

AN ANALYSIS OF SNELL'S PRINCIPLES OF EQUITY.

FOUNDED ON THE TENTH EDITION. With Notes thereon.

By E. E. BLYTH, LL.D., Solicitor.

"Mr. Blyth's book will undoubtedly be very useful to readers of Snell."—*Law Times.*

"This is an admirable analysis of a good treatise—read with Snell, this little book will be found very profitable to the student."—*Law Journal.*

In 8vo, price 2s., sewed,

QUESTIONS ON EQUITY.

FOR STUDENTS PREPARING FOR EXAMINATION.

FOUNDED ON THE NINTH EDITION OF

SNELL'S "PRINCIPLES OF EQUITY."

By W. T. WAITE,

BARRISTER-AT-LAW, HOLT SCHOLAR OF THE HONOURABLE SOCIETY OF GRAY'S INN.

Second Edition, in one volume, 8vo, price 18s., cloth,

PRINCIPLES OF CONVEYANCING.

AN ELEMENTARY WORK FOR THE USE OF STUDENTS.

By HENRY C. DEANE,

OF LINCOLN'S INN, BARRISTER-AT-LAW, SOMETIME LECTURER TO THE INCORPORATED LAW SOCIETY OF THE UNITED KINGDOM.

"*We hope to see this book, like Snell's Equity, a standard class-book in all Law Schools where English law is taught.*"—CANADA LAW JOURNAL.

"We like the work, it is well written and is an excellent student's book, and being only just published, it has the great advantage of having in it all the recent important enactments relating to conveyancing. It possesses also an excellent index."—*Law Students' Journal.*

"Will be found of great use to students entering upon the difficulties of Real Property Law. It has an unusually exhaustive index covering some fifty pages."—*Law Times.*

"In the parts which have been re-written, Mr. Deane has preserved the same pleasant style marked by simplicity and lucidity which distinguished his first edition. After 'Williams on Real Property,' there is no book which we should so strongly recommend to the student entering upon Real Property Law as Mr. Deane's 'Principles of Conveyancing,' and the high character which the first edition attained has been fully kept up in this second."—*Law Journal.*

Fourth Edition, in 8vo, price 10s., cloth,

A SUMMARY OF THE

LAW & PRACTICE IN ADMIRALTY.

FOR THE USE OF STUDENTS.

By EUSTACE SMITH,

OF THE INNER TEMPLE; AUTHOR OF "A SUMMARY OF COMPANY LAW."

"The book is well arranged, and forms a good introduction to the subject."—*Solicitors' Journal.*
"It is however, in our opinion, a well and carefully written little work, and should be in the hands of every student who is taking up Admiralty Law at the Final."—*Law Students' Journal.*
"Mr. Smith has a happy knack of compressing a large amount of useful matter in a small compass. The present work will doubtless be received with satisfaction equal to that with which his previous 'Summary' has been met."—*Oxford and Cambridge Undergraduates' Journal.*

Third Edition, in 8vo, price 7s. 6d., cloth,

A SUMMARY OF THE

LAW AND PRACTICE IN THE ECCLESIASTICAL COURTS.

FOR THE USE OF STUDENTS.

By EUSTACE SMITH,

OF THE INNER TEMPLE; AUTHOR OF "A SUMMARY OF COMPANY LAW," AND "A SUMMARY OF THE LAW AND PRACTICE IN ADMIRALTY."

"His object has been, as he tells us in his preface, to give the student and general reader a fair outline of the scope and extent of ecclesiastical law, of the principles on which it is founded, of the Courts by which it is enforced, and the procedure by which these Courts are regulated. We think the book well fulfils its object. Its value is much enhanced by a profuse citation of authorities for the propositions contained in it."—*Bar Examination Journal.*

Fourth Edition, in 8vo, price 7s. 6d., cloth,

AN EPITOME OF THE LAWS OF PROBATE AND DIVORCE,

FOR THE USE OF STUDENTS FOR HONOURS EXAMINATION.

By J. CARTER HARRISON, SOLICITOR.

"The work is considerably enlarged, and we think improved, and will be found of great assistance to students."—*Law Students' Journal.*

Sixth Edition. In one volume, 8vo, price 20s., cloth,

PRINCIPLES OF THE COMMON LAW.

INTENDED FOR THE USE OF STUDENTS AND THE PROFESSION.

SIXTH EDITION.

By JOHN INDERMAUR, Solicitor,

AUTHOR OF "A MANUAL OF THE PRACTICE OF THE SUPREME COURT,"
"EPITOMES OF LEADING CASES," AND OTHER WORKS.

"The student will find in Mr. Indermaur's book a safe and clear guide to the Principles of Common Law."—*Law Journal,* 1892.

"The present edition of this elementary treatise has been in general edited with praiseworthy care. The provisions of the statutes affecting the subjects discussed, which have been passed since the publication of the last edition, are clearly summarised, and the effect of the leading cases is generally very well given. In the difficult task of selecting and distinguishing principle from detail, Mr. Indermaur has been very successful; the leading principles are clearly brought out, and very judiciously illustrated."—*Solicitors' Journal.*

"The work is acknowledged to be one of the best written and most useful elementary works for Law Students that has been published."—*Law Times.*

"The praise which we were enabled to bestow upon Mr. Indermaur's very useful compilation on its first appearance has been justified by a demand for a second edition."—*Law Magazine.*

"We were able, four years ago, to praise the first edition of Mr. Indermaur's book as likely to be of use to students in acquiring the elements of the law of torts and contracts. The second edition maintains the character of the book."—*Law Journal.*

"Mr. Indermaur renders even law light reading. He not only possesses the faculty of judicious selection, but of lucid exposition and felicitous illustration. And while his works are all thus characterised, his 'Principles of the Common Law' especially displays those features. That it has already reached a second edition, testifies that our estimate of the work on its first appearance was not unduly favourable, highly as we then signified approval; nor needs it that we should add anything to that estimate in reference to the general scope and execution of the work. It only remains to say, that the present edition evinces that every care has been taken to insure thorough accuracy, while including all the modifications in the law that have taken place since the original publication; and that the references to the Irish decisions which have been now introduced are calculated to render the work of greater utility to practitioners and students, *both* English and Irish."—*Irish Law Times.*

"*This work, the author tells us in his Preface, is written mainly with a view to the examinations of the Incorporated Law Society; but we think it is likely to attain a wider usefulness. It seems, so far as we can judge from the parts we have examined, to be a careful and clear outline of the principles of the common law. It is very readable; and not only students, but many practitioners and the public, might benefit by a perusal of its pages.*"—Solicitors' Journal.

WORKS FOR LAW STUDENTS. 25

Fifth Edition, in 8vo, price 12s. 6d., cloth,

A MANUAL OF THE PRACTICE OF THE SUPREME COURT OF JUDICATURE,
IN THE QUEEN'S BENCH AND CHANCERY DIVISIONS.
Intended for the use of Students and the Profession.
By JOHN INDERMAUR, Solicitor.

"The second edition has followed quickly upon the first, which was published in 1878. This fact affords good evidence that the book has been found useful. It contains sufficient information to enable the student who masters the contents to turn to the standard works on practice with advantage."—*Law Times.*

"This is a very useful student's book. It is clearly written, and gives such information as the student requires, without bewildering him with details. The portion relating to the Chancery Division forms an excellent introduction to the elements of the practice, and may be advantageously used, not only by articled clerks, but also by pupils entering the chambers of equity draftsmen."—*Solicitors' Journal.*

Seventh Edition, in 8vo, price 6s., cloth,

AN EPITOME OF LEADING COMMON LAW CASES;
WITH SOME SHORT NOTES THEREON.

Chiefly intended as a Guide to "SMITH'S LEADING CASES." By JOHN INDERMAUR, Solicitor (Clifford's Inn Prizeman, Michaelmas Term, 1872).

"We have received the third edition of the 'Epitome of Leading Common Law Cases,' by Mr. Indermaur, Solicitor. The first edition of this work was published in February, 1873, the second in April, 1874; and now we have a third edition dated September, 1875. No better proof of the value of this book can be furnished than the fact that in less than three years it has reached a third edition."—*Law Journal.*

Seventh Edition, in 8vo, price 6s., cloth,

AN EPITOME OF LEADING CONVEYANCING AND EQUITY CASES;
WITH SOME SHORT NOTES THEREON, FOR THE USE OF STUDENTS.
By JOHN INDERMAUR, Solicitor, Author of "An Epitome of Leading Common Law Cases."

"We have received the second edition of Mr. Indermaur's very useful Epitome of Leading Conveyancing and Equity Cases. The work is very well done."—*Law Times.*

"The Epitome well deserves the continued patronage of the class—Students—for whom it is especially intended. Mr. Indermaur will soon be known as the 'Students' Friend.'"—*Canada Law Journal.*

Fifth Edition, in 8vo, price 5s. 6d., cloth,

SELF-PREPARATION FOR THE FINAL EXAMINATION.
CONTAINING A COMPLETE COURSE OF STUDY, WITH STATUTES, CASES AND QUESTIONS;
And intended for the use of those Articled Clerks who read by themselves.
By JOHN INDERMAUR, Solicitor.

"In this edition Mr. Indermaur extends his counsels to the whole period from the Intermediate examination to the Final. His advice is practical and sensible: and if the course of study he recommends is intelligently followed, the articled clerk will have laid in a store of legal knowledge more than sufficient to carry him through the Final Examination."—*Solicitors' Journal.*

"This book contains recommendations as to how a complete course of study for the above examination should be carried out, with reference to the particular books to be read *seriatim*. We need only remark that it is essential for a student to be set on the right track in his reading, and that anyone of ordinary ability, who follows the course set out by Mr. Indermaur, ought to pass with great credit."—*Law Journal.*

Fourth Edition, in 8vo, price 8s., cloth,

SELF-PREPARATION FOR THE INTERMEDIATE EXAMINATION,

As it at present exists on Stephen's Commentaries. Containing a complete course of Study, with Statutes, Questions, and Advice as to portions of the book which may be omitted, and of portions to which special attention should be given; also the whole of the Questions and Answers at the Intermediate Examinations which have at present been held on Stephen's Commentaries, and intended for the use of all Articled Clerks who have not yet passed the Intermediate Examination. By JOHN INDERMAUR, Author of "Principles of Common Law," and other works.

In 8vo, 1875, price 6s., cloth,

THE STUDENTS' GUIDE TO THE JUDICATURE ACTS,
AND THE RULES THEREUNDER:
Being a book of Questions and Answers intended for the use of Law Students.
By JOHN INDERMAUR, Solicitor.

Fifth Edition, in Crown 8vo, price 12s. 6d., cloth,

AN EPITOME OF CONVEYANCING STATUTES,

EXTENDING FROM 13 EDW. I. TO THE END OF 55 & 56 VICTORIÆ. Fifth Edition, with Short Notes. By GEORGE NICHOLS MARCY, of Lincoln's Inn, Barrister-at-Law.

Second Edition. In 8vo, price 26s., cloth,

A NEW LAW DICTIONARY,

AND INSTITUTE OF THE WHOLE LAW;

EMBRACING FRENCH AND LATIN TERMS AND REFERENCES TO THE AUTHORITIES, CASES, AND STATUTES.

SECOND EDITION, revised throughout, and considerably enlarged.

By ARCHIBALD BROWN,

M.A. EDIN. AND OXON., AND B.C.L. OXON., OF THE MIDDLE TEMPLE, BARRISTER-AT-LAW; AUTHOR OF THE "LAW OF FIXTURES," "ANALYSIS OF SAVIGNY'S OBLIGATIONS IN ROMAN LAW," ETC.

Reviews of the Second Edition.

"*So far as we have been able to examine the work, it seems to have been most carefully and accurately executed, the present Edition, besides containing much new matter, having been thoroughly revised in consequence of the recent changes in the law; and we have no doubt whatever that it will be found extremely useful, not only to students and practitioners, but to public men, and men of letters.*"—IRISH LAW TIMES.

"*Mr. Brown has revised his Dictionary, and adapted it to the changes effected by the Judicature Acts, and it now constitutes a very useful work to put into the hands of any student or articled clerk, and a work which the practitioner will find of value for reference.*" —SOLICITORS' JOURNAL.

"*It will prove a reliable guide to law students, and a handy book of reference for practitioners.*"—LAW TIMES.

In Royal 8vo., price 5s., cloth,

ANALYTICAL TABLES

OF

THE LAW OF REAL PROPERTY;

Drawn up chiefly from STEPHEN'S BLACKSTONE, with Notes.

By C. J. TARRING, of the Inner Temple, Barrister-at-Law.

CONTENTS.

TABLE I. Tenures.	TABLE V. Uses.
,, II. Estates, according to quantity of Tenants' Interest.	,, VI. Acquisition of Estates in land of freehold tenure.
,, III. Estates, according to the time at which the Interest is to be enjoyed.	,, VII. Incorporeal Hereditaments.
,, IV. Estates, according to the number and connection of the Tenants.	,, VIII. Incorporeal Hereditaments.

"*Great care and considerable skill have been shown in the compilation of these tables, which will be found of much service to students of the Law of Real Property.*"—*Law Times.*

Sixth Edition, in 8vo, price 20s., cloth,

PRINCIPLES OF THE CRIMINAL LAW.

INTENDED AS A LUCID EXPOSITION OF THE SUBJECT FOR THE USE OF STUDENTS AND THE PROFESSION.

By SEYMOUR F. HARRIS, B.C.L., M.A. (Oxon.),

AUTHOR OF "A CONCISE DIGEST OF THE INSTITUTES OF GAIUS AND JUSTINIAN."

SIXTH EDITION.

By C. L. ATTENBOROUGH, of the Inner Temple, Barrister-at-Law.

REVIEWS.

"The characteristic of the present Edition is the restoration to the book of the character of 'a concise exposition' proclaimed by the title-page. Mr. Attenborough has carefully pruned away the excrescences which had arisen in successive editions, and has improved the work both as regards terseness and clearness of exposition. In both respects it is now an excellent student's book. The text is very well broken up into headings and paragraphs, with short marginal notes—the importance of which, for the convenience of the student, is too often overlooked."—*Solicitors' Journal.*

"We think the book—always a favourite with students—has got a new lease of life, and will now prove the only text book which most men will care to study until they get beyond the examination stage of their existence. . . . On the whole our verdict is that the new Edition is distinctly a success, and we have no hesitation in commending it to the student as the best text book that exists for his purposes."—*Law Students' Journal.*

"*The favourable opinion we expressed of the first edition of this work appears to have been justified by the reception it has met with. Looking through this new Edition, we see no reason to modify the praise we bestowed on the former Edition. The recent cases have been added and the provisions of the Summary Jurisdiction Act are noticed in the chapter relating to Summary Convictions. The book is one of the best manuals of Criminal Law for the student.*"—SOLICITORS' JOURNAL.

"*There is no lack of Works on Criminal Law, but there was room for such a useful handbook of Principles as Mr. Seymour Harris has supplied. Accustomed, by his previous labours, to the task of analysing the law, Mr. Harris has brought to bear upon his present work qualifications well adapted to secure the successful accomplishment of the object which he had set before him. That object is not an ambitious one, for it does not pretend to soar above utility to the young practitioner and the student. For both these classes, and for the yet wider class who may require a book of reference on the subject, Mr. Harris has produced a clear and convenient Epitome of the Law. A noticeable feature of Mr. Harris's work, which is likely to prove of assistance both to the practitioner and the student, consists of a Table of Offences, with their legal character, their punishment, and the statute under which it is inflicted, together with a reference to the pages where a Statement of the Law will be found.*"—LAW MAGAZINE AND REVIEW.

"This work purports to contain 'a concise exposition of the nature of crime, the various offences punishable by the English law, the law of criminal procedure, and the law of summary convictions,' with tables of offences, punishments, and statutes. The work is divided into four books. Book I. treats of crime, its divisions and essentials; of persons capable of committing crimes; and of principals and accessories. Book II. deals with offences of a public nature; offences against private persons; and offences against the property of individuals. Each crime is discussed in its turn, with as much brevity as could well be used consistently with a proper explanation of the legal characteristics of the several offences. Book III. explains criminal procedure, including the jurisdiction of Courts, and the various steps in the apprehension and trial of criminals from arrest to punishment. This part of the work is extremely well done, the description of the trial being excellent, and thoroughly calculated to impress the mind of the uninitiated. Book IV. contains a short sketch of 'summary convictions before magistrates out of quarter sessions.' The table of offences at the end of the volume is most useful, and there is a very full index. Altogether we must congratulate Mr. Harris on his adventure."—*Law Journal.*

"*Mr. Harris has undertaken a work, in our opinion, so much needed that he might diminish its bulk in the next edition by obliterating the apologetic preface. The appearance of his volume is as well timed as its execution is satisfactory. The author has shown an ability of omission which is a good test of skill, and from the overwhelming mass of the criminal law he has discreetly selected just so much only as a learner needs to know, and has presented it in terms which render it capable of being easily taken into the mind.*"— SOLICITORS' JOURNAL.

Second Edition, in crown 8vo, price 5s. 6d., cloth,

THE STUDENTS' GUIDE TO BANKRUPTCY;

Being a Complete Digest of the Law of Bankruptcy in the shape of Questions and Answers, and comprising all Questions asked at the Solicitors' Final Examinations in Bankruptcy since the Bankruptcy Act, 1883, and all important Decisions since that Act. By JOHN INDERMAUR, Solicitor, Author of "Principles of Common Law," &c., &c.

In 12mo, price 5s. 6d., cloth,

A CONCISE TREATISE ON THE LAW OF BILLS OF SALE,

FOR THE USE OF LAWYERS, LAW STUDENTS, & THE PUBLIC.

Embracing the Acts of 1878 and 1882. Part I.—Of Bills of Sale generally. Part II.—Of the Execution, Attestation, and Registration of Bills of Sale and satisfaction thereof. Part III.—Of the Effects of Bills of Sale as against Creditors. Part IV.—Of Seizing under, and Enforcing Bills of Sale. Appendix, Forms, Acts, &c. By JOHN INDERMAUR, Solicitor.

"The object of the book is thoroughly practical. Those who want to be told exactly what to do and where to go when they are registering a bill of sale will find the necessary information in this little book."—*Law Journal*.

In 8vo, price 2s. 6d., cloth,

A COLLECTION OF LATIN MAXIMS,

LITERALLY TRANSLATED.

INTENDED FOR THE USE OF STUDENTS FOR ALL LEGAL EXAMINATIONS.

"The book seems admirably adapted as a book of reference for students who come across a Latin maxim in their reading."—*Law Journal*.

In one volume, 8vo, price 9s., cloth,

LEADING STATUTES SUMMARISED,

FOR THE USE OF STUDENTS.

By ERNEST C. THOMAS,

BACON SCHOLAR OF THE HON. SOCIETY OF GRAY'S INN, LATE SCHOLAR OF TRINITY COLLEGE, OXFORD; AUTHOR OF "LEADING CASES IN CONSTITUTIONAL LAW BRIEFLY STATED."

Second Edition, in 8vo, enlarged, price 6s., cloth,

LEADING CASES IN CONSTITUTIONAL LAW

BRIEFLY STATED, WITH INTRODUCTION AND NOTES.

By ERNEST C. THOMAS,

BACON SCHOLAR OF THE HON. SOCIETY OF GRAY'S INN, LATE SCHOLAR OF TRINITY COLLEGE, OXFORD.

"Mr. E. C. Thomas has put together in a slim octavo a digest of the principal cases illustrating Constitutional Law, that is to say, all questions as to the rights or authority of the Crown or persons under it, as regards not merely the constitution and structure given to the governing body, but also the mode in which the sovereign power is to be exercised. In an introductory essay Mr. Thomas gives a very clear and intelligent survey of the general functions of the Executive, and the principles by which they are regulated; and then follows a summary of leading cases."—*Saturday Review*.

"Mr. Thomas gives a sensible introduction and a brief epitome of the familiar leading cases."—*Law Times*.

In 8vo, price 8s., cloth,

AN EPITOME OF HINDU LAW CASES. With

Short Notes thereon. And Introductory Chapters on Sources of Law, Marriage, Adoption, Partition, and Succession. By WILLIAM M. P. COGHLAN, Bombay Civil Service, late Judge and Sessions Judge of Tanna.

Second Edition, in crown 8vo, price 12s. 6d., cloth,

THE BANKRUPTCY ACT, 1883,

WITH NOTES OF ALL THE CASES DECIDED UNDER THE ACT;

THE CONSOLIDATED RULES AND FORMS, 1886; THE DEBTORS ACT, 1869, SO FAR AS APPLICABLE TO BANKRUPTCY MATTERS, WITH RULES AND FORMS THEREUNDER; THE BILLS OF SALE ACTS, 1878 AND 1882;

Board of Trade Circulars and Forms, and List of Official Receivers; Scale of Costs, Fees, and Percentages, 1886; Orders of the Bankruptcy Judge of the High Court; and a Copious Index.

BY WILLIAM HAZLITT, ESQ., AND RICHARD RINGWOOD, M.A.,
SENIOR REGISTRAR IN BANKRUPTCY, OF THE MIDDLE TEMPLE, ESQ., BARRISTER-AT-LAW.

Second Edition, by R. RINGWOOD, M.A., Barrister-at-Law.

"This is a very handy edition of the Act and Rules. . . . . . The cross references and marginal references to corresponding provisions of the Act of 1869 are exceedingly useful. . . . . There is a very full index, and the book is admirably printed."—*Solicitors' Journal*.

Part I., price 7s. 6d., sewed,

LORD WESTBURY'S DECISIONS IN THE EUROPEAN ARBITRATION. Reported by FRANCIS S. REILLY, of Lincoln's Inn, Barrister-at-Law.

Parts I., II., and III., price 25s., sewed,

LORD CAIRNS'S DECISIONS IN THE ALBERT ARBITRATION. Reported by FRANCIS S. REILLY, of Lincoln's Inn, Barrister-at-Law.

Second Edition, in royal 8vo, price 30s., cloth,

A TREATISE ON

THE STATUTES OF ELIZABETH AGAINST FRAUDULENT CONVEYANCES.

THE BILLS OF SALE ACTS 1878 AND 1882 AND THE LAW OF VOLUNTARY DISPOSITIONS OF PROPERTY.

BY THE LATE H. W. MAY, B.A. (Ch. Ch. Oxford),

Second Edition, thoroughly revised and enlarged, by S. WORTHINGTON WORTHINGTON, of the Inner Temple, Barrister-at-Law. Editor of the "Married Women's Property Acts," 5th edition, by the late J. R. GRIFFITH.

"In conclusion, we can heartily recommend this book to our readers, not only to those who are in large practice, and who merely want a classified list of cases, but to those who have both the desire and the leisure to enter upon a systematic study of our law."—*Solicitors' Journal*.

"As Mr. Worthington points out, since Mr. May wrote, the 'Bills of Sale Acts' of 1878 and 1882 have been passed; the 'Married Women's Property Act, 1882' (making settlements by married women void as against creditors in cases in which similar settlements by a man would be void), and the 'Bankruptcy Act, 1883.' These Acts and the decisions upon them have been handled by Mr. Worthington in a manner which shows that he is master of his subject, and not a slavish copyist of sections and head-notes, which is a vicious propensity of many modern compilers of text-books. His Table of Cases (with reference to all the reports), is admirable, and his Index most exhaustive."—*Law Times*.

"The results of the authorities appear to be given well and tersely, and the treatise will we think be found a convenient and trustworthy book of reference."—*Law Journal*.

"Mr. Worthington's work appears to have been conscientious and exhaustive."—*Saturday Review*.

"Examining Mr. May's book, we find it constructed with an intelligence and precision which render it entirely worthy of being accepted as a guide in this confessedly difficult subject. The subject is an involved one, but with clean and clear handling it is here presented as clearly as it could be. . . . On the whole, he has produced a very useful book of an exceptionally scientific character."—*Solicitors' Journal*.

"The subject and the work are both very good. The former is well chosen, new, and interesting; the latter has the quality which always distinguishes original research from borrowed labours."—*American Law Review*.

"We are happy to welcome his (Mr. May's) work as an addition to the, we regret to say, brief catalogue of law books conscientiously executed. We can corroborate his own description of his labours, 'that no pains have been spared to make the book as concise and practical as possible, without doing so at the expense of perspicuity, or by the omission of any important points.'"—*Law Times*.

In one volume, medium 8vo., price 38s., Cloth ; or in Half-Roxburgh, 42s.,

A HISTORY OF THE FORESHORE

AND THE LAW RELATING THERETO.

WITH A HITHERTO UNPUBLISHED TREATISE BY LORD HALE, LORD HALE'S "DE JURE MARIS," AND THE THIRD EDITION OF HALL'S ESSAY ON THE

RIGHTS OF THE CROWN IN THE SEA-SHORE.

WITH NOTES, AND AN APPENDIX RELATING TO FISHERIES.

By STUART A. MOORE, F.S.A.,

OF THE INNER TEMPLE, BARRISTER-AT-LAW.

"This work is nominally a third edition of the late Mr. Hall's essay on the rights of the Crown in the Sea-shore, but in reality is an absolutely new production, for out of some 900 odd pages Hall's essay takes up but 227. Mr. Moore has written a book of great importance, which should mark an epoch in the history of the rights of the Crown and the subject in the *litus maris*, or foreshore of the kingdom. Hall's treatise (with Loveland's notes) is set out with fresh notes by the present editor, who is anything but kindly disposed towards his author, for his notes are nothing but a series of exposures of what he deems to be Hall's errors and misrepresentations. Mr. Moore admits his book to be a brief for the opposite side of the contention supported by Hall, and a more vigorous and argumentive treatise we have scarcely ever seen. Its arguments are clearly and broadly disclosed, and supported by a wealth of facts and cases which show the research of the learned author to have been most full and elaborate. . . . There is no doubt that this is an important work, which must have a considerable influence on that branch of the law with which it deals. That law is contained in ancient and most inaccessible records; these have now been brought to light, and it may well be that important results to the subject may flow therefrom. The Profession, not to say the general public, owe the learned author a deep debt of gratitude for providing ready to hand such a wealth of materials for founding and building up arguments. Mr. Stuart Moore has written a work which must, unless his contentions are utterly unfounded, at once become the standard text-book on the law of the Sea-shore."—*Law Times*, Dec. 1st.

"Mr. Stuart Moore in his valuable work on the Foreshore."—*The Times*.

"Mr. Stuart Moore's work on the title of the Crown to the land around the coast of England lying between the high and low water-mark is something more than an ordinary law book. It is a history, and a very interesting one, of such land and the rights exercised over it from the earliest times to the present day; and a careful study of the facts contained in the book and of the arguments brought forward can scarcely fail to convince the reader of the inaccuracy of the theory, now so constantly put forward by the Crown, that without the existence of special evidence to the contrary, the land which adjoins riparian property, and which is covered at high tide, belongs to the Crown and not to the owner of the adjoining manor. The list which Mr. Moore gives of places where the question of foreshore has been already raised, and of those as to which evidence on the subject exists amongst the public records, is valuable, though by no means exhaustive; and the book should certainly find a place in the library of the lord of every riparian manor."—*Morning Post*.

In one volume, 8vo, price 12s., cloth,

A TREATISE ON THE LAW RELATING TO THE

POLLUTION AND OBSTRUCTION OF WATER COURSES;

TOGETHER WITH A BRIEF SUMMARY OF THE VARIOUS SOURCES OF RIVERS POLLUTION.

By CLEMENT HIGGINS, M.A., F.C.S.,

OF THE INNER TEMPLE, BARRISTER-AT-LAW.

"As a compendium of the law upon a special and rather intricate subject, this treatise cannot but prove of great practical value, and more especially to those who have to advise upon the institution of proceedings under the Rivers Pollution Prevention Act, 1876, or to adjudicate upon those proceedings when brought."—*Irish Law Times*.

"We can recommend Mr. Higgins' Manual as the best guide we possess."—*Public Health*.

"County Court Judges, Sanitary Authorities, and Riparian Owners will find in Mr. Higgins' Treatise a valuable aid in obtaining a clear notion of the Law on the Subject. Mr. Higgins has accomplished a work for which he will readily be recognised as having special fitness on account of his practical acquaintance both with the scientific and the legal aspects of his subject."—*Law Magazine and Review*.

"The volume is very carefully arranged throughout, and will prove of great utility both to miners and to owners of land on the banks of rivers."—*The Mining Journal*.

"Mr. Higgins writes tersely and clearly, while his facts are so well arranged that it is a pleasure to refer to his book for information; and altogether the work is one which will be found very useful by all interested in the subject to which it relates."—*Engineer*.

"A compact and convenient manual of the law on the subject to which it relates."—*Solicitors' Journal*.

In 8vo, Fourth Edition, price 25s., cloth,

MAYNE'S TREATISE
ON
THE LAW OF DAMAGES.
FOURTH EDITION.
BY

JOHN D. MAYNE,
OF THE INNER TEMPLE, BARRISTER-AT-LAW;

AND

LUMLEY SMITH,
OF THE INNER TEMPLE, Q.C.

"Few books have been better kept up to the current law than this treatise. The earlier part of the book was remodelled in the last edition, and in the present edition the chapter on Penalties and Liquidated Damages has been re-written, no doubt in consequence of, or with regard to, the elaborate and exhaustive judgment of the late Master of the Rolls in *Wallis v. Smith* (31 W. R. 214; L. R. 21 Ch. D. 243). The treatment of the subject by the authors is admirably clear and concise. Upon the point involved in *Wallis v. Smith* they say 'The result is that an agreement with various covenants of different importance is not to be governed by any inflexible rule peculiar to itself, but is to be dealt with as coming under the general rule, that the intention of the parties themselves is to be considered. If they have said that in the case of any breach a fixed sum is to be paid, then they will be kept to their agreement, unless it would lead to such an absurdity or injustice that it must be assumed that they did not mean what they said.' This is a very fair summary of the judgments in *Wallis v. Smith*, especially of that of Lord Justice Cotton ; and it supplies the nearest approach which can be given at present to a rule for practical guidance. We can heartily commend this as a carefully edited edition of a thoroughly good book."—*Solicitors' Journal.*

"The editors have, with their well-known care, eliminated much obsolete matter, and revised and corrected the text in accordance with the recent changes in procedure and legislation. The chapter on penalties and liquidated damages has been to a great extent re-written, and a new chapter has been added on breach of statutory obligations. As of former editions of this valuable work, we can but speak of it with strong commendation as a most reliable authority on a very important branch of our law—the Right to Damages as the result of an Action at Law."—*Law Journal.*

"*During the twenty-two years which have elapsed since the publication of this well-known work, its reputation has been steadily growing, and it has long since become the recognised authority on the important subject of which it treats.*"—LAW MAGAZINE AND REVIEW.

"This edition of what has become a standard work has the advantage of appearing under the supervision of the original author as well as of Mr. Lumley Smith, the editor of the second edition. The result is most satisfactory. Mr. Lumley Smith's edition was ably and conscientiously prepared, and we are glad to find that the reader still enjoys the benefit of his accuracy and learning. At the same time the book has doubtless been improved by the reappearance of its author as co-editor. The earlier part, indeed, has been to a considerable extent entirely rewritten.

"Mr. Mayne's remarks on damages in actions of tort are brief. We agree with him that in such actions the courts are governed by far looser principles than in contracts; indeed, sometimes it is impossible to say they are governed by any principles at all. In actions for injuries to the person or reputation, for example, a judge cannot do more than give a general direction to the jury to give what the facts proved in their judgment required. And, according to the better opinion, they may give damages 'for example's sake,' and mulct a rich man more heavily than a poor one. In actions for injuries to property, however, 'vindictive' cr 'exemplary' damages cannot, except in very rare cases, be awarded, but must be limited, as in contract, to the actual harm sustained.

"It is needless to comment upon the arrangement of the subjects in this edition, in which no alteration has been made. The editors modestly express a hope that all the English as well as the principal Irish decisions up to the date have been included, and we believe from our own examination that the hope is well founded. We may regret that, warned by the growing bulk of the book, the editors have not included any fresh American cases, but we feel that the omission was unavoidable. We should add that the whole work has been thoroughly revised."—*Solicitors' Journal.*

"*This text-book is so well known, not only as the highest authority on the subject treated of but as one of the best text-books ever written, that it would be idle for us to speak of it in the words of commendation that it deserves. It is a work that no practising lawyer can do without.*"—CANADA LAW JOURNAL.

In crown 8vo, price 4s. 6d., cloth,

ABSTRACT DRAWING. Containing Instructions on
the Drawing of Abstracts of Title, and an Illustrative Appendix. By C. E. SCOTT, Solicitor.

"This little book is intended for the assistance of those who have the framing of abstracts of title entrusted to their care. It contains a number of useful rules, and an illustrative appendix."—*Law Times.*
"A handy book for all articled clerks."—*Law Students' Journal.*
"Solicitors who have articled clerks would save themselves much trouble if they furnished their clerks with a copy of this little book before putting them on to draft an abstract of a heap of title deeds."—*Law Notes.*
"The book ought to be perused by all law students and articled clerks."—*Red Tape.*

Second Edition, in crown 8vo, price 7s., cloth,

THE LAW RELATING TO CLUBS.
BY THE LATE JOHN WERTHEIMER, BARRISTER-AT-LAW.
Second Edition, by A. W. CHASTER, Barrister-at-Law.

"A convenient handbook, drawn up with great judgment and perspicuity."—*Morning Post.*
"Both useful and interesting to those interested in club management."—*Law Times.*
"Mr. Wertheimer's history of the cases is complete and well arranged."—*Saturday Review.*

"This is a very neat little book on an interesting subject. The law is accurately and well expressed."—*Law Journal.*
"This is a very handy and complete little work. This excellent little treatise should lie on the table of every club."—*Pump Court.*

In 8vo, price 2s., sewed,

TABLE of the FOREIGN MERCANTILE LAWS and CODES
in Force in the Principal States of EUROPE and AMERICA. By CHARLES LYON-CAEN, Professeur agrégé à la Faculté de Droit de Paris; Professeur à l'Ecole libre des Sciences politiques. Translated by NAPOLEON ARGLES, Solicitor, Paris.

In 8vo, price 1s., sewed,

A GUIDE TO THE FRENCH LAWS OF 1889, ON NATION-
ALITY AND MILITARY SERVICE, as affecting British Subjects. By A. PAVITT, Solicitor, Paris.

In one volume, demy 8vo, price 10s. 6d., cloth,

PRINCIPLES OF THE LAW OF STOPPAGE IN TRANSITU,
RETENTION, and DELIVERY. By JOHN HOUSTON, of the Middle Temple, Barrister-at-Law.

In 8vo, price 10s., cloth,

THE TRIAL OF ADELAIDE BARTLETT FOR
MURDER; Complete and Revised Report. Edited by EDWARD BEAL, B.A., of the Middle Temple, Barrister-at-Law. With a Preface by EDWARD CLARKE, Q.C., M.P.

In 8vo, price 10s. 6d., cloth,
A REPORT OF THE CASE OF

THE QUEEN v. GURNEY AND OTHERS,
In the Court of Queen's Bench before the Lord Chief Justice COCKBURN. With Introduction, containing History of the Case, and Examination of the Cases at Law and Equity applicable to it. By W. F. FINLASON, Barrister-at-Law.

In royal 8vo, price 10s. 6d., cloth,

THE PRACTICE OF EQUITY BY WAY OF REVIVOR AND SUPPLEMENT.
With Forms of Orders and Appendix of Bills. By LOFTUS LEIGH PEMBERTON, of the Chancery Registrar's Office.

In 8vo, price 6s. 6d., cloth,

THE ANNUAL DIGEST OF MERCANTILE CASES FOR THE YEAR 1886.

BEING A DIGEST OF THE DECISIONS OF THE ENGLISH, SCOTCH AND IRISH COURTS ON MATTERS RELATING TO COMMERCE.

By JAMES A. DUNCAN, M.A., LL.B., Trin. Coll., Camb.,

AND OF THE INNER TEMPLE, BARRISTER-AT-LAW.

"We hope the present issue may be the first of a series which will naturally increase in value with the progress of time."—*Saturday Review.*

"There can only be one opinion, and that a very decided one indeed, in favour of the value of this book to men of business and to members of the legal profession."—*Liverpool Mercury.*

"A work of such handy reference, well indexed, and containing the essence of a year's decisions will be found a valuable addition to office libraries."—*Liverpool Daily Post.*

*** *The Annual Digest of Mercantile Cases, for* 1885, *can also be had, price* 6s., *cloth.*

THE LAW AND PRACTICE OF ELECTION PETITIONS,

With an Appendix containing the Parliamentary Elections Acts, the Corrupt and Illegal Practices Prevention Acts, the General Rules of Procedure made by the Election Judges in England, Scotland, and Ireland, Forms of Petitions, &c. Third Edition. By HENRY HARDCASTLE, of the Inner Temple, Barrister-at-Law.

"Mr. Hardcastle gives us an original treatise with foot-notes, and he has evidently taken very considerable pains to make his work a reliable guide. We can thoroughly recommend Mr. Hardcastle's book as a concise manual on the law and practice of election petitions."—*Law Times.*

Vols. I., II., & III., price 73s.; and Vol. IV., Pts. I. to IV., price 14s.,

REPORTS OF THE DECISIONS OF THE

JUDGES FOR THE TRIAL OF ELECTION PETITIONS

IN ENGLAND AND IRELAND.

PURSUANT TO THE PARLIAMENTARY ELECTIONS ACT, 1868.

By EDWARD LOUGHLIN O'MALLEY AND HENRY HARDCASTLE.

*** *Vol. IV. Parts III. and IV. Edited by* J. S. SANDARS, *Barrister-at-Law.*

In 8vo, price 12s., cloth,

THE LAW OF FIXTURES,

IN THE PRINCIPAL RELATION OF

LANDLORD AND TENANT,

AND IN ALL OTHER OR GENERAL RELATIONS.

FOURTH EDITION.

By ARCHIBALD BROWN, M.A. Edin. and Oxon., and B.C.L. Oxon.

OF THE MIDDLE TEMPLE, BARRISTER-AT-LAW.

"A new chapter has been added with reference to the Law of Ecclesiastical Fixtures and Dilapidations. The book is worthy of the success it has achieved."—*Law Times.*

"The treatise is commendable as well for originality as for laboriousness."—*Law Journal.*

Stevens & Haynes' Series of Reprints of the Early Reporters.

SIR BARTHOLOMEW SHOWER'S PARLIAMENTARY CASES.

In 8vo, 1876, price 4*l.* 4*s.*, best calf binding,

SHOWER'S CASES IN PARLIAMENT
RESOLVED AND ADJUDGED UPON PETITIONS & WRITS OF ERROR.

FOURTH EDITION.
CONTAINING ADDITIONAL CASES NOT HITHERTO REPORTED.

REVISED AND EDITED BY

RICHARD LOVELAND LOVELAND,

OF THE INNER TEMPLE, BARRISTER-AT-LAW; EDITOR OF "KELYNG'S CROWN CASES," AND "HALL'S ESSAY ON THE RIGHTS OF THE CROWN IN THE SEASHORE."

"Messrs. STEVENS & HAYNES, the successful publishers of the Reprints of Bellewe, Cooke, Cunningham, Brookes's New Cases, Choyce Cases in Chancery, William Kelynge and Kelyng's Crown Cases, determined to issue a new or fourth Edition of Shower's Cases in Parliament.

"The volume, although beautifully printed on old-fashioned Paper, in old-fashioned type, instead of being in the quarto, is in the more convenient octavo form, and contains several additional cases not to be found in any of the previous editions of the work.

"These are all cases of importance, worthy of being ushered into the light of the world by enterprising publishers.

"Shower's Cases are models for reporters, even in our day. The statements of the case, the arguments of counsel, and the opinions of the Judges, are all clearly and ably given.

"This new edition with an old face of these valuable reports, under the able editorship of R. L. Loveland, Esq., should, in the language of the advertisement, 'be welcomed by the profession, as well as enable the custodians of public libraries to complete or add to their series of English Law Reports.'"—*Canada Law Journal.*

BELLEWE'S CASES, T. RICHARD II.

In 8vo, 1869, price 3*l.* 3*s.*, bound in calf antique,

LES ANS DU ROY RICHARD LE SECOND.

Collect' ensembl' hors les abridgments de Statham, Fitzherbert et Brooke. Per RICHARD BELLEWE, de Lincolns Inne. 1585. Reprinted from the Original Edition.

"No public library in the world, where English law finds a place, should be without a copy of this edition of Bellewe."—*Canada Law Journal.*

"We have here a *fac-simile* edition of Bellewe, and it is really the most beautiful and admirable reprint that has appeared at any time. It is a perfect gem of antique printing, and forms a most interesting monument of our early legal history. It belongs to the same class of works as the Year Book of Edward I. and other similar works which have been printed in our own time under the auspices of the Master of the Rolls; but is far superior to any of them, and is in this respect highly creditable to the spirit and enterprise of private publishers. The work is an important link in our legal history; there are no year books of the reign of Richard II., and Bellewe supplied the only substitute by carefully extracting and collecting all the cases he could find, and he did it in the most convenient form—that of alphabetical arrangement in the order of subjects, so that the work is a digest as well as a book of law reports. It is in fact a collection of cases of the reign of Richard II., arranged according to their subjects in alphabetical order. It is therefore one of the most intelligible and interesting legal memorials of the Middle Ages."—*Law Times.*

CUNNINGHAM'S REPORTS.

In 8vo, 1871, price 3*l.* 3*s.*, calf antique,

CUNNINGHAM'S (T.) Reports in K. B., 7 to 10 Geo. II.; to which is prefixed a Proposal for rendering the Laws of England clear and certain, humbly offered to the Consideration of both Houses of Parliament. Third edition, with numerous Corrections. BY THOMAS TOWNSEND BUCKNILL, Barrister-at-Law.

"The instructive chapter which precedes the cases, entitled 'A proposal for rendering the Laws of England clear and certain,' gives the volume a degree of peculiar interest, independent of the value of many of the reported cases. That chapter begins with words which ought, for the information of every people, to be printed in letters of gold. They are as follows: 'Nothing conduces more to the peace and prosperity of every nation than good laws and the due execution of them.' The history of the civil law is then rapidly traced. Next a history is given of English Reporters, beginning with the reporters of the Year Books from 1 Edw. III. to 12 Hen. VIII.—being near 200 years—and afterwards to the time of the author."—*Canada Law Journal.*

STEVENS & HAYNES, BELL YARD, TEMPLE BAR. 35

Stevens and Haynes' Series of Reprints of the Early Reporters.

CHOYCE CASES IN CHANCERY.

In 8vo, 1870, price 2l. 2s., calf antique,

THE PRACTICE OF THE HIGH COURT OF CHANCERY.

With the Nature of the several Offices belonging to that Court. And the Reports of many Cases wherein Relief hath been there had, and where denyed.

"This volume, in paper, type, and binding (like 'Bellewe's Cases') is a fac-simile of the antique edition. All who buy the one should buy the other."—*Canada Law Journal.*

In 8vo, 1872, price 3l. 3s., calf antique,

SIR G. COOKE'S COMMON PLEAS REPORTS
IN THE REIGNS OF QUEEN ANNE, AND KINGS GEORGE I. AND II.

The Third Edition, with Additional Cases and References contained in the Notes taken from L. C. J. EYRE'S MSS. by Mr. Justice NARES, edited by THOMAS TOWNSEND BUCKNILL, of the Inner Temple, Barrister-at-Law.

"Law books never can die or remain long dead so long as Stevens and Haynes are willing to continue them or revive them when dead. It is certainly surprising to see with what facial accuracy an old volume of Reports may be produced by these modern publishers, whose good taste is only equalled by their enterprise."—*Canada Law Journal.*

BROOKE'S NEW CASES WITH MARCH'S TRANSLATION.

In 8vo, 1873, price 4l. 4s., calf antique,

BROOKE'S (Sir Robert) New Cases in the time of Henry VIII., Edward VI., and Queen Mary, collected out of BROOKE'S Abridgement, and arranged under years, with a table, together with MARCH'S (John) *Translation of* BROOKE'S New Cases in the time of Henry VIII., Edward VI., and Queen Mary, collected out of BROOKE'S Abridgement, and reduced alphabetically under their proper heads and titles, with a table of the principal matters. In one handsome volume. 8vo. 1873.

"Both the original and the translation having long been very scarce, and the mispaging and other errors in March's translation making a new and corrected edition peculiarly desirable, Messrs. Stevens and Haynes have reprinted the two books in one volume, uniform with the preceding volumes of the series of Early Reports."—*Canada Law Journal.*

KELYNGE'S (W.) REPORTS.

In 8vo, 1873, price 4l. 4s., calf antique,

KELYNGE'S (William) Reports of Cases in Chancery, the King's Bench, &c., from the 3rd to the 9th year of his late Majesty King George II., during which time Lord King was Chancellor, and the Lords Raymond and Hardwicke were Chief Justices of England. To which are added, seventy New Cases not in the First Edition. Third Edition. In one handsome volume. 8vo. 1873.

KELYNG'S (SIR JOHN) CROWN CASES.

In 8vo, 1873, price 4l. 4s., calf antique,

KELYNG'S (Sir J.) Reports of Divers Cases in Pleas of the Crown in the Reign of King Charles II., with Directions to Justices of the Peace, and others; to which are added, Three Modern Cases, viz., Armstrong and Lisle, the King and Plummer, the Queen and Mawgridge. Third Edition, *containing several additional Cases never before printed*, together with a TREATISE UPON THE LAW AND PROCEEDINGS IN CASES OF HIGH TREASON, first published in 1793. The whole carefully revised and edited by RICHARD LOVELAND LOVELAND, of the Inner Temple, Barrister-at-Law.

"We look upon this volume as one of the most important and valuable of the unique reprints of Messrs. Stevens and Haynes. Little do we know of the mines of legal wealth that lie buried in the old law books. But a careful examination, either of the reports or of the treatise embodied in the volume now before us, will give the reader some idea of the good service rendered by Messrs. Stevens and Haynes to the profession. . . . Should occasion arise, the Crown prosecutor, as well as counsel for the prisoner, will find in this volume a complete *vade mecum* of the law of high treason and proceedings in relation thereto."—*Canada Law Journal.*

Second Edition, in 8vo, price 26s., cloth,

A CONCISE TREATISE ON

PRIVATE INTERNATIONAL JURISPRUDENCE,

BASED ON THE DECISIONS IN THE ENGLISH COURTS.

By JOHN ALDERSON FOOTE,

OF LINCOLN'S INN, BARRISTER-AT-LAW; CHANCELLOR'S LEGAL MEDALLIST AND SENIOR WHEWELL SCHOLAR OF INTERNATIONAL LAW, CAMBRIDGE UNIVERSITY, 1873; SENIOR STUDENT IN JURISPRUDENCE AND ROMAN LAW, INNS OF COURT EXAMINATION, HILARY TERM, 1874.

"This work seems to us likely to prove of considerable use to all English lawyers who have to deal with questions of private international law. Since the publication of Mr. Westlake's valuable treatise, twenty years ago, the judicial decisions of English courts bearing upon different parts of this subject have greatly increased in number, and it is full time that these decisions should be examined, and that the conclusions to be deduced from them should be systematically set forth in a treatise. Moreover, Mr. Foote has done this well."—*Solicitors' Journal.*

"Mr. Foote has done his work very well, and the book will be useful to all who have to deal with the class of cases in which English law alone is not sufficient to settle the question."—*Saturday Review,* March 8, 1879.

"The author's object has been to reduce into order the mass of materials already accumulated in the shape of explanation and actual decision on the interesting matter of which he treats; and to construct a framework of private international law, not from the *dicta* of jurists so much as from judicial decisions in English Courts which have superseded them. And it is here, in compiling and arranging in a concise form this valuable material, that Mr. Foote's wide range of knowledge and legal acumen bear such good fruit. As a guide and assistant to the student of international law, the whole treatise will be invaluable; while a table of cases and a general index will enable him to find what he wants without trouble."—*Standard.*

"The recent decisions on points of international law (and there have been a large number since Westlake's publication) have been well stated. So far as we have observed, no case of any importance has been omitted, and the leading cases have been fully analysed. The author does not hesitate to criticise the grounds of a decision when these appear to him to conflict with the proper rule of law. Most of his criticisms seem to us very just. . . . . On the whole, we can recommend Mr. Foote's treatise as a useful addition to our text-books, and we expect it will rapidly find its way into the hands of practising lawyers."—*The Journal of Jurisprudence and Scottish Law Magazine.*

"Mr. Foote has evidently borne closely in mind the needs of Students of Jurisprudence as well as those of the Practitioners. For both, the fact that his work is almost entirely one of Case-law will commend it as one useful alike in Chambers and in Court."—*Law Magazine and Review.*

"Mr. Foote's book will be useful to the student. . . . . One of the best points of Mr. Foote's book is the 'Continuous Summary,' which occupies about thirty pages, and is divided into four parts—Persons, Property, Acts, and Procedure. Mr. Foote remarks that these summaries are not in any way intended as an attempt at codification. However that may be, they are a digest which reflects high credit on the author's assiduity and capacity. They are 'meant merely to guide the student;' but they will do much more than guide him. They will enable him to get such a grasp of the subject as will render the reading of the text easy and fruitful."—*Law Journal.*

"This book is well adapted to be used both as a text-book for students and a book of reference for practising barristers."—*Bar Examination Journal.*

"This is a book which supplies the want which has long been felt for a really good modern treatise on Private International Law adapted to the every-day requirements of the English Practitioner. The whole volume, although designed for the use of the practitioner, is so moderate in size—an octavo of 500 pages only—and the arrangement and development of the subject so well conceived and executed, that it will amply repay perusal by those whose immediate object may be not the actual decisions of a knotty point but the satisfactory disposal of an examination paper."—*Oxford and Cambridge Undergraduates' Journal.*

"Since the publication, some twenty years ago, of Mr. Westlake's Treatise, Mr. Foote's book is, in our opinion, the best work on private international law which has appeared in the English language. . . The work is executed with much ability, and will doubtless be found of great value by all persons who have to consider questions on private international law."—*Athenæum.*

THE
Law Magazine and Review,
AND
QUARTERLY DIGEST OF ALL REPORTED CASES.

Price FIVE SHILLINGS each Number.

No. CCXVIII. (Vol. 1, No. I. of the New QUARTERLY Series.) November, 1875.
  No. CCXIX. (Vol. 1, 4th Series No. II.) February, 1876.

N.B.—These two Numbers are out of print.

No. CCXX.   (Vol. 1, 4th Series No. III.)   For May, 1876.
No. CCXXI.   (Vol. 1, 4th Series No. IV.)   For August, 1876.

Nos. CCXXII. to CCXLV. (Vol. 2, 4th Series, to Vol. 7, 4th Series, Nos. V. to XXVIII.), November, 1876, to August, 1882.

Nos. CCXLVI. to CCXLIX. (Vol. 8, 4th Series Nos. XXIX. to XXXII.), November, 1882, to August, 1883.

Nos. CCL. to CCLIII. (Vol. 9, 4th Series, Nos. XXXIII. to XXXVI.), November, 1883, to August, 1884.

Nos. CCLIV. to CCLVII. (Vol. 9, 4th Series, Nos. XXXVII. to XL.), November, 1884, to August, 1885.

Nos. CCLVIII. to CCLXI. (Vol. X., 4th Series, Nos. XLI. to XLIV.), November, 1885, to August, 1886.

Nos. CCLXII. to CCLXV. (Vol. XI., 4th Series, Nos. XLV. to XLVIII.), November, 1886, to August, 1887.

Nos. CCLXVI., to CCLXIX. (Vol. XII., 4th Series, Nos. XLIX. to LII.), November, 1887, to August, 1888.

Nos. CCLXX. to CCLXXIII. (Vol. XIII., 4th Series, Nos. LIII. to LVI.), November, 1888, to August, 1889.

No. CCLXXIV. to CCLXXVII. (Vol. XIV., 4th Series, Nos. LVII. to LX.), November, 1889, to August, 1890.

No. CCLXXVIII. to CCLXXXI. (Vol. XV., 4th Series, Nos. LXI. to LXIV.), November, 1890, to August, 1891.

No. CCLXXXII to CCLXXXV. (Vol. XVI., 4th Series, Nos. LXV. to LXVIII.). November, 1891, to August, 1892.

An Annual Subscription of 20s., paid in advance to the Publishers, will secure the receipt of the **LAW MAGAZINE**, free by post, within the United Kingdom, or for 24s. to the Colonies and Abroad.

Fifth Edition, in one vol., 8vo. *In preparation.*

A TREATISE ON HINDU LAW AND USAGE.

By JOHN D. MAYNE, of the Inner Temple, Barrister-at-Law, Author of "A Treatise on Damages," &c.

"A new work from the pen of so established an authority as Mr. Mayne cannot fail to be welcome to the legal profession. In his present volume the late Officiating Advocate-General at Madras has drawn upon the stores of his long experience in Southern India, and has produced a work of value alike to the practitioner at the Indian Bar, or at home, in appeal cases, and to the scientific jurist.

"To all who, whether as practitioners or administrators, or as students of the science of jurisprudence, desire a thoughtful and suggestive work of reference on Hindu Law and Usage, we heartily recommend the careful perusal of Mr. Mayne's valuable treatise."—*Law Magazine and Review.*

In 8vo, 1877, price 15s., cloth,

A DIGEST OF HINDU LAW,

AS ADMINISTERED IN THE COURTS OF THE MADRAS PRESIDENCY.

ARRANGED AND ANNOTATED

By H. S. CUNNINGHAM, M.A., Advocate-General, Madras.

DUTCH LAW.

In 2 Vols., Royal 8vo, price 90s., cloth,

VAN LEEUWEN'S COMMENTARIES ON THE ROMAN-DUTCH LAW. Revised and Edited with Notes in Two Volumes by C. W. DECKER, Advocate. Translated from the original Dutch by J. G. KOTZÉ, LL.B., of the Inner Temple, Barrister-at-Law, and Chief Justice of the Transvaal. With Facsimile Portrait of DECKER from the Edition of 1780.

** Vol. II. can be had separately, price 50s.

BUCHANAN (J.), Reports of Cases decided in the Supreme Court of the CAPE OF GOOD HOPE. 1868, 1869, 1870-73, and 74. Bound in Three Vols. Royal 8vo.

——————— 1875, 1876, 1879, etc.

MENZIES' (W.), Reports of Cases decided in the Supreme Court of the CAPE OF GOOD HOPE. Vol. I., Vol. II., Vol. III.

BUCHANAN (J.), Index and Digest of Cases decided in the Supreme Court of the CAPE OF GOOD HOPE, reported by the late Hon. WILLIAM MENZIES. Compiled by JAMES BUCHANAN, Advocate of the Supreme Court. In One Vol., royal 8vo.

In 8vo, 1878, cloth,

PRECEDENTS IN PLEADING: being Forms filed of Record in the Supreme Court of the Colony of the Cape of Good Hope. Collected and Arranged by JAMES BUCHANAN.

In Crown 8vo, price 31s. 6d., boards,

THE INTRODUCTION TO DUTCH JURISPRUDENCE OF HUGO GROTIUS, with Notes by Simon van Groenwegen van der Made, and References to Van der Keesel's Theses and Schorer's Notes. Translated by A. F. S. MAASDORP, B.A., of the Inner Temple, Barrister-at-Law.

In 12mo, price 15s. *net*, boards,

SELECT THESES ON THE LAWS OF HOLLAND & ZEELAND.

Being a Commentary of Hugo Grotius' Introduction to Dutch Jurisprudence, and intended to supply certain defects therein, and to determine some of the more celebrated Controversies on the Law of Holland. By DIONYSIUS GODEFRIDUS VAN DER KESSEL, Advocate, and Professor of the Civil and Modern Laws in the Universities of Leyden. Translated from the original Latin by C. A. LORENZ, of Lincoln's Inn, Barrister-at-Law. Second Edition, With a Biographical Notice of the Author by Professor J. DE WAL, of Leyden.

THE
Bar Examination Annual
FOR 1893.

(In Continuation of the Bar Examination Journal.)

EXAMINATION PAPERS, 1892.
    FOR PASS, HONORS, AND BARSTOW SCHOLARSHIP.
RESULT OF EXAMINATIONS.
NAMES OF SUCCESSFUL CANDIDATES.
EXAMINATION REGULATIONS FOR 1893.
A GUIDE TO THE BAR.
LEADING DECISIONS AND STATUTES OF 1892.
NEW BOOKS AND NEW EDITIONS.

W. D. EDWARDS, LL.B.,
OF LINCOLN'S INN, BARRISTER-AT-LAW.

Now published, in 8vo, price 18s. each, cloth,

THE BAR EXAMINATION JOURNAL, VOLS. IV., V.,
VI., VII., VIII., IX. & X. Containing the Examination Questions and Answers from Easter Term, 1878, to Hilary Term, 1892, with List of Successful Candidates at each examination, Notes on the Law of Property, and a Synopsis of Recent Legislation of importance to Students, and other information.

BY A. D. TYSSEN AND W. D. EDWARDS, Barristers-at-Law.

Fifth Edition. In 8vo, price 9s. cloth,

A SUMMARY OF JOINT STOCK COMPANIES' LAW.

BY T. EUSTACE SMITH,
OF THE INNER TEMPLE, BARRISTER-AT-LAW.

"The author of this hand-book tells us that, when an articled student reading for the final examination, he felt the want of such a work as that before us, wherein could be found the main principles of law relating to joint-stock companies . . . Law students may well read it ; for Mr. Smith has very wisely been at the pains of giving his authority for all his statements of the law or of practice, as applied to joint-stock company business usually transacted in solicitors 'chambers. In fact, Mr. Smith has by his little book offered a fresh inducement to students to make themselves—at all events, to some extent—acquainted with company law as a separate branch of study."—*Law Times.*

"These pages give, in the words of the Preface, 'as briefly and concisely as possible, a general view both of the principles and practice of the law affecting companies.' The work is excellently printed, and authorities are cited ; but in no case is the very language of the statutes copied. The plan is good, and shows both grasp and neatness, and, both amongst students and laymen, Mr. Smith's book ought to meet a ready sale."—*Law Journal.*

"The book is one from which we have derived a large amount of valuable information, and we can heartily and conscientiously recommend it to our readers."—*Oxford and Cambridge Undergraduates' Journal.*

In 8vo, Sixth Edition, price 9s., cloth,

THE MARRIED WOMEN'S PROPERTY ACTS;

1870, 1874, 1882 and 1884,

WITH COPIOUS AND EXPLANATORY NOTES, AND AN APPENDIX OF THE ACTS RELATING TO MARRIED WOMEN.

By ARCHIBALD BROWN, M.A., Edinburgh and Oxon., and the Middle Temple, Barrister-at-Law. Being the Sixth Edition of The Married Women's Property Acts. By the late J. R. GRIFFITHS, B.A. Oxon., of Lincoln's Inn, Barrister-at-Law.

"Upon the whole, we are of opinion that this is the best work upon the subject which has been issued since the passing of the recent Act. Its position as a well-established manual of acknowledged worth gives it at starting a considerable advantage over new books; and this advantage has been well maintained by the intelligent treatment of the Editor."—*Solicitors' Journal.*

"The notes are full, but anything rather than tedious reading, and the law contained in them is good, and verified by reported cases. . . . A distinct feature of the work is its copious index, practically a summary of the marginal headings of the various paragraphs in the body of the text. This book is worthy of all success."—*Law Magazine.*

In 8vo, price 12s., cloth,

THE LAW OF NEGLIGENCE.

SECOND EDITION.

By ROBERT CAMPBELL, of Lincoln's Inn, Barrister-at-Law, and Advocate of the Scotch Bar.

"No less an authority than the late Mr. Justice Willes, in his judgment in *Oppenheim v. White Lion Hotel Co.*, characterised Mr. Campbell's 'Law of Negligence' as a 'very good book;' and since very good books are by no means plentiful, when compared with the numbers of indifferent ones which annually issue from the press, we think the profession will be thankful to the author of this new edition brought down to date. It is indeed an able and scholarly treatise on a somewhat difficult branch of law, in the treatment of which the author's knowledge of Roman and Scotch Jurisprudence has stood him in good stead. We confidently recommend it alike to the student and the practitioner."—*Law Magazine.*

In royal 8vo,

AN INDEX TO TEN THOUSAND PRECEDENTS

IN CONVEYANCING AND TO COMMON AND COMMERCIAL FORMS. Arranged in Alphabetical order with Subdivisions of an Analytical Nature; together with an Appendix containing an Abstract of the Stamp Act, 1870, with a Schedule of Duties; the Regulations relative to, and the Stamp Duties payable on, Probates of Wills, Letters of Administration, Legacies, and Successions. By WALTER ARTHUR COPINGER, of the Middle Temple, Barrister-at-Law.

BIBLIOTHECA LEGUM.

In 12mo (nearly 400 pages), price 2s., cloth,

A CATALOGUE OF LAW BOOKS. Including all the Reports

in the various Courts of England, Scotland, and Ireland; with a Supplement to December, 1884. By HENRY G. STEVENS and ROBERT W. HAYNES, Law Publishers.

In small 4to, price 2s., cloth, beautifully printed, with a large margin, for the special use of Librarians,

A CATALOGUE OF THE REPORTS IN THE VARIOUS COURTS OF THE UNITED KINGDOM OF GREAT BRITAIN AND IRELAND. *ARRANGED BOTH IN ALPHA-BETICAL & CHRONOLOGICAL ORDER.* By STEVENS & HAYNES, Law Publishers.

Second Edition, much enlarged. In 8vo. *In preparation.*

CHAPTERS ON THE
LAW RELATING TO THE COLONIES.

To which is appended a TOPICAL INDEX of CASES DECIDED in the PRIVY COUNCIL on Appeal from the Colonies, the Channel Islands and the Isle of Man, reported in Acton, Knapp, Moore, the Law Journal Reports, and the Law Reports.

By CHARLES JAMES TARRING,

OF THE INNER TEMPLE, ASSISTANT JUDGE H. B. M SUP. CONSULAR COURT FOR THE OTTOMAN DOMINION, AND H. M. CONSUL, CONSTANTINOPLE.

CONTENTS.

TABLE OF CASES CITED.
TABLE OF STATUTES CITED.
Introductory.—Definition of a Colony.
Chapter I.—The laws to which the Colonies are subject.
Chapter II.—The Executive.
    Section 1.—The Governor.
    Section 2.—The Executive Council.
Chapter III.—The Legislative power.
    Section 1.—Crown Colonies.
    Section 2.—Privileges and powers of colonial Legislative Assemblies.
Chapter IV.—The Judiciary and Bar.

Chapter V.—Appeals from the Colonies.
Chapter VI.—Section 1.—Imperial Statutes relating to the Colonies in general.
    Section 2.—Imperial Statutes relating to particular Colonies.

TOPICAL INDEX OF CASES.
INDEX OF TOPICS OF ENGLISH LAW DEALT WITH IN THE CASES.
INDEX OF NAMES OF CASES.
GENERAL INDEX.

In 8vo, price 10s., cloth,

THE TAXATION OF COSTS IN THE CROWN OFFICE.

COMPRISING A COLLECTION OF
BILLS OF COSTS IN THE VARIOUS MATTERS TAXABLE IN THAT OFFICE;
INCLUDING
COSTS UPON THE PROSECUTION OF FRAUDULENT BANKRUPTS, AND ON APPEALS FROM INFERIOR COURTS;

TOGETHER WITH
A TABLE OF COURT FEES,
AND A SCALE OF COSTS USUALLY ALLOWED TO SOLICITORS, ON THE TAXATION OF COSTS ON THE CROWN SIDE OF THE QUEEN'S BENCH DIVISION OF THE HIGH COURT OF JUSTICE.

By FREDK. H. SHORT,
CHIEF CLERK IN THE CROWN OFFICE.

"This is decidedly a useful work on the subject of those costs which are liable to be taxed before the Queen's Coroner and Attorney (for which latter name that of 'Solicitor' might now well be substituted), or before the master of the Crown Office; in fact, such a book is almost indispensable when preparing costs for taxation in the Crown Office, or when taxing an opponent's costs. Country solicitors will find the scale relating to bankruptcy prosecutions of especial use, as such costs are taxed in the Crown Office. The 'general observations' constitute a useful feature in this manual."—*Law Times.*

"This book contains a collection of bills of costs in the various matters taxable in the Crown Office. When we point out that the only scale of costs available for the use of the general body of solicitors is that published in Mr. Corner's book on 'Crown Practice' in 1844, we have said quite enough to prove the utility of the work before us.

"In them Mr. Short deals with 'Perusals,' 'Copies for Use,' 'Affidavits,' 'Agency,' 'Correspondence,' 'Close Copies,' 'Counsel,' 'Affidavit of Increase,' and kindred matters; and adds some useful remarks on taxation of 'Costs in Bankruptcy Prosecutions,' '*Quo Warranto,*' '*Mandamus,*' 'Indictments,' and 'Rules.'

"We have rarely seen a work of this character better executed, and we feel sure that it will be thoroughly appreciated."—*Law Journal.*

"The recent revision of the old scale of costs in the Crown Office renders the appearance of this work particularly opportune, and it cannot fail to be welcomed by practitioners. Mr. Short gives, in the first place, a scale of costs usually allowed to solicitors on the taxation of costs in the Crown Office, and then bills of costs in various matters. These are well arranged and clearly printed."—*Solicitors' Journal.*

Just Published, in 8vo, price 7s. 6d., cloth,

BRITISH CONSULAR JURISDICTION IN THE EAST,

WITH TOPICAL INDICES OF CASES ON APPEAL FROM, AND
RELATING TO, CONSULAR COURTS AND CONSULS;
Also a Collection of Statutes concerning Consuls.

By C. J. TARRING, M.A.,
ASSISTANT-JUDGE OF H.B.M. SUPREME CONSULAR COURT FOR THE LEVANT.

In one volume, 8vo, price 8s. 6d., cloth,
A COMPLETE TREATISE UPON THE

NEW LAW OF PATENTS, DESIGNS, & TRADE MARKS,

CONSISTING OF THE PATENTS, DESIGNS, AND TRADE MARKS ACT,
1883, WITH THE RULES AND FORMS, FULLY ANNOTATED
WITH CASES, &c.

And a Statement of the Principles of the Law upon those subjects, with a Time Table
and Copious Index.

By EDWARD MORTON DANIEL,
OF LINCOLN'S INN, BARRISTER-AT-LAW, ASSOCIATE OF THE INSTITUTE OF PATENT AGENTS.

In 8vo, price 8s., cloth,

The TRADE MARKS REGISTRATION ACT, 1875,

And the Rules thereunder; THE MERCHANDISE MARKS ACT, 1862, with an
Introduction containing a SUMMARY OF THE LAW OF TRADE MARKS,
together with practical Notes and Instructions, and a copious INDEX. By
EDWARD MORTON DANIEL, of Lincoln's Inn, Barrister-at-Law.

Second Edition, in one volume, 8vo, price 16s., cloth,
A CONCISE TREATISE ON THE

STATUTE LAW OF THE LIMITATIONS OF ACTIONS.

With an Appendix of Statutes, Copious References to English, Irish, and American Cases,
and to the French Code, and a Copious Index.

By HENRY THOMAS BANNING, M.A.,
OF THE INNER TEMPLE, BARRISTER-AT-LAW.

"The work is decidedly valuable."—*Law Times.*

"Mr. Banning has adhered to the plan of printing the Acts in an appendix, and making his book a running treatise on the case-law thereon. The cases have evidently been investigated with care and digested with clearness and intellectuality."—*Law Journal.*

In 8vo, price 1s., sewed,
AN ESSAY ON THE

ABOLITION OF CAPITAL PUNISHMENT.

*Embracing more particularly an Enunciation and Analysis of the Principles of Law as
applicable to Criminals of the Highest Degree of Guilt.*

By WALTER ARTHUR COPINGER,
OF THE MIDDLE TEMPLE, ESQ., BARRISTER-AT-LAW.

Sixth Edition, in 8vo, price 31s. 6d., cloth,

THE INDIAN CONTRACT ACT, No. IX., of 1872.

TOGETHER
WITH AN INTRODUCTION AND EXPLANATORY NOTES, TABLE OF
CONTENTS, APPENDIX, AND INDEX.

By H. S. CUNNINGHAM AND H. H. SHEPHERD,
BARRISTERS-AT-LAW.

Second Edition, in 8vo, price 15s., cloth,

LEADING CASES and OPINIONS on INTERNATIONAL LAW

COLLECTED AND DIGESTED FROM
ENGLISH AND FOREIGN REPORTS, OFFICIAL DOCUMENTS, PARLIAMENTARY PAPERS, and other Sources.

With **NOTES** and **EXCURSUS**, Containing the Views of the Text Writers on the Topics referred to, together with Supplementary Cases, Treaties, and Statutes; and Embodying an Account of some of the more important International Transactions and Controversies.

By PITT COBBETT, M.A., D.C.L.,
OF GRAY'S INN, BARRISTER-AT-LAW, PROFESSOR OF LAW, UNIVERSITY OF SYDNEY, N.S.W.

"The book is well arranged, the materials well selected, and the comments to the point. Much will be found in small space in this book."—*Law Journal.*

"The notes are concisely written and trustworthy. . . . The reader will learn from them a great deal on the subject, and the book as a whole seems a convenient introduction to fuller and more systematic works."—*Oxford Magazine.*

Second Edition, in royal 8vo. 1100 pages, price 45s., cloth,

STORY'S COMMENTARIES ON EQUITY JURISPRUDENCE.

Second English Edition, from the Twelfth American Edition.

By W. E. GRIGSBY, LL.D. (Lond.), D.C.L. (Oxon.),
AND OF THE INNER TEMPLE, BARRISTER-AT-LAW.

"It is high testimony to the reputation of Story, and to the editorship of Dr. Grigsby, that another edition should have been called for. . . . The work has been rendered more perfect by additional indices."—*Law Times.*

Second Edition, in 8vo, price 8s., cloth,

THE PARTITION ACTS, 1868 & 1876.

A Manual of the Law of Partition and of Sale, in Lieu of Partition. With the Decided Cases, and an Appendix containing Judgments and Orders. By W. GREGORY WALKER, B.A., of Lincoln's Inn, Barrister-at-Law.

"This is a very good manual—practical, clearly written, and complete. The subject lends itself well to the mode of treatment adopted by Mr. Walker, and in his notes to the various sections he has carefully brought together the cases, and discussed the difficulties arising upon the language of the different provisions."—*Solicitors' Journal.*

Second Edition, in 8vo, price 22s. cloth,

A TREATISE ON THE

LAW AND PRACTICE RELATING TO INFANTS.

By ARCHIBALD H. SIMPSON, M.A.,
OF LINCOLN'S INN, BARRISTER-AT-LAW, AND FELLOW OF CHRIST'S COLLEGE, CAMBRIDGE.

SECOND EDITION. By E. J. ELGOOD, B.C.L., M.A., of Lincoln's Inn, Barrister-at-Law.

"Mr. Simpson's book comprises the whole of the law relating to infants, both as regards their persons and their property, and we have not observed any very important omissions. The author has evidently expended much trouble and care upon his work, and has brought together, in a concise and convenient form, the law upon the subject down to the present time."—*Solicitors' Journal.*

"Its law is unimpeachable. We have detected no errors, and whilst the work might have been done more scientifically, it is, beyond all question, a compendium of sound legal principles."—*Law Times.*

"Mr. Simpson has arranged the whole of the Law relating to Infants with much fulness of detail, and yet in comparatively little space. The result is due mainly to the businesslike condensation of his style. Fulness, however, has by no means been sacrificed to brevity; and, so far as we have been able to test it, the work omits no point of any importance, from the earliest cases to the last. In the essential qualities of clearness, completeness, and orderly arrangement it leaves nothing to be desired.

"Lawyers in doubt on any point of law or practice will find the information they require, if it can be found at all, in Mr. Simpson's book, and a writer of whom this can be said may congratulate himself on having achieved a considerable success."—*Law Magazine,* February, 1876.

In one volume, royal 8vo, 1877, price 30s., cloth,

THE DOCTRINES & PRINCIPLES OF THE LAW OF INJUNCTIONS.

By WILLIAM JOYCE,
OF LINCOLN'S INN, BARRISTER-AT-LAW.

"Mr. Joyce, whose learned and exhaustive work on 'The Law and Practice of Injunctions' has gained such a deservedly high reputation in the Profession, now brings out a valuable companion volume on the 'Doctrines and Principles' of this important branch of the Law. In the present work the Law is enunciated in its abstract rather than its concrete form, as few cases as possible being cited; while at the same time no statement of a principle is made unsupported by a decision, and for the most part the very language of the Courts has been adhered to. Written as it is by so acknowledged a master of his subject, and with the conscientious carefulness that might be expected from him, this work cannot fail to prove of the greatest assistance alike to the Student—who wants to grasp principles freed from their superincumbent details—and to the practitioner, who wants to refresh his memory on points of doctrine amidst the oppressive details of professional work."—*Law Magazine and Review.*

BY THE SAME AUTHOR.

In two volumes, royal 8vo, 1872, price 70s., cloth,

THE LAW & PRACTICE OF INJUNCTIONS.
EMBRACING
ALL THE SUBJECTS IN WHICH COURTS OF EQUITY AND COMMON LAW HAVE JURISDICTION.

By WILLIAM JOYCE,
OF LINCOLN'S INN, BARRISTER-AT-LAW.

REVIEWS.

"A work which aims at being so absolutely complete, as that of Mr. Joyce upon a subject which is of almost perpetual recurrence in the Courts, cannot fail to be a welcome offering to the profession, and doubtless, it will be well received and largely used, for it is as absolutely complete as it aims at being. . . . . This work is, therefore, eminently a work for the practitioner, being full of practical utility in every page, and every sentence, of it. . . . . We have to congratulate the profession on this new acquisition to a digest of the law, and the author on his production of a work of permanent utility and fame."— *Law Magazine and Review.*

"Mr. Joyce has produced, not a treatise, but a complete and compendious *exposition* of the Law and Practice of Injunctions both in equity and common law.

"Part III. is devoted to the practice of the Courts. Contains an amount of valuable and technical matter nowhere else collected.

"From these remarks it will be sufficiently perceived what elaborate and painstaking industry, as well as legal knowledge and ability, has been necessary in the compilation of Mr. Joyce's work. No labour has been spared to save the practitioner labour, and no research has been omitted which could tend towards the elucidation and exemplification of the general principles of the Law and Practice of Injunctions."—*Law Journal.*

"He does not attempt to go an inch beyond that for which he has express written authority; he allows the cases to speak, and does not speak for them.

"The work is something more than a treatise on the Law of Injunctions. It gives us the general law on almost every subject to which the process of injunction is applicable. Not only English, but American decisions are cited, the aggregate number being 3,500, and the statutes cited 160, whilst the index is, we think, the most elaborate we have ever seen—occupying nearly 200 pages. The work is probably entirely exhaustive."—*Law Times.*

"This work, considered either as to its matter or manner of execution, is no ordinary work. It is a complete and exhaustive treatise both as to the law and the practice of granting injunctions. It must supersede all other works on the subject. The terse statement of the practice will be found of incalculable value. We know of no book as suitable to supply a knowledge of the law of injunctions to our common law friends as Mr. Joyce's exhaustive work. It is alike indispensable to members of the Common Law and Equity Bars. Mr. Joyce's great work would be a casket without a key unless accompanied by a good index. His index is very full and well arranged. We feel that this work is destined to take its place as a standard text-book, and *the* text-book on the particular subject of which it treats. The author deserves great credit for the very great labour bestowed upon it. The publishers, as usual, have acquitted themselves in a manner deserving of the high reputation they bear."—*Canada Law Journal.*

Third Edition, in 8vo, price 20s., cloth,

A TREATISE UPON

THE LAW OF EXTRADITION,

WITH THE CONVENTIONS UPON THE SUBJECT EXISTING BETWEEN ENGLAND AND FOREIGN NATIONS,

AND THE CASES DECIDED THEREON.

By SIR EDWARD CLARKE,
OF LINCOLN'S INN, S.-G., Q.C., M.P.

"Mr. Clarke's accurate and sensible book is the best authority to which the English reader can turn upon the subject of Extradition."—*Saturday Review.*

"The opinion we expressed of the merits of this work when it first appeared has been fully justified by the reputation it has gained. It is seldom we come across a book possessing so much interest to the general reader and at the same time furnishing so useful a guide to the lawyer."—*Solicitors' Journal.*

"The appearance of a second edition of this treatise does not surprise us. It is a useful book, well arranged and well written. A student who wants to learn the principles and practice of the law of extradition will be greatly helped by Mr. Clarke. Lawyers who have extradition business will find this volume an excellent book of reference. Magistrates who have to administer the extradition law will be greatly assisted by a careful perusal of 'Clarke upon Extradition.' This may be called a warm commendation, but those who have read the book will not say it is unmerited."—*Law Journal.*

THE TIMES of September 7, 1874, in a long article upon "Extradition Treaties," makes considerable use of this work and writes of it as "*Mr. Clarke's useful Work on Extradition.*"

In 8vo, price 2s. 6d., cloth,

TABLES OF STAMP DUTIES

FROM 1815 TO 1878.

By WALTER ARTHUR COPINGER,
OF THE MIDDLE TEMPLE, ESQUIRE, BARRISTER-AT-LAW; AUTHOR OF "THE LAW OF COPYRIGHT IN WORKS OF LITERATURE AND ART," "INDEX TO PRECEDENTS IN CONVEYANCING," "TITLE DEEDS," &C.

"We think this little book ought to find its way into a good many chambers and offices."—*Solicitors' Journal.*

"This book, or at least one containing the same amount of valuable and well-arranged information, should find a place in every Solicitor's office. It is of especial value when examining the abstract of a large number of old title-deeds."—*Law Times.*

"His *Tables of Stamp Duties, from 1815 to 1878*, have already been tested in Chambers, and being now published, will materially lighten the labours of the profession in a tedious department, yet one requiring great care."—*Law Magazine and Review.*

In one volume, 8vo, price 14s., cloth,

TITLE DEEDS:

THEIR CUSTODY, INSPECTION, AND PRODUCTION, AT LAW, IN EQUITY, AND IN MATTERS OF CONVEYANCING,

Including Covenants for the Production of Deeds and Attested Copies; with an Appendix of Precedents, the Vendor and Purchaser Act, 1874, &c., &c., &c. By WALTER ARTHUR COPINGER, of the Middle Temple, Barrister-at-Law; Author of "The Law of Copyright" and "Index to Precedents in Conveyancing."

"The literary execution of the work is good enough to invite quotation, but the volume is not large, and we content ourselves with recommending it to the profession."—*Law Times.*

"A really good treatise on this subject must be essential to the lawyer; and this is what we have here. Mr. Copinger has supplied a much-felt want, by the compilation of this volume. We have not space to go into the details of the book; it appears well arranged, clearly written, and fully elaborated. With these few remarks we recommend his volume to our readers."—*Law Journal.*

Third Edition, in 8vo, considerably enlarged, price 36s., cloth,

THE LAW OF COPYRIGHT

In Works of Literature and Art; including that of the Drama, Music, Engraving, Sculpture, Painting, Photography, and Ornamental and Useful Designs; together with International and Foreign Copyright, with the Statutes Relating thereto, and References to the English and American Decisions. By WALTER ARTHUR COPINGER, of the Middle Temple, Barrister-at-Law.

"Mr. Copinger's book is very comprehensive, dealing with every branch of his subject, and even extending to copyright in foreign countries. So far as we have examined, we have found all the recent authorities noted up with scrupulous care, and there is an unusually good index. These are merits which will, doubtless, lead to the placing of this edition on the shelves of the members of the profession whose business is concerned with copyright; and deservedly, for the book is one of considerable value."—*Solicitors' Journal.*

Third Edition, in One large Volume, 8vo, price 32s., cloth,

A MAGISTERIAL AND POLICE GUIDE:

BEING THE LAW
RELATING TO THE

PROCEDURE, JURISDICTION, AND DUTIES OF MAGISTRATES AND POLICE AUTHORITIES,

IN THE METROPOLIS AND IN THE COUNTRY.

With an Introduction showing the General Procedure before Magistrates both in Indictable and Summary Matters.

By HENRY C. GREENWOOD,
STIPENDIARY MAGISTRATE FOR THE DISTRICT OF THE STAFFORDSHIRE POTTERIES; AND

TEMPLE CHEVALIER MARTIN,
CHIEF CLERK TO THE MAGISTRATES AT LAMBETH POLICE COURT, LONDON;
AUTHOR OF "THE LAW OF MAINTENANCE AND DESERTION," "THE NEW FORMULIST," ETC.

Third Edition. Including the SESSION 52 & 53 Vict., and the CASES DECIDED in the SUPERIOR COURTS to the END OF THE YEAR 1889, *revised and enlarged.*

By TEMPLE CHEVALIER MARTIN.

"A second edition has appeared of Messrs. Greenwood and Martin's valuable and comprehensive magisterial and police Guide, a book which Justices of the peace should take care to include in their Libraries."—*Saturday Review.*

"Hence it is that we rarely light upon a work which commands our confidence, not merely by its research, but also by its grasp of the subject of which it treats. The volume before us is one of the happy few of this latter class, and it is on this account that the public favour will certainly wait upon it. We are moreover convinced that no effort has been spared by its authors to render it a thoroughly efficient and trustworthy guide."—*Law Journal.*

"Magistrates will find a valuable handbook in Messrs. Greenwood and Martin's 'Magisterial and Police Guide,' of which a fresh Edition has just been published."—*The Times.*

"A very valuable introduction, treating of proceedings before Magistrates, and largely of the Summary Jurisdiction Act, is in itself a treatise which will repay perusal. We expressed our high opinion of the Guide when it first appeared, and the favourable impression then produced is increased by our examination of this Second Edition."—*Law Times.*

"For the form of the work we have nothing but commendation. We may say we have here our ideal law book. It may be said to omit nothing which it ought to contain."—*Law Times.*

"This handsome volume aims at presenting a comprehensive magisterial handbook for the whole of England. The mode of arrangement seems to us excellent, and is well carried out."—*Solicitors' Journal.*

"The *Magisterial and Police Guide*, by Mr. Henry Greenwood and Mr. Temple Martin, is a model work in its conciseness, and, as far as we have been able to test it, in completeness and accuracy. *It ought to be in the hands of all who, as magistrates or otherwise, have authority in matters of police.*"—*Daily News.*

"*This work is eminently practical, and supplies a real want. It plainly and concisely states the law on all points upon which Magistrates are called upon to adjudicate, systematically arranged, so as to be easy of reference. It ought to find a place on every Justice's table, and we cannot but think that its usefulness will speedily ensure for it as large a sale as its merits deserve.*"—*Midland Counties Herald.*

"The exceedingly arduous task of collecting together all the enactments on the subject has been ably and efficiently performed, and the arrangement is so methodical and precise that one is able to lay a finger on a Section of an Act almost in a moment. It is wonderful what a mass of information is comprised in so comparatively small a space. We have much pleasure in recommending the volume not only to our professional, but also to our general readers; nothing can be more useful to the public than an acquaintance with the outlines of magisterial jurisdiction and procedure."—*Sheffield Post.*

In one thick volume, 8vo, price 32s., cloth,

THE LAW OF RAILWAY COMPANIES.

Comprising the Companies Clauses, the Lands Clauses, the Railways Clauses Consolidation Acts, the Railway Companies Act, 1867, and the Regulation of Railways Act, 1868; with Notes of Cases on all the Sections, brought down to the end of the year 1868; together with an Appendix giving all the other material Acts relating to Railways, and the Standing Orders of the Houses of Lords and Commons; and a copious Index. By HENRY GODEFROI, of Lincoln's Inn, and JOHN SHORTT, of the Middle Temple, Barristers-at-Law.

In a handy volume, crown 8vo, 1870, price 10s. 6d., cloth,

THE LAW OF SALVAGE,

As administered in the High Court of Admiralty and the County Courts; with the Principal Authorities, English and American, brought down to the present time; and an Appendix, containing Statutes, Forms, Table of Fees, etc. By EDWYN JONES, of Gray's Inn, Barrister-at-Law.

In crown 8vo, price 4s., cloth,

A HANDBOOK OF THE

LAW OF PARLIAMENTARY REGISTRATION.

WITH AN APPENDIX OF STATUTES AND FULL INDEX.

By J. R. SEAGER, REGISTRATION AGENT.

In 8vo, price 5s., cloth,

THE LAW OF PROMOTERS OF PUBLIC COMPANIES.

By NEWMAN WATTS,

OF LINCOLN'S INN, BARRISTER-AT-LAW.

"Some recent cases in our law courts, which at the time attracted much public notice, have demonstrated the want of some clear and concise exposition of the powers and liabilities of promoters, and this task has been ably performed by Mr. Newman Watts."—*Investor's Guardian.*

"Mr. Watts has brought together all the leading decisions relating to promoters and directors, and has arranged the information in a very satisfactory manner, so as to readily show the rights of different parties and the steps which can be legally taken by promoters to further interests of new companies."—*Daily Chronicle.*

Second Edition, in One Vol., 8vo, price 12s., cloth,

A COMPENDIUM OF ROMAN LAW,

FOUNDED ON THE INSTITUTES OF JUSTINIAN; together with Examination Questions Set in the University and Bar Examinations (with Solutions), and Definitions of Leading Terms in the Words of the Principal Authorities. Second Edition. By GORDON CAMPBELL, of the Inner Temple, M.A., late Scholar of Exeter College, Oxford; M.A., LL.D., Trinity College, Cambridge: Author of "An Analysis of Austin's Jurisprudence, or the Philosophy of Positive Law."

In 8vo, price 7s. 6d., cloth,

TITLES TO MINES IN THE UNITED STATES,

WITH THE

STATUTES AND REFERENCES TO THE DECISIONS OF THE COURTS RELATING THERETO.

By W. A. HARRIS, B.A. OXON.,

OF LINCOLN'S INN, BARRISTER-AT-LAW; AND OF THE AMERICAN BAR.

INDEX

To the Names of Authors and Editors of Works enumerated in this Catalogue.

ALDRED (P. F.), page 21.
ARGLES (N.), 32.
ATTENBOROUGH (C. L.), 27.
BALDWIN (E. T.), 15.
BANNING (H. T.), 42
BEAL (E.), 32.
BELLEWE (R.), 34.
BEVEN (T.) 14.
BLYTH (E. E.), 22.
BRICE (SEWARD), 9, 16.
BROOKE (SIR R.), 35.
BROWN (ARCHIBALD), 20, 22, 26, 33, 40.
BROWNE (J. H. BALFOUR), 19.
BUCHANAN (J.), 38.
BUCKLEY (H. B.), 17.
BUCKNILL (T. T.), 34, 35.
CAMPBELL (GORDON), 47.
CAMPBELL (ROBERT), 9, 40.
CARMICHAEL (C. H. E.), 21.
CECIL (LORD R.), 11.
CHASTER (A. W.), 32.
CLARKE (EDWARD), 45.
COBBETT (PITT), 43.
COGHLAN (W. M.), 28.
COOKE (SIR G.), 35.
COOKE (HUGH), 10.
COPINGER (W. A.), 40, 42, 45.
CORNER (R. J.), 10.
CRAIES (W. F.), 6, 9.
CUNNINGHAM (H. S.), 38, 42.
CUNNINGHAM (JOHN), 7.
CUNNINGHAM (T.), 34.
DANIEL (E. M.), 42.
DARLING (C. J.), 18.
DEANE (H. C.), 23.
DE WAL (J.), 38.
DUNCAN (J. A.), 33.
EDWARDS (W. D.), 16, 39.
ELGOOD (E. J.), 6, 18, 43.
ELLIOTT (G.), 14.
EMDEN (A.), 8, 11.
EVERSLEY (W. P.), 9.
FINLASON (W. F.), 32.
FOA (E.), 11.
FOOTE (J. ALDERSON), 36.
FORBES (U. A.), 18.
FORSYTH (W.), 14.
FROST (R.), 12.
GIBBS (F. W.), 10.
GODEFROI (H.), 47.
GREENWOOD (H. C.), 46.
GRIFFITH (J. R.), 40.
GRIGSBY (W. E.), 43.
GROTIUS (HUGO), 38.
HALL (R. G.), 30.
HANSON (A.), 10.
HARDCASTLE (H.), 9, 33.
HARRIS (SEYMOUR F.), 20, 27.
HARRIS (W. A.), 47.
HARRISON (J. C.), 23.
HARWOOD (R. G.), 10.
HAZLITT (W.), 29.
HIGGINS (C.), 30.

HOUSTON (J.), 32.
HUDSON (A. A.), 12.
HURST (J.), 11.
INDERMAUR (JOHN), 24, 25, 28.
JONES (E.), 47.   JOYCE (W.), 44.
KAY (JOSEPH), 17.
KELKE (W. H.), 6.
KELYNG (SIR J.), 35.
KELYNGE (W.), 35.
KOTZÉ (J. G.), 38.
LLOYD (EYRE), 13.
LOCKE (J.), 32.
LORENZ (C. A.), 38.
LOVELAND (R. L.), 30, 34, 35.
MAASDORP (A. F. S.), 38.
MACASKIE (S. C.), 7.
MARCH (JOHN), 35.
MARCY (G. N.), 26.
MARSH (THOMAS), 21.
MARTIN (TEMPLE C.), 7, 46.
MATTINSON (M. W.), 7.
MAY (H. W.), 29.
MAYNE (JOHN D.), 31, 38.
MELLOR (F. H.), 10.
MENZIES (W.), 38.
MOORE (S. A.), 30.
O'MALLEY (E. L.), 33.
PAVITT (A.), 32.
PEILE (C. J.), 7.
PEMBERTON (L. L.), 18, 32.
PHIPSON (S. L.), 20.
PORTER (J. B.), 6.
REILLY (F. S.), 29.
RINGWOOD (R.), 13, 15, 29.
SALKOWSKI (C.), 14.
SALMOND (J. W.), 13.
SAVIGNY (F. C. VON), 20.
SCOTT (C. F.), 32.
SEAGER (J. R.), 47.
SHORT (F. H.), 10, 41.
SHORTT (JOHN), 47.
SHOWER (SIR B.), 34.
SIMPSON (A. H.), 43.
SLATER (J.), 7.
SMITH (EUSTACE), 23, 39.
SMITH (F. J.), 6.
SMITH (LUMLEY), 31.
SNELL (E. H. T.), 22.
STORY, 43.
TARRING (C. J.), 26, 41, 42.
TASWELL-LANGMEAD, 21.
THOMAS (ERNEST C.), 28.
TYSSEN (A. D.), 39.
VAN DER KEESEL (D. G.), 38.
VAN LEEUWEN, 38.
WAITE (W. T.), 22.
WALKER (W. G.), 6, 18, 43.
WATTS (C. N.), 47.
WERTHEIMER (J.), 32.
WHITEFORD (F. M.), 20.
WHITFIELD (E. E.), 14.
WILLIAMS (S. E.), 7.
WORTHINGTON (S. W.), 29.

www.ingramcontent.com/pod-product-compliance
Lightning Source LLC
Chambersburg PA
CBHW031736230426
43669CB00007B/360